PYRENEES COSTA BRAVA

51 ROUTES ON FOOT, BY BICYCLE AND IN KAYAK

Texts and photographs by
Sergi Lara

Kayaks in the bay of Port de la Selva

PYRENEES OF GIRONA
COSTA BRAVA

51 ROUTES ON FOOT, BY BICYCLE AND IN KAYAK

PYRENEES OF GIRONA
COSTA BRAVA
51 ROUTES ON FOOT, BY BICYCLE AND IN KAYAK

The lands of Girona have been a crossroads for the majority of European cultures. It is then, since time immemorial, an authentic region of passing, surrounded by some of the most important geographic systems of the continent. On one side, the Pyrenean range, fitted between the Iberian peninsula and Europe; and on the other side, the Costa Brava, one of the most extraordinary parts of the Mediterranean coast, a result precisely of the geographic convulsion caused by the fold of the Pyrenees and the reliefs of the coastal massifs. To close the magical triangle of this territory on its western flank an equally exceptional series of inland massifs stands out. Here we come across mountains such as Montseny, Guillerías, Collsacabra and Puigsacalm, maximum exponents of the rich biodiversity of the lands of Girona, as well as the excellent models of geographic space. Neither should we forget some spots that occupy a central position, such as the volcanic area of La Garrotxa, the extensive massifs of Les Gavarres or the agricultural plain of Alt Empordà. And to complete this complex framework of structures, two short rivers, but of major importance within the history of Catalonia: the rivers Ter and Fluvià.

With just a quick revision we can immediately see that we are before a unique territory, with one third of its surface protected under classifications of Natural Park or Space of Natural Interest; in total, twenty natural reserves that make up an immense green belt. Inland, the central spaces and the courses of the rivers provide many access routes and leisure activities. Furthermore, the very large number of towns and villages with remote origins, before the Roman period in some cases, enables the coming together of the cultural heritage with the natural spots to be one of the most sensational in the world. For this reason, and for the infinite number of hiking routes, active tourism in this part of the continent makes its inhabitants really privileged people. We can safely say that doing routes in the Pyrenees of Girona and the Costa Brava, whether on foot, by bike or in kayak in the sea, is a veritable gift for both body and soul. If we add to all of this a favourable climate, with many nuances according to the time of the year, the many support services and the presence of the finest gastronomies on the planet, we can plan an unbeatable emotional experience at any time of year.

PRACTICAL ADVICE AND SAFETY IN THE MOUNTAIN

Two fundamental elements to safely deal with any trip, however easy or short it is, are being in good physical shape and knowledge of the natural world that lets us interpret the terrain on a map. The speed you go or the choice of route are very personal questions, but without doubt the decisions must be thought about according to the capabilities and know-how of each person, and not risking taking on levels higher than those demanded. Checking the weather, which sometimes does not fulfil the forecast until we reach our destination, is an aspect that must also be very much taken into account. In this sense, if conditions are not good, it is better to know to go back in time to avoid problems. The landscape and the mountain will always be there, and it is in no way the same to enjoy the marvels that nature offers us during a splendid day, whether in summer or winter, than trying to do it on a bad day. It is also true that both in the mountains and at sea, sudden changes in the weather are not an exception, and for this very reason we should be prepared and be in both good physical form and have good equipment in order to react in the best way possible.

BEFORE SETTING OUT

It is well worth joining a federation and consequently having insurance cover in one of the policies considered in the respective regulations of the mountain federations (in the Catalan case, the FEEC together with its clubs or associated entities). You should also carry documentation and plan for possible alternatives, as well as inform beforehand the place you are going and, if possible, make the trip with colleagues in the same condition or of the same level. The main federations in Catalonia and Spain are:

TYPES OF PATHS AND SIGNPOSTING

Long-distance paths (GR)

Short-distance paths (PR)

Local paths (SL)

Itineràrnia network

Route of the River Ter

Green Ways

Pirinexus network

Cycle-touring

MTB routes

WEATHER SERVICES

Meteorological Service of Catalonia
www.meteo.cat

State Meteorological Agency
www.aemet.es

French Meteorological Service
www.meteo.fr

Federation of Excursionist Entities of Catalonia
www.feec.cat.
Spanish Federation of Mountain Sports and Climbing
www.fedme.es.

LEVELS OF DIFFICULTY FOR WALKING CONSIDERED IN THIS GUIDE

• **Trekking**
Medium-high physical requirement on routes with technical sections.

• **Path walking**
Medium physical requirement on routes that require care.

• **Nordic walking**
Medium physical requirement on routes with comfortable sections.

WHAT TO DO IN CASE OF EMERGENCY

1 Do not act hastily or commit a possible negligence.
2 Control the pulse, the level of consciousness and respiration.
3 Observe the eyes (pupils), possible fractures and haemorrhages.
4 Side positioning of the injured person without giving them water.
5 Hyperextension of the head for unblocking respiratory tracts.
6 Fit out a minimum of space for shelter, comfort and signalling.
7 Telephone message A: injured, age, place, state of consciousness and injuries.
8 Telephone message B: weather conditions and place of accident.
9 Position A before a helicopter: I need help (arms raised / Y-yes).
10 Position B before a helicopter: Everything alright (one arm up and one down / N-no).

EMERGENCIES
TEL. 112

RECOMMENDED BASIC TREKKING EQUIPMENT

- Altimeter and compass
- Bottle of water of 1.5 litres
- Telescopic stick for trekking, walking or Nordic walking
- First-aid kit
- Fleece jersey
- Hat and gloves
- Waterproof and windproof jacket
- Front torch with change of batteries
- Cartographic map
- Repair material (duct tape, bootlaces and thread)
- Varied but energy-giving food
- Quality summer mountain socks
- Rucksack with 40-50 litres' capacity
- Long and short mountain or sports trousers
- Mountain boots with resistant sole and good protection
- Thermal shirt and cotton T-shirt
- Sunglasses and solar protection

BASIC EQUIPMENT FOR KAYAKING IN THE SEA

- Cold drink and hot drink in a flask
- Sealed bags with dry clothes, food, light, radio and telephone
- Kayak of fibre or plastic with closed compartments bow and stern
- Nautical map or plasticised cartographic map
- Rope of 10 metres, tapes for repairs and detachable spare oar
- Pumps or old slippers
- Sponge and pump to pump out water
- Lifesaving jacket with whistle incorporated and windproof jacket
- Neoprene suit or similar, neoprene gloves and technical T-shirts

▲ Cala Giverola

▼ Stop-off in the bay of Llorell

▲ Pyrenean landscape of La Cerdanya

▼ Peak of Puigpedrós in spring

Walking routes in the
PYRENEES

From the county of La Cerdanya to the massif of the Albera, the routes chosen connect or are close to the main long-distance path that crosses the Pyrenees on its southern side, the mythical GR-11 or Trans-Pyrenean Walk. The range of suggestions takes us from the high mountain peaks to the Mediterranean woods, through a fantastic collection of routes to enjoy the best mountaineering. We should say, however, that the routes in the high mountain areas are recommendations during the period in which the terrain is practically free of snow –from late spring to mid-autumn. Therefore in no way do we suggest this guide to provide more technical experiences that greater mountaineering skills at all levels demand. The Pyrenees, as a whole, require being in good physical condition and proven knowledge of orientation and meteorology, since you must always be prepared for any unforeseen situation, however trivial. Although the routes follow popular itineraries, the natural setting is wild, and before adversity things can become very complicated.

On the one hand we have the possibility of enjoying high routes, over precipices and craggy peaks, which must be tackled in optimum weather conditions. On the other hand, the low mountain routes, amid dense woods and sudden fractures of the land, also require concentration and good map-reading. Generally speaking, then, no trip should be taken lightly. As a reward, we will enjoy the panoramas and experiences that will stay fixed in our memories forever and will almost certainly make us even more enthusiastic mountain lovers. In this sense, the recommendation is to ignore the concept that rules the popular mountain races, that has nothing to do with the philosophy of a guide like this one, where what we propose is to enjoy all the details of the landscape, without this meaning you have to walk slowly. Quite the contrary, in the Pyrenees it is always preferable to carefully control the walking and resting time, but always conserving enough energy to avoid possible injuries and other problems that arise due to overexertion.

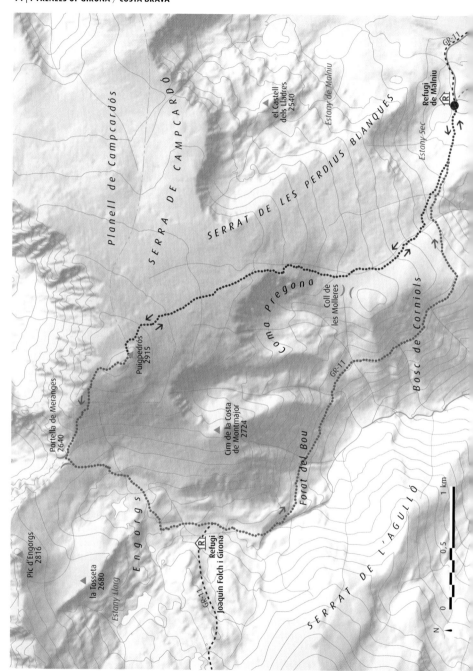

1
THE MASSIF OF PUIGPEDRÓS
1

▲ The valley of la Llosa in autumn

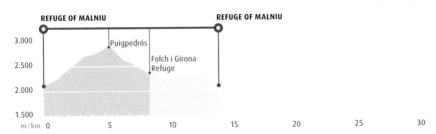

Methods
Path walking, trekking

Distance
9 km

Duration
3 - 4 h

Gradients
+800m / -800 m

A gateway of the central Pyrenees, this massif concentrates all the typical high mountain spots, through cirques of glacial origin with many lakes, alpine meadows and coniferous woods. We suggest an easy there and back route to climb to the peak of Puigpedrós, while the circular route via the cirque of Engorgs we only recommend for experienced trekkers.

ROUTE

With access from the village of **Meranges** (1,540 m) along a wide forest track of 9,5 km –the first 6 asphalted–, the historic **refuge of Malniu** (2,140 m) is the starting and return point of the route. It is a staffed refuge that offers meals

▲ The valley of the river Duran towards Malniu

from the end of spring until the beginning of autumn. You have to pay a fee for using the car parking space. There is also a large camping area with fantastic meadow views. The path up to the peak of Puigpedrós starts alongside the pretty **Lake Sec** (2,145 m), in a beautiful high mountain setting. For the first metres we follow the route of the GR-11 path, until coming to a sign that tells us the direction to take to begin this climb, although we have to go through a rather confusing area between rocks, shrubs and streams. Heading northwest, we find ourselves above some projections and the main stream until coming out to some large grassy knolls. From here we can make out the peak in the distance, and enjoy a com-

fortable approach via small peat bogs. In the last section of the climb we reach the vast rocky space that gives its name to this emblematic mountain (its name in Catalan means "stony mountain"), with a final climb through large blocks of rock. The peak of **Puigpedrós** (2,914 m) stands over the French border, very close to the frontier with Andorra, and as well as being the highest point in the Girona lands, it could also be said is the most remote. To return, we repeat the route the other way to the refuge of Malniu. It is highly recommendable to complete the trip with the visit to the **lake of Malniu** (2,260 m), which is hidden between dense coniferous woods.

1

TOUR AROUND THE CIRQUE OF ENGORGS
(only for experienced trekkers)

◄ V ►

Distance
14 km

Duration
5 - 7 h

Gradients
+1,000 m / -1,000 m

From the peak of Puigpedrós, you have to drop in a north-west direction along a wide slope between blocks of rock and dry grass, taking as a reference point the pass of the **Portella de Meranges** (2,640 m). Once here, we complete the descent via a lovely valley, where different streams come together, to the foot of the majestic **cirque of Engorgs**, occupied by a series of different-sized lakes. On the other side of the main stream is the **Folch i Girona refuge** (2,375 m), of free use and very useful in case of necessity, from where it links up with the GR-11 path to return to the refuge of Malniu. In the opposite direction to this refuge, the GR-path offers one of the most spectacular sections of the mythical Trans-Pyrenean crossing via the cirque of Engorgs and the sensational **valley of La Llosa** to the Andorran frontier. At the beginning of our path back, we cross some meadows and then set off on a rocky descent to the left of the rough course of the **river Duran**. We should take care at some points where there is a danger of landslides. We follow the red and white markers of the Trans-Pyrenean path at all times, which takes us along a long journey through disperse woods. Here we are forced to undertake some rather demanding manoeuvres to cross some fallen trees, as well as a series of abrupt streams with waterfalls. On reaching a pretty **meadow** (2,200 m), we set off on a steady climb to go around the long spur that we have had in sight throughout the return path. We thus reach a **pass** (2,300 m) from where there is a good view of the refuge of Malniu on the horizon. From here we embark on a very exciting and pleasant descent, between more meadows and woods, a final section in which we can savour the whole trip that we are about to complete.

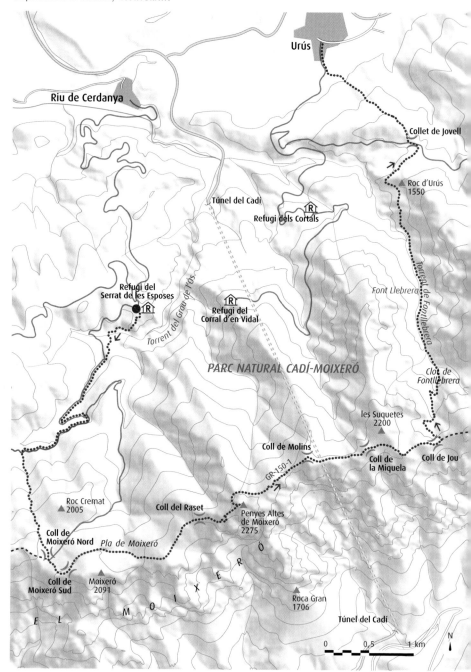

Urús

Collet de Jovell

Roc d'Urús
1550

Túnel del Cadí

Refugi dels Cortals

Riu de Cerdanya

Font Llebrera

Torrent de Fontllebrera

Refugi del
Serrat de les Esposes

Refugi del
Corral d'en Vidal

Torrent del Grau de l'Os.

Clot de
Fontllebrera

PARC NATURAL CADÍ-MOIXERÓ

les Suquetes
2200

Coll de Molins

Coll de Jou

Coll de
la Miquela

GR-150-1

Roc Cremat
2005

Coll del Raset

Penyes Altes
de Moixeró
2275

Coll de
Moixeró Nord

Pla de Moixeró

Ó

Coll de
Moixeró Sud

Moixeró
2091

X   E   R

Roca Gran
1706

M   O   I

Túnel del Cadí

E   L

0   0.5   1 km

N

2 THE MOIXERÓ RANGE

▲ High part of the Moixeró range

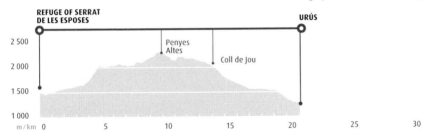

Methods
Path walking, trekking

Distance
22 km

Duration
7 - 9 h

Gradients
+1,100 m / -1,370 m

The Cadí-Moixeró Natural Park was created in 1983 and covers an extensive territory marked by imposing geological faults, with impressive ravines and channels of calcareous rock. Our one-way route along the Moixeró range enables us to enjoy exceptional meadows and woods, all of which offer a very complete itinerary of great beauty.

ROUTE

The starting point of our route is the **refuge of Serrat de les Esposes** (1,510 m), accessible with vehicle along a comfortable forest track of 7 km from the village of **Riu de Cerdanya** (1,180 m), very close to the north opening of the

Cadí Tunnel. The one-way nature of the route means we must have two vehicles, or make a transfer by taxi from the village of Urús, the final point of the trip. It is highly recommendable to spend the night in the refuge, which is staffed and offers meals throughout the summer season. For the first third our route follows the section of crossing known as *Cavalls del Vent* (Horses of the Wind), which joins the refuges of the Cadí-Moixeró Natural Park, signposted with orange marks. From the turn in the track beside the refuge, we find the marks of this path and start a descent through some pretty meadows and an area of shrubs until the **stream of Grau de l'Ós** (1,420 m). Here we are before a wonderful spot, surrounded by crags of calcareous rock, the remains of old dry stone walls and pastureland. We then climb a little to come out on a forest track

that negotiates the same stream and which we follow for 3 kilometres. Some way higher up, the track crosses the stream and there is a pair of zigzags to gain height, always within a fantastic wood with a great variety of deciduous and high mountain species. We thus reach a small meadow on the left, where a dry stream drops. We should pay attention to the orange markers on rocks and trees. Here we embark on the longest and most demanding climb on the route, which has a series of short zigzags on stony ground, but always under the cover of an extensive conifer wood. This climb culminates in the **Coll de Moixeró Nord** (1,979 m), from where we take in the highest part of the Moixeró range, one of the most select spaces of the Pyrenees.

The continuation of the path leads us directly to the **Coll de Moixeró Sud** (1,972 m),

▲ **Coll del Raset**

in a really memorable section. Below us we leave behind an old shepherd's cabin, while ahead of us, to the east, we take in an immense carpet of grass. On our right, close-up is the **Pic de Moixeró** (2,091 m) while we cross the **Pla de Moixeró** (2,003 m), a spot where the cattle usually gather in the summer. On this second third of the route we follow the red and white markers of the GR-150 path, always on the line of the crest of the Moixeró range. We immediately drop down to the **Coll del Raset** (2,059 m), leaving on the right the beginning of the fantastic *Camí de la Canal de la Serp* (the Snake's Canal Path) towards the town of Bagà. From here we enter conifer woods again and start a strong climb with points on which we have to scramble with our hands, since the path progresses along the reliefs of rock that cover the upper part of the range and which culminate in the mythical **Penyes Altes de Moixeró** (2,279 m). The south slope of these crags has an impressive rocky wall, with a superb panorama overlooking the Cadí range and the massif of Pedraforca. Our route always continues eastwards, towards the Pic de la Tosa d'Alp, identifiable for being the highest point of the ski resorts of Masella and La Molina. From the Penyes Altes we must go back a little and take the red and white marked path again. We then undertake a descending bypass along a craggy area as far as the **Coll de Molins** (2,060 m), and from here up towards the **Coll de la Miquela** (2,162 m), with technical points on more rock projections. The last

section that follows the crest is much more comfortable, alternating between meadows and woods until the historic pass of the **Coll de Jou** (2,024 m). Here we change direction completely to head north, towards the village of Urús. We use the short-distance path (white and yellow markers), which coincides with an old path that crosses the range. We set off on a steep descent with zigzags until reaching the **Clot de Fontllebrera** (1,720 m), a point where the slope levels out and the path is wider and easier going. Further below we reach the lovely spot of the **Font Llebrera** (1,520 m), which feeds the **Fontllebrera stream.** A little further on we come to a fence and start the climb via what is known as **Roca d'Urús** (1,550 m), a craggy and spectacular cliff over the **valley of Fontllebrera**. We then enjoy a pleasant path through the wood, which culminates in the crossroads of paths of the **Coll de Jovell** (1,520 m), where we should pay careful attention to the signposted path that descends straight steeply through the final dense wood. The quiet village of **Urús** (1,240 m) appears in the middle of a plain that dominates the whole valley of the Cerdanya. The village features an old washhouse with fountain, as well as its Romanesque-style church.

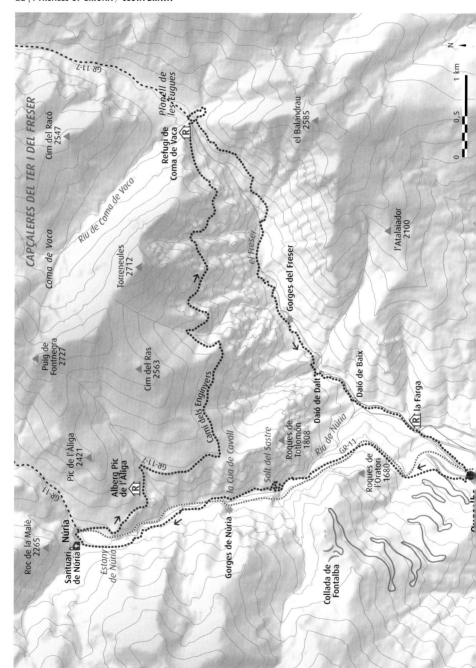

3

THE GORGES OF NÚRIA AND THE FRESER

▲ The sanctuary of Núria in autumn

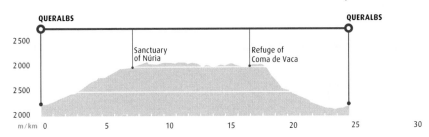

Methods
Path walking, trekking

Distance
25 km

Duration
8 - 10 h

Gradients
+1,350 m / -1,350 m

Located at the foot of one of the most emblematic Pyrenean destinations of the whole range, the demanding route proposed can be divided into three sections. The first, the climb up the historic path across the rocky gorges of Núria; the second, the unforgettable path over the gorges of the Freser, and the third, the fantastic descent that follows the course of the river Freser.

ROUTE

Arriving in the village of **Queralbs** (1,220 m), with its splendid 11th century church of Sant Jaume, we find the signpost of the GR-11 towards the sanctuary of Núria (red and white markers), which we follow throughout the section that negotiates the course of the river Núria, using the historic path that for so many centuries was covered by shepherds and hermits. Although today the rack train has distorted this landscape between abrupt mountains, it cannot be denied that the outline of the path still conserves a major part of its attractiveness due to the accumulation of reliefs and landscapes concentrated in the impressive **gorges of Núria**. The large walls of the **Roques de Totlomón**, the drop of the **Salt del Sastre** (1,600 m) or the **waterfall of the Cua de Cavall** (1,750 m), are some of these spots that make the climb up the popular really fun, marked by the signs of the Trans-Pyrenean Walk. In the end, the arrival to the **Sanctuary of Núria** (1,970 m) is

thrilling, despite being a spot excessively cared for as a symbol of pro-Catalan feeling with Christian roots, as the tiny **hermitage** confirms devoted to Saint Gil, the first inhabitant of this spot around the year 700 AD. Once this section of the route has been covered, you undoubtedly fancy stretching out on the well-cared for grass for a while, which surrounds the artificial lake constructed in 1956. The large complex of the sanctuary was established during the first third of the 20th century, although the original guesthouse, of which nothing remains, dates back to 1162. Today the Sanctuary of Núria is above all a high mountain tourist spot, with a hotel-restaurant with all comforts, as well as some alpine skiing slopes, done here since 1921. In 1931 the rack train entered into service, with stations in Ribas de Freser, Queralbs and the sanctuary itself. Even though the **valley of Núria** is one of the prides of the Catalan government –in fact it is owned by the Generalitat de Catalunya–, it is chiefly a major mountainous zone, with five small valleys of glacial origin that come together on the same plain as the sanctuary, where there is no lack of obligatory paths to climb up to peaks and passes. In fact the irregular perimeter that makes up these peaks, which coincides with the frontier crest and which can be covered on foot in its entirety, is known as the **Olla de Núria**, or pot. To continue on our route we must climb a grassy slope heading southeast, towards the visible location of the **Pic de l'Àliga** hostel (2,120 m), which coincides with a section of ski slope with a cable-car

▲ The way between Queralbs and the Sanctuary of Núria

▲ **Spectacular views from the "Camí dels Enginyers"**

above. A variant of the GR-11 leaves from below this hostel, known popularly as the *Camí dels Enginyers* (Engineers' Path), which flanks the **valley of the Freser** by its high part, with the **Pic de Torreneules** (2,711 m) in the highest part and the **Pic de Balandrau** (2,584 m) on the other side. It is a long and spectacular path, with some brusque descents and climbs that cross streams and spurs which at some points even have chains to help pass along. With this in mind, it is best to avoid this path if there is snow or ice, which may remain until early summer or appear in the first days of autumn. The final destination, the **refuge of Coma de Vaca** (1,995 m), stands out for the beauty of its location, a flat area of grass

where several streams converge. The origin of the refuge is connected to the old hydro-electric plant that gave its name to the path we have followed since the Sanctuary of Núria. The final and direct descent across the **gorges of the Freser** is within a very rocky setting, although the closeness of waterfalls and the forest cover help keep cool during the hottest days. The path comes out on a cemented track and from here to the **La Farga hostel** (1,170 m), alongside the road leading to Queralbs.

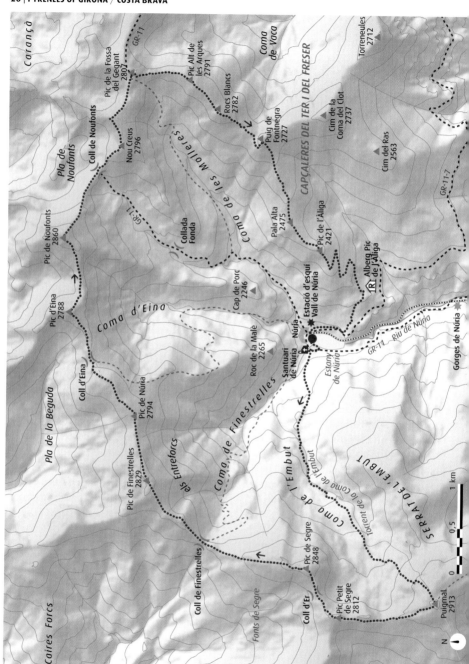

Carançà

GR-11

Pic de la Fossa
del Gegant
2807

Pic Alt de
les Arques
2791

Coma
de Vaca

Torreneules
2712

Coll de Noufonts

Rocs Blancs
2782

Puig de
Fodinegra
2727

Cim de la
Coma del Clot
2737

CAPÇALERES DEL TER I DEL FRESER

Pla de
Noufonts

Nou Creus
2796

Cim del Ras
2563

GR-11-7

Pic de Noufonts
2860

GR-11

Coma de les Molleres

Collada
Fonda

Pala Alta
2475

Pic de l'Àliga
2421

Alberg Pic
de l'Àliga

Pic d'Eina
2788

Coma d'Eina

Cap de Porc
2246

Estació d'esquí
Vall de Núria

R

Núria

GR-11 — Riu de Núria

Gorges de Núria

Coll d'Eina

Roc de la Malè
2265

Santuari
de Núria

Pla de la Beguda

Pic de Núria
2794

Estany
de Núria

els Entreforcs

Coma de Finestrelles

Coma de l'Embut

Pic de Finestrelles
2829

Torrent de la Coma de l'Embut

SERRAT DE L'EMBUT

Caires Forcs

Pic de Segre
2848

1 km

0.5

Coll de Finestrelles

Pic Petit
de Segre
2812

0

Coll d'Er

Fonts de Segre

Puigmal
2913

N

4 THE OLLA DE NÚRIA

4

▲ On the Coll de Noucreus

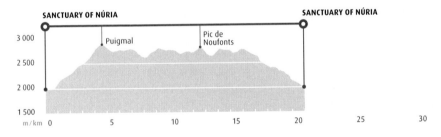

Methods
Path walking, trekking

Distance
21 km

Duration
7 - 9 h

Gradients
+1,950 m / -1,950 m

The Sanctuary of Núria is without doubt the most emblematic destination of the Pyrenees of Girona, surrounded by an exceptional mountain perimeter. The popular high mountain circuit that links all the peaks of this perimeter is rightly the leitmotiv of our route, which has many points to cut it short and adapt it to each person's interests or needs.

ROUTE

Our starting and return point is the **Sanctuary of Núria** (1,970 m) using before and after the historic rack train that climbs up to this spot from the villages of Ribes de Freser and Queralbs, a mountain train line opened in 1931 that enabled an increase and improvement in the tourist facilities linked to the sanctuary itself. The choice of direction of the walk firstly takes us up towards the main peak of the series –Puigmal–, from where we can go along the Olla de Núria to the point we wish. We should take into account that doing the whole route across fifteen peaks of over 2,000 metres requires a great physical effort and may also end up being very dangerous in case of unstable weather or with risk of rainfall. The start of the path to Puigmal is next to the camping area, and immediately negotiates a steep slope diagonally to enter into the wild **stream of La Coma de l'Embut**. For a few moments we move inside this space among abrupt reliefs, but gradually the slopes widen to become a much more open climb, within a marvellous high mountain setting. In the final part we must face a steep slope between large rocks that ends at the very peak of **Puigmal** (2,913 m), the ceiling of the region, with a sensational 360° panoramic view. From here begins the series of peaks and passes that mark the frontier crest, always with the valleys of the French side to the north. In the first section we climb the **Pic Petit del Segre** (2,812 m) and the **Pic del Segre** (2,848 m), until the **Coll de Finestrelles** (2,604 m), the first pass from where we can descend directly to the Sanctuary of Núria. We then embark on a tough climb to the **Pic de Finestrelles** (2,829 m), and from here another much gentler one to the **Pic de Núria** (2,794 m).

Next comes the **Coll de Núria** (2,684 m) –also called the Coll d'Eina–, where the main path passes, between the town of Eina, on the French side, and the Sanctuary of Núria. At this point we have now covered half of the Olla de Núria and should think carefully if we are capable of completing the rest of the route, with constant climbs and descents of craggy peaks. The next section covers the **Pic d'Eina** (2,789 m) and the **Pic de Noufonts** (2,867 m) until the **Coll de Noufonts** (2,658 m), the third pass from which you can go down to the sanctuary. We leave to the side an old stone refuge, which may be useful in case of need, and we climb to the **Pic de Noucreus** (2,799 m). Immediately we reach the dramatic **Coll de Noucreus** (2,795 m), where we find the new iron crosses that commemorate the death of a group of people when they tried to cross

▲ **In the area around Puigmal**

▲ Walkers around the Sanctuary of Núria

this pass during a storm. A little further on we reach the **Pic de la Fossa del Gegant** (2,808 m), which speaks to us of legendary times, with a spectacular panoramic view over the **cirque of Carançà**. On the Coll de Noucreus we have the last chance to go down directly to the Sanctuary of Núria – recommendable-, starting right here the return via the rough crest of the **Serra del Mig**, which closes the Olla de Núria on its eastern flank. We head southwest and go over, one after the other, the **Pic Alt de les Arques** (2,791 m), the **Pic Baix de les Arques** (2,782 m), the **Pic de Rocs Blancs** (2,765 m) and the **Pic de Font Negre** (2,722 m). From this last peak we have to embark on the steep descent with sensational views, pass-ing the **Pic de la Pala** (2,475 m) and the **Pic de l'Àliga** (2,471 m), with a final part over the outline of the ski slopes of the small resort of the valley of Núria until the popu-lar **Pic de l'Àliga** hostel (2,120 m), and from here to the sanctuary.

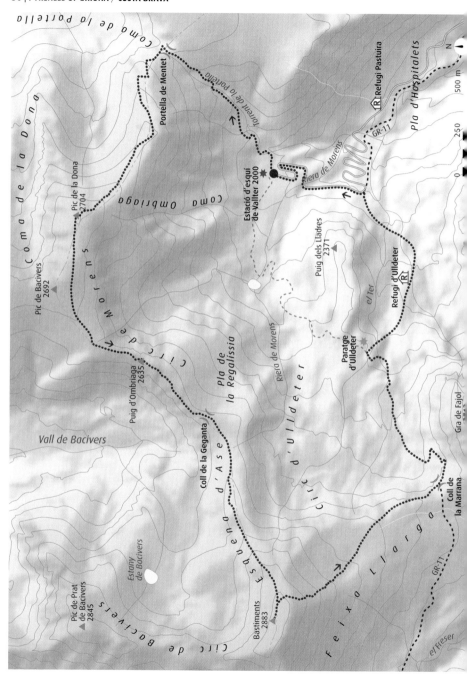

Coma de la Portella

Coma de la Dona

Portella de Mentet

Torrent de la Portella

Refugi Pastuira ®

Pla d'Hospitalets

N

500 m

250

0

Pic de la Dona
2704

Coma Ombriaga

Estació d'esquí
de Vallter 2000

Riera de Morens

GR-11

Pic de Bacivers
2692

Circ de Morens

Puig dels Lladres
2371

el Ter

Refugi d'Ulldeter ®

Puig d'Ombriaga
2635

Pla de
la Regalissia

Riera de Morens

Paratge
d'Ulldeter

Vall de Bacivers

Coll de la Geganta

Circ d'Ulldeter

Gra de Fajol

Estany
de Bacivers

Esquena d'Ase

Coll de
la Marrana

Pic de Prat
de Bacivers
2845

Bastiments
2883

Feixa llarga

GR-11

Circ de Bacivers

el Freser

5 THE CIRQUE OF ULLDETER

▲ **Pic de Bastiments**

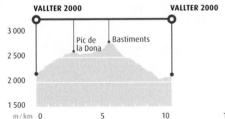

Methods
Path walking, trekking

Distance
11 km

Duration
4-5 h

Gradients
+950 m / -950 m

Thanks to the road that goes to the Vallter 2000 ski resort, the trekker has great accessibility to embark on this magnificent circular route. Despite the presence of modern infrastructures, the high mountain landscape is impressive and enables us to enjoy a marvellous half-day walk at the end of the valley of Camprodón.

ROUTE

The starting and arrival point is the final car park of **the Vallter 2000 ski resort** (2,150 m), which is also where the road ends that comes from Camprodón and Setcases. The signposted path leaves from behind the main services building of the resort as far as the pass of the **Portella de Mentet** (2,412 m), which initially goes through a small wood of black pines and then negotiates a ravine with a steep slope. On the final part of the climb, we leave another path on the right to the peaks of Roca Colom and Costabona. Once at the pass we discover the French side, and the path drops towards the village of Mentet. From here we always follow the path that goes all along the frontier crest as far as the Pic de Bastiments, which also marks the perimeter of the cirque of Ulldeter. First we climb up to the **Pic de la Dona** (2,704 m), from where there are some fantastic views, with the **valley of Mentet** on one side and the **valley of Bacivers** on the other.

We then set off on the most pleasant and comfortable section of the route, over extensive knolls, to the **Coll de la Geganta** (2,607 m), with the solitary **cirque of Bacivers** at our feet. From this point we face the toughest and most difficult section, with a steep climb over a slippery area of large rocks, where our path makes short zigzags. We thus reach a large iron cross, and a little higher up, the peak of the **Pic de Bastiments** (2,883 m). Towards the south we take in the whole of the **valley of the Freser**, in a mountain area of great purity, confirmed by the presence in the area of many herds of chamois, as well as colonies of vultures. The downward path towards the extensive Coll de la Marrana is steep to begin with, among unstable rocks, and a gentler end part over meadows of dry grass, where it is a pleasure

to relax while taking in all the reliefs of the **cirque of Ulldeter**.

On the **Coll de la Marrana** (2,530 m) we connect with the route of the GR-11 path, coming from the Sanctuary of Núria, which we follow for a while in the direction towards the refuge of Ulldeter. Initially, we start up another very steep descent, although the path makes zigzags over a more stable terrain. We thus reach a flat area, where a water spring marks the birth of the river Ter. We are at the spot known as **Ulldeter** (2,395 m). Once here, for a few moments we enter into the area of the Vallter 2000 ski resort, with several ski slopes all around. On the left we leave a track that leads directly to the main car park of the resort, but the recommendation to enjoy the wild nature a little more is to continue along the GR-11 path, passing beneath the channels of the **Pic Gra de Fajol** (2,712 m) to the door of the **refuge of Ulldeter** (2,235 m), surrounded by a fantastic wood of black pines. The history of this popular refuge dates back to 1909, with an original emplacement close to the spot of Ull de Ter, where you can still see some remains of old demolished walls. The current building, from 1959, offers accommodation and meals throughout the year. The downhill path to the road of the Vallter 2000 ski resort passes to the left of the **river Ter** and comes out on a large bend (2,080 m), from where, to end the circuit, the last few remaining metres are on gently rising asphalt.

5

▲ The cirque of Bacivers from the Pic de la Dona   ▼ Climbing towards the Pic de Bastiments

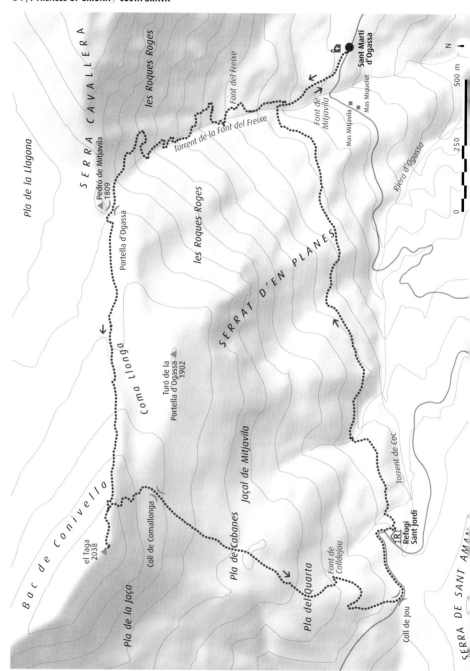

6 THE TAGA AND THE SERRA CAVALLERA

6

▲ Panorama of the village of Bruguera

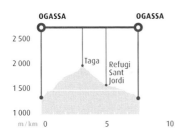

Methods
Path walking, trekking

Distance
8 km

Duration
3 - 4 h

Gradients
+750 m / -750 m

This series of mountains marks the limit of peaks higher than 2,000 metres in the lands of Girona, providing numerous routes and excellent access. Due to the steep gradients that must be tackled, the basic route up to the peak of the Taga requires a good level of fitness, although the grassy terrain and some magnificent views are just rewards for the effort.

ROUTE

To find the starting and arrival point of the route you have to take the road that joins Sant Joan de les Abadesses and the small village of **Ogassa** (1,000 m). From here we go along a mountain road in good condition, but always steep, until reaching a fork at the foot of the imposing wall of the **Serra Cavallera**. On the right we leave the diversion of a cemented track in the direction of the church of Sant Martí de Surroca and Camprodon. We have to take the track in the opposite direction, also cemented and with very steep sections that leads to the **church of Sant Martí d'Ogassa** (1,320 m). Here there is a small parking space and the beginning of a very direct path to the Pic del Taga, which is above us. We always follow the yellow markings, and at the beginning we negotiate a stony path with some electrified fencing to control the cattle, which we must close again after passing through. On reaching some meadows, we come to a water trough and the surprising spot of the **Font del Freixe** (1,500 m),

with a large area of boxwood trees that cover a large part of spot. Being careful to follow the markings on a rather maze-like and winding path, we climb a series of steep slopes along a majestic grassy side, situated between the mountain of the Taga on the left and the Serra Cavallera on the right. The outline of zigzags help overcome this climb considerably, culminating in the pass of the **Portella d'Ogassa** (1,792 m), where there is a crossroads of paths. Heading west, always over extensive meadows, we complete the rest of the climb to the large cross that crowns the **Pic del Taga** (2,038 m), a first-class geodesic apex that provides a full panorama of all of the valley of Ribes from a bird's eye view. From here we descend directly south and on a steep slope, over the

▲ Church of Sant Martí de Surroca

6

▲ Wakers descending from the Pic del Taga to the Coll de Jou

side of grassy meadows that requires care in not slipping.

Half way down we cross the **plain of Cabanes** (1,794 m), a good point to rest the legs and take in new views of the area. We finally reach the pass of the **Coll de Jou** (1,635 m), where the continuation of the cemented track continues that joins Ogassa with the pretty village of **Bruguera** (1,200 m), a hidden spot surrounded by fantastic bends. On the other side of the track, from the Coll de Jou itself, a path leaves tempting you to climb up to the peak of the **Puig de Sant Amand** (1,851 m), very popular with walkers from the county of Ripollès and which conceals some interesting reliefs of calcareous rock. We return towards Sant Martí d'Ogassa, along a path that goes a little below the pass, very close to the rustic **refuge of Sant Jordi** (1,600 m), and which crosses the streams that feed **Riera d'Ogassa**. We thus advance all along the south side of the Taga mountain, leaving a little below us the rural tourism guest house of **Mas de Mitjavila** (1,310 m), with an option of leaving the cemented track at this point or continue the encirclement to the **stream of the Font del Freixe** (1,400 m). Once here we repeat the path that we started out on in the opposite direction.

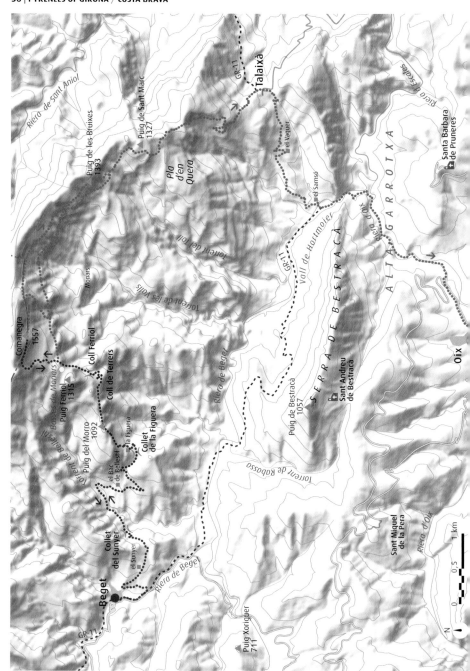

7 THE MASSIF OF COMANEGRA

▲ On the Cingle del Pujant del Llop

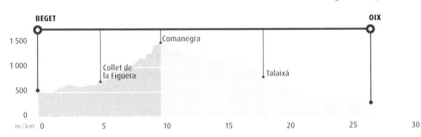

Methods
Path walking, trekking

Distance
20 km (route there and back)

Duration
6-7 h

Gradients
+1,300 m / -1,300 m

Between the village of Beget and the valley of Sant Aniol extends the wildest pat pf the Alta Garrotxa area, which also concentrates the highest altitudes, with suggestions for routes that provide two options. The first consists of climbing to the peak of the Puig de Comanegra with a route there and back. The second is a full crossing via the peaks of the massif to the village of Oix.

ROUTE

Hidden in a corner separated from the world until just a few decades ago, the village of **Beget** (540 m) reflects the charac-ter of the Alta Garrotxa very well, an authentic no-man's land. To arrive there we have two bendy roads, from either Camprodón or from Oix. In the latter case, it is worth thinking about using two vehicles, one in each village, to ensure the start and end of the route as a one-way crossing. It is also a good idea to reserve rooms in one of the guest houses we find in the different districts of the area. In any case, the visit to Beget, before or after the trip, takes us to one of the best-conserved Pyrenean villages, which features a remarkable Romanesque church devoted to Saint Cristobal, within a network of narrow streets and stone houses spread between two streams that make up the **Riera de Beget**. To find the beginning of the route it is best to take the path parallel to the stream until coming out at the road from Oix. A little

further on the climb starts on the forest track that leads to the **El Sunyer** country guesthouse (630 m). The track continues a few kilometres more at the foot of the massif of Comanegra. On crossing the **Collet del Sunyer** (670 m), the track descends a little to cross the **stream of Bellestil**, an area from which you get a really good perspective of this part of the massif. On restarting the climb along the same track, we leave on our left the entrance to **Mas del Bac de Bellestil** (700 m), a point where the slope sharpens with a series of zigzags. We thus reach the **Collet de la Figuera** (860 m), a pretty spot from where we no longer follow the route of the track.

On the left, from the Collet de la Figuera, we find the yellow markers of the signposted

▲ Sant Cristòfol de Beget

path to Comanegra, with an initial part of gentle bends until the ruins of **Mas de la Figuera** (900 m). From here on we should pay attention finding the markers through a holm-oak wood. We set off on a very steep climb among the spectacular crags of rock of the **Puig del Morro** (1,092 m). The first rest comes on reaching the **Coll de Terrers** (1,097 m), from where a memorable section begins along an aesthetic spur among varied vegetation that leads us to the **Coll Ferriol de Baix** (1,140 m), and from here to the **Coll Ferriol** (1,192 m), after a steep slope. Before us is the prominent **Puig Ferriol** (1,315 m). To climb it we have to deal with a new series of steep slopes through a fantastic wood of mixed species. On ending this climb, we set off on the extensive meadows that surround the reservoir of **Monars** (1,280 m), a historic cattle point at the foot of the Puig de Comanegra, accessible via a forest track that comes from the village of Rocabruna. Once here, the direct climb to the peak of the highest point in the county of La Garrotxa –the **Puig de Comanegra** (1,557 m)–, requires following the path with green and orange markers that negotiate the large slopes of grass on the southern side of the mountain, with a final section over a rocky landscape under the cover of a beech wood, now on the northern or French side. To return to Beget we retrace our way out, although we have a possible variant signposted from the reservoir of Monars, along a path that drops to the old village of Monars, and from here along a spectacular ravine until reencountering the track from the Collet de la Figuera.

FROM THE PUIG DE COMANEGRA TO OIX VIA THE PUIG DE SANT MARC AND TALAIXÀ ◄ V

Distance
27 km (Route BEGET – OIX)

Duration
8 - 10 h

Gradients
+1,500 m / -1,620 m

This variant of the trip is only recommendable for experienced trekkers and when having a large margin of daylight. If you have climbed up to the Puig de Comanegra, you should take the path that follows the whole crest southeast, firstly through the magical beech woods that cover the north side, then over extensive knolls of grass. If you have not climbed to Comanegra, from the reservoir of Monars you should go to the end of the forest track, where an indicator shows a path below the abovementioned crest of peaks of which the Puig de Sant Marc also forms a part. The two paths link up on going through the area of the **Puig de les Bruixes** (1,393 m), where we recover the yellow marks as the only route guide to Talaixà. The climb to the peak of the

Puig de Sant Marc (1,327 m) is also optional, though we recommend it in order to appreciate what is considered the best panorama over the peaks and valleys of the Alta Garrotxa, one of the most remote and wildest spaces on the whole Pyrenean range. Below the impressive calcareous crag of this peak we cross the last beech wood along a winding maze-like path.

The arrival to the bucolic spot of the **Pla d'en Quera** (1,210 m) reveals a small plateau of grass with equally privileged views. From here we set off on a technically difficult descent along a small channel of rock that is given the name of **Pujant del Llop** (1,150 m), below which we meet up with the very dense holm-oak and oak wood again. Our path, always with the guidance of the yellow marks, outlines a steep descent through the wood, until coming to an area of old terraces. Here we should pay attention on passing some crossroads. The path then goes back into a very dense wood, until reaching the ruins of the old village of **Talaixà** (760 m), with its church as an emblem and a small walkers' refuge that invites us to take a rest. Once here, we link up with the GR-11 path (red and white marks), returning to Beget, passing by **Mas del Vaquer** (610 m). Having reached this enclave, we go along a forest track for quite a while until coming to the path again on the left. On the final descent to reach the end of the mysterious **valley of Hortmoier** we enjoy the richness of the forest, though being very careful not to slip. The final point of the descent is the popular **walkway of Samsó** (370 m), recently remodelled to make it easier to cross the bed of the **stream of Beget**. A little further on we come to the forest track that leads to Oix, and therefore stop following the GR-11 path. Ahead of us, to Oix, we have the last 4 km of the route, always on the forest track, which in the first section crosses the sensational cliffs of the **Grau d'Escales**, where the stream of Beget and the **stream of Oix** meet, which at the same time divides the **Serra de Bestracà** and the **crest of Ferran**. A little further on we drop down to a spectacular bridge of medieval origin, from where we start a steady climb to a rural guesthouse and the road between Beget and Oix. A few metres before ending the trip in the small village of **Oix** (420 m), we pass beneath its elegant medieval castle, within a very calm mountainous setting with a great deal of character.

▲ Contemplating Comanegra from the Puig de les Bruixes

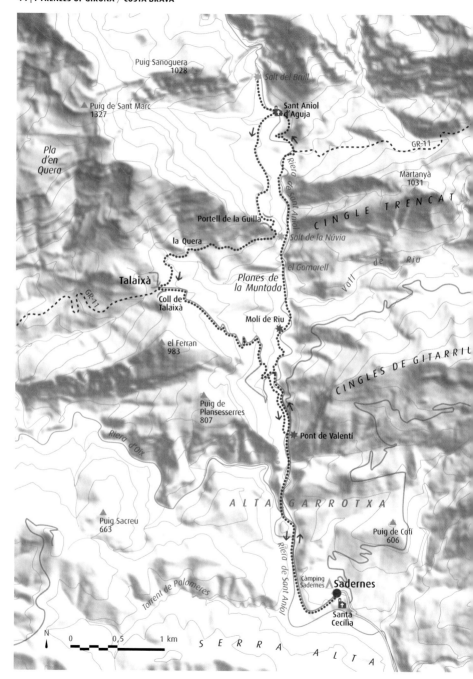

Puig Sanoguera
1028

Salt del Brull

Puig de Sant Marc
1327

Sant Aniol
d'Aguja

GR-11

Martanyà
1031

Pla
d'en
Quera

CINGLE TRENCAT

Portell de la Guilla

la Quera

Salt de la Núvia

de Riu

el Gomarell

volt

Planes de
la Muntada

Talaixà

Coll de
Talaixà

GR-11

Molí de Riu

el Ferran
983

CINGLES DE GITARRIL

Puig de
Plansesserres
807

Pont de Valentí

Riera d'Oix

ALTA GARROTXA

Puig Sacreu
663

Riera de Sant Aniol

Puig de Cofí
606

Camping
Sadernes

Sadernes

Santa
Cecília

Torrent de Palomeres

SERRA ALTA

N

0   0,5   1 km

8

THE VALLEY OF SANT ANIOL

▲ General panorama of the valley of Sant Aniol

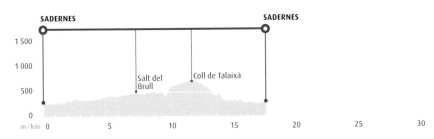

Methods
Path walking, trekking

Distance
18 km

Duration
5-6 h

Gradients
+650 m / -650 m

Located in the heart of the Natural Space of the Alta Garrotxa, it is one of the most popular destinations of the Girona Pyrenees. Precisely for this reason, we do not recommend making this trip during the summer, due to the large influx of visitors. Spring and autumn are ideal times to enjoy all the magic of this valley, although you should take care on some sections of the path, irregular and stony.

ROUTE

With access via a good road from the village of Montagut, the enclave of **Sadernes** (300 m) is the entrance to the valley, where there is a popular hostel-restaurant, a campsite and a

Romanesque-style church devoted to Saint Cecilia. The road ends in Sadernes and a forest track begins that for the first kilometres has a series of parking spaces for vehicles. Even though we can use these car parks to save 2.5 km of track, we set the start and end of the route in Sadernes. Immersed in an extraordinary setting of calcareous walls, where climbing is a very common activity, we cover the first section on the track, which crosses the **stream of Sant Aniol** a couple of times over bridges. We thus reach the historic **bridge of Valentí** (330 m), of medieval origin, which we leave on our left (we don't have to cross it). A little further ahead we come across a chain*, leaving on the right the branch of track that climbs to the

▲ **Well in the stream of Sant Aniol**

heights of the massif of Bassegoda via the valley of Riu. We continue straight to negotiate the stream of Sant Aniol, which we cross shortly after to progress through an area between fields and woods. We must follow the yellow markers at all times, ignoring the signs to Talaixà on the left, which is where we propose returning by. After passing alongside the ruins of the **Molí de Riu** (350 m), we cross the spot of **Les Planes de la Muntada** and reach the astonishing **reservoir of El Gomarell** (360 m). Here we must cross the stream again to the other side by a stony pass, starting a spectacular section along the inside of a gorge. The route becomes very slippery and requires a great deal of care. Halfway along we come to a **hanging bridge** (400 m) which allows us to pass from one side of the river to the other, although we immediately cross back via a pass over stones.

Further on we connect with the GR-11 path (red and white marks), always staying close to the stream of Sant Aniol until coming to the last walkway that takes us to **Sant Aniol d'Aguja** (440 m), an old monastic complex that dates back to the 11th century, with a hermitage and the remains of an old guesthouse reconverted into a walkers' refuge. The path leaves from a popular fountain to the spot of the **Salt del Brull** (500 m), some 10 minutes away, which stands out for the large waterfall in the middle of a gorge. Once again in Sant Aniol d'Aguja, we set off again along the GR-11 path to the old village of Talaixà, enjoying a spectacular route that flanks a series of rocky reliefs above the val-

▲ Talaixà

ley of Sant Aniol. This section features the pass of the **Portell de la Guilla** (560 m), where there is a series of short descents and climbs, and above all the pass of the **Salt de la Núvia** (550 m), a natural balcony between majestic slopes. At this very point we have a path that drops directly to Les Planes de la Muntada, very useful in case we need to cut short the route. However, we continue along the GR-11 path, with a constant climb that will take us past the ruins of the old settlement of **La Quera** (660 m), and later the pass of the **Coll de Talaixà** (760 m). The old village of Talaixà appeared documented for the first time in 872 and still had 139 inhabitants in 1918. From then on it was gradually abandoned, until recently a couple of houses

were recovered on the Coll de Talaixà itself, which include a walkers' refuge. Following the signs, we leave the GR-11 to begin the return journey to Sadernes along the route that goes to the bridge of Valentí, on a path signposted with green and orange marks that has many zigzags through the wood. In the low part we pass some crosses and forks until re-meeting the forest track of the start of the route.

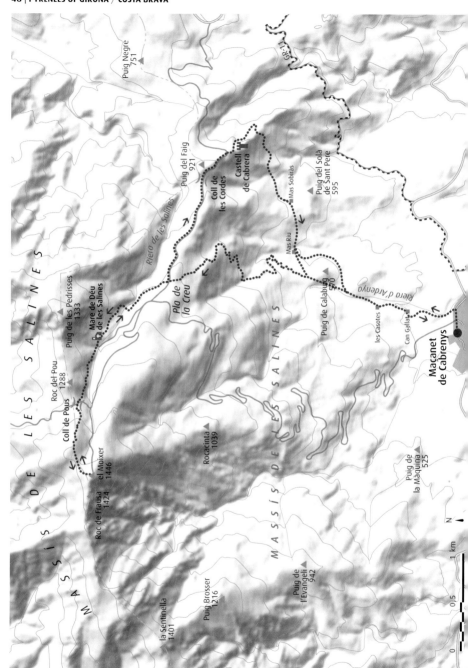

9 THE MASSIF OF LES SALINES

▲ Sanctuary of Les Salines

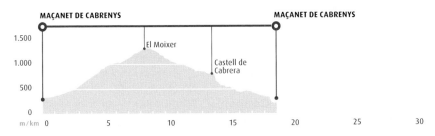

Methods
Path walking, trekking

Distance
19 km

Duration
6-7 h

Gradients
+1,100 m / -1,100 m

Circular route on a massif recognised as a Space of Natural Interest, which represents a veritable biological island with an outstanding presence of Mediterranean and sub-humid woods of great value. A loop that links up the GR-11 and GR-10 trans-Pyrenean paths favours the recovery of historical memory in a region that no longer recognises the old frontiers.

ROUTE

Situated between two streams at the foot of the massif, the village of **Maçanet de Cabrenys** (370 m) still possesses all the structure of the fortified precinct of medieval origin,

▲ Maçanet de Cabrenys

with a lovely network of alleyways and an outstanding 12th-century church. To find the start of our route you have to go along Carrer Tramuntana to the **stream of Ardenya**. Once here we can enjoy a landscape beneath the shelter of a lovely coppice until reaching a corner, where we leave to the right the start of the popular forest track for vehicles, of 12 km, to the sanctuary of Salines. Following carefully the markers with the characteristic red and white strips of the long-distance GR path, we begin to walk along the *Camí Vell* (Old Way), which continues negotiating the course of the stream of Ardenya. In a moment we cross a wide meadow with the farm of **Can Gallat** (390 m) on the right, but we immediately enter a delightful cork wood

with the usual presence of flocks of sheep driven by the last shepherds in the region. Shortly after the pretty **farmhouse of Les Casotes** (430 m) appears, where we enjoy a short section of path between old dry stone walls that comes out above the stream of Ardenya, which we cross to continue along a narrow and rocky path that flanks the **Puig de Calabuig** (570 m). We leave a marked path on the right that comes from the castle of Cabrera, which is the way back for us. Half way up we cross the **stream of Clot de les Cadiretes** (720 m), from where we set off on a path with continuous zigzags and steep gradient, within a magical wood decorated by large blocks of granite. Further on we come out into a clearing of the wood with remains of terraces of an old farmhouse, where *El Roc de l'Ermità* (The Rock of the Hermit) is, a large block that was used by the hermits of the sanctuary of Les Salines as a watchtower to take in the lands of Empordá.

A little higher we reach the **Pla de la Creu** (1,030 m), where we come across a forest track that joins the sanctuary of Les Salines and the village of Vajol, passing through the entrance to the castle of Cabrera, a route that we must follow after the not-to-be-missed visit to the sanctuary. Following the signs to France, we cross the track and go through a magnificent wood of wild pines, which shortly after becomes a phenomenal terrace. Just here we come across the beautiful course of the **stream of Les Salines** (1,030 m), where we should be careful of the rock surface and the dead leaves, which make the way a little slippery. Higher up we reach the **Font dels Tres Raigs** or *spring of the Three Spouts* (1,070 m), from where fresh water always springs. From here, some steps take us to the entrance of the historic **sanctuary of Les Salines** (1,080 m), surrounded by a bucolic meadow to which some herds of oxen occasionally come to graze, following a millenary tradition, since the name tells us that it was here where the local cowherds gathered the cattle to give them salt during the periods of transhumance. The origin of the site dates back to 1271, it was partially destroyed in 1590 due to religious wars, and completely restored throughout the 18th century.

The complex is made up of a church and rectory, a guesthouse that opens as a bar on holidays, and also a rustic walkers' refuge of free use. A little further on, beside the entrance track, is a small **cave** where, according to popular tradition, the image of a Virgin appeared.

The marked path to the **Coll dels Pous** (1,289 m) leads to the French side. We should ignore the marks of the GR-10 to follow at all times the yellow marks of a diffuse path through a dense beech wood. On the left appears a cemented track that culminates in the highest point of the massif, the **Pic Moixer** (1,446 m), crowned by a television booster station. We return once more the sanctuary, and from here to the forest track of the Pla de la Creu we head towards the castle of Cabrera, with a gradual descent to the **Coll de les Cordes** (900 m), where we begin to enjoy magnificent panoramas over the plain of Empordà and the gulf of Roses. Shortly after on the right appears the path to the remains of the **castle of Cabrera** (850 m), from the 11th century, which stands over a spectacular natural watchtower of rock. Paying attention to the yellow markers, we embark on a steep descent to the other side of the castle buttress, until coming to an easy path that passes through some surprising sand formations and comes out alongside the ruins of the **Mas del Sobiràs** (590 m). Further on we cross the **stream of the Clot del Dotres** (510 m), within a thick wood, with the pretty **Mas Riu** on the other side of a meadow. We immediately reach the crossroads of paths alongside the stream of Ardenya, from where we just have to retrace our steps of the outward journey.

▲ **Way of the sanctuary of Les Salines**

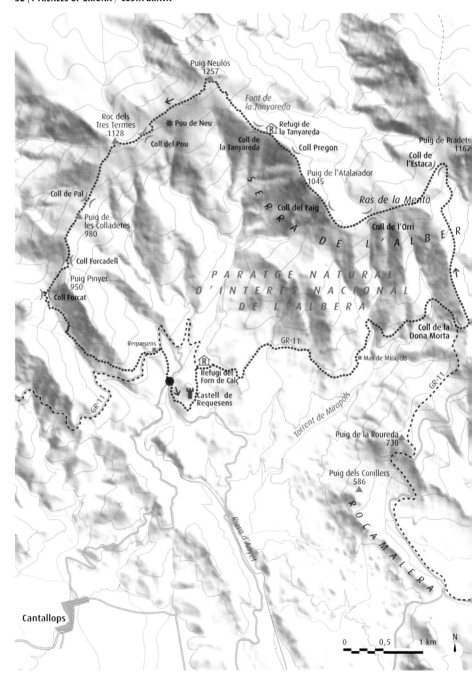

Puig Neulós
1257

Font de
la Tanyareda

Roc dels
Tres Termes
1128

Pou de Neu

Refugi de
la Tanyareda

Coll del Pou

Coll de
la Tanyareda

Coll Pregon

Puig de Pradets
1167

Coll de
l'Estaca

Puig de l'Atalaiador
1045

Coll de Pal

SERRA

Ras de la Menta

Coll del Faig

Coll de l'Orri

Puig de
les Colladetes
980

DE L'ALBER

Coll Forcadell

PARATGE NATURAL

Puig Pinyer
950

D'INTERÈS NACIONAL

Coll Forcat

DE L'ALBERA

Coll de la
Dona Morta

Requesens

GR-11

Mas de Miràpols

Refugi del
Forn de Calç

GR-11

GR-11

Castell de
Requesens

Torrent de Miràpols

Puig de la Roureda
730

Puig dels Conillers
586

R O C A M A L E R A

Riera d'Anyet

Cantallops

0   0,5   1 km

N

10 THE VALLEY OF REQUESENS AND PUIG NEULÓS

10

▲ Crossing beech woods in the area of Mirapols

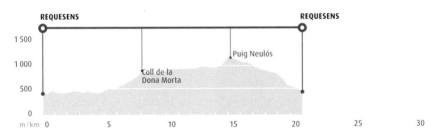

Methods
Path walking, trekking

Distance
21 km

Duration
7-8 h

Gradients
+1,100 m / -1,100 m

A high level circular route, in the heart of the Natural Park of L'Albera, it requires solid trekking know-how to be able to interpret a terrain with a lot of biodiversity. The route goes through many spots full of items of historical heritage that show very ancient human activity in harmony with the wild nature.

ROUTE

Planning this route requires going by private vehicle from the village of **Cantallops** (185 m), where you should take the popular forest track for 6 km to the castle of Requesens, emblematic in the region. The starting and return point is the fork of tracks besiode the lovely **stream of Requesens** (400 m), enjoying a wood repopulated 150 years ago, with species such as chestnut, poplar, plantain and even cedar. We find the branch path right here that climbs straight to what is called the "Cantina" of Requesens. On the right, below, we leave the branch to the village of Sant Climent de Sescebes, and on the right, above, the way to the castle. Following the markers, we climb through a fantastic holm-oak wood, first along a track and then a path with yellow markers, to the foot of the large wall of the **castle of Requesens** (515 m).

The origin of this fortification dates back to the 11th century, even though it was the end of the 19th century when it was completely rebuilt, giving it its monumental

▲ Castle of Requesens

stamp, although this did not avoid it being abandoned throughout the 20th century.

According to where we arrive, we must follow the wall to the last bend of the entrance track, from where a path leaves that goes to the refuge of the Forn de Calç slightly downhill, through another holm-oak coppice. On reaching a pretty pine grove, we come to a crossroads. We must link up on the right with the GR-11 path (red and white markers). A little further on we discover the surprising **refuge of the Forn de Calç** (480 m), situated on top of a monumental 17th-century lime kiln. We follow the route of the GR-11 at all times, starting a long section of track that gradually narrows until reaching the **Mas de Mirapols** (500 m), a settlement of medieval origin and currently abandoned.

On crossing the **stream of Mirapols** we start a lovely section of rising path, in a wild wood among ferns, hazelnut trees, oaks and beech trees. On reaching the **Coll de la Dona Morta** (700 m) we come to a marvellous oak wood and find a sign that marks the way to the Coll de l'Estaca (link with GR-10 and PR-C71). The opposite direction, towards the village of Vilamaniscle, tells us we are no longer following the route of the GR-11. To complete this connecting loop between the two paths that involve crossing the Pyrenees in their entirety, we recover the yellow markers once again. We thus head directly north. On the first section we flank the mountainous side until dropping to a secondary crest. On reaching a spectacular panoramic view, above some delightful granite formations, we can make out the now-

▲ Castle of Requesens

distant silhouette of the castle of Requesens. From here on we have to be very careful not to lose the markers, since the path becomes less defined on going through meadows and woods within an ecosystem of great richness. In any case, we always have on our right the enclosure that borders the large **estate of the Baussitges area**, where we discover a pretty stone cabin a little higher up. Now and again we encounter a steep ramp, with the appearance of other attractive rock formations and the remains of the outline of an old cattle route. Much care is required when coming to a dense beech wood, since here we have to find a passing point through the abovementioned enclosure, to reach an extensive meadow, turning slightly to the right. Crossing this point, we suddenly come to a new stone cabin and a plaque that recalls the ambush suffered by the two *maquis* –old guerrilla fighters and smugglers-, that took place her on the 26th of August 1949.

A little further up we can make out in the distance the marvellous pass of the Coll de l'Estaca, with the **Puig de Pradets** (1,167 m) and the **Puig dels Quatre Termes** (1,156 m) on the right. Before, though, we must cross a beech wood and an area of brambles until coming out to a slope in open country. Once at the **Coll de l'Estaca** (1,030 m), we cross an old enclosure that marks the line of the frontier, where there is a path indicator. From this moment on we follow the route of the GR-10 and PR-C71 paths heading west, alternating the red and white, and yellow markers and wooden posts over the **crest of the massif of the Albera**. To start, we cross the extensive knoll of grass known as the **Ras de la Menta** (1,065 m), just at the edge of a series of high category beech woods, adapted to the conditions that the climate imposes here. After completing a long crossing through fantastic alpine meadows with the view of the large telecommunication tower that crowns the Puig Neulós on the horizon, we reach the **Coll de l'Orri** (980 m). We then enter a beech wood and enjoy a very pleasant section of path to the **Coll del Faig** (990 m).

At the Coll del Faig we come to a new path indicator and the border stone no. 584, from where we go along a series of small climbs and drops in a magical beech wood. On our right we discover the **refuge of the Tanyareda** (1,050 m), hidden in the wood and useful if necessary. A little further on we reach the historic **spring of the Tanyareda** (1,060 m), at the foot of the large stretch of grass of the upper slopes of Puig Neulós, with a drinking trough for the livestock. We immediately tackle a steep climb to the peak of **Puig Neulós** (1,257 m), the highest point of the massif of La Albera, with a large French telecommunications tower on the side. From here we drop down beside the line of meadows that cover the crest, heading southwest, leaving on the right the road to the telecommunications tower, and to the left the frontier valley. We thus reach the **Coll del Pou de Neu** or *Snow Well* (1,110 m), the starting point of a forest track that con-

nects Puig Neulós with Requesens, and where we recommend spending a few minutes on the other side of the border fence. The reason is the discovery of the fantastic snow well, which is where its name comes from. A marked path leads us directly, in less than five minutes, to see this small work of 17th-century engineering.

A little further on we reach a bend in the road, leaving on the left the **Roc dels Tres Termes** (1,128 m). Here we should pay attention, since we stop following the GR-10 path to be guided by only the yellow path markers of the Short-Distance path to La Jonquera. We embark on a demanding descent on rocky buttresses, first through pine woods and then through beech woods, until reaching the solitary spot of **Coll Forcat** (830 m). Following the mandatory indicator, we return towards the valley of Requesens on an old path that turns into a stony forest track, always under the cover of the wood. We finally reach **Requesens** (510 m), an old farm settlement with a sanctuary dated 1704 devoted to the virgin of Requesens. The destination is also known for a farm that safeguards the conservation of the Albera cow and a historic "cantina" that serves homemade cooking. We reencounter the red and white marks of the GR-11 path, to the refuge of Forn de Calç, which comes out above the stream of Requesens, the point where we had set out on the route.

▲▼ Beech wood between Coll de L'Estaca and Puig Neulós

10

Walking routes between the rivers FLUVIÀ and TER

The inland areas of Girona have a series of massifs of a great biological and scenic richness. They also show a set of structures that clearly symbolises the great geological convulsion that represents the formation of the Iberian Peninsula and the rising of the Pyrenees. Between this range and the coastal range, the Serralada Litoral Catalana, we discover what is called the Serralada Transversal, which as its name suggests establishes the physical connection between two of the most important mountainous systems in the Catalan territory. The result of this structural fusion is the series of most important series of crags in Catalonia and one of the most important in Europe. The tectonic faults responsible for these spectacular enjambements also provided the existence of the hydrographic network that defines the whole territory from the peaks of the Pyrenees to the mouths of the rivers of the Costa Brava. With its 208 kilometres in length, the river Ter is the main river in Girona, a geographical symbol that extends from the Pyrenean frontier to the Mediterranean Sea, after making an improbable turn between the massif of Montseny and the Serralada Transversal. The second longest river is the Fluvià, at 97 kilometres, which springs from the buttresses of the Serralada Transversal and crosses the main volcanic space of the Iberian Peninsula –the volcanic zone of La Garrotxa–, before its end in the Natural Park of the Aiguamolls de l'Empordà.

From the walker's point of view, the Ruta del Ter, which literally follows the course of the river from the beginning to the end, is a basic tool for linking the natural spaces and villages that make up the heartlands of Girona. It is, without doubt, the two GR paths linked to the Pre-Pyrenees, the GR-1 and GR-2, which enable the most original routes to be outlined. In any case, our selection uses mainly short-distance paths, which in all the cases establish thematic routes or to cover emblematic geographic points.

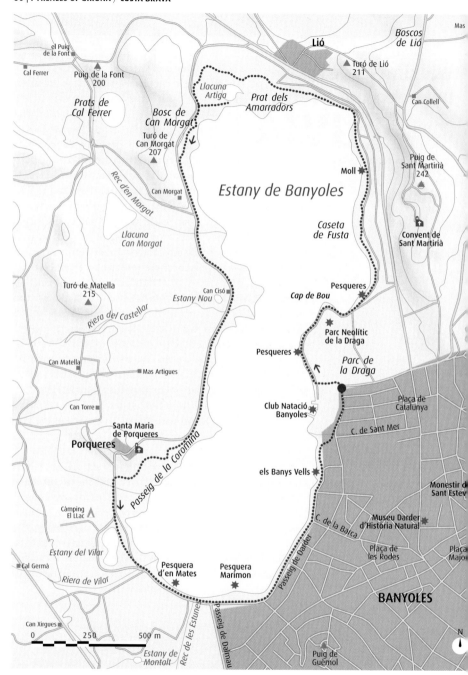

Boscos
de Lió

Mas

Lió

Turó de Lió
211

Can Collell

el Puig
de la Font

Cal Ferrer

Puig de la Font
200

Prats de
Cal Ferrer

Bosc de
Can Morgat

Llacuna
Artiga

Prat dels
Amarradors

Turó de
Can Morgat
207

Puig de
Sant Martirià
242

Moll

Rec d'en Morgat

Can Morgat

Estany de Banyoles

Llacuna
Can Morgat

Caseta
de Fusta

Convent de
Sant Martirià

Turó de Matella
215

Can Cisó

Estany Nou

Pesqueres

Cap de Bou

Parc Neolític
de la Draga

Riera del Castellar

Can Matella

Mas Artigues

Pesqueres

Parc de
la Draga

Can Torre

Santa Maria
de Porqueres

Porqueres

Passeig de la Coromina

Club Natació
Banyoles

Plaça de
Catalunya

C. de Sant Mer

Càmping
El Llac

els Banys Vells

Monestir d
Sant Estev

Estany del Vilar

Cal Germà

Pesquera
d'en Mates

Pesquera
Marimon

C. de la Barca

Museu Darder
d'Història Natural

Plaça de
les Rodes

Plaça
Majo

Riera de Vilar

Passeig de Darder

BANYOLES

Can Xirgues

0   250   500 m

Estany de
Montalt

Rec de les Estune

Passeig de Dalmau

Puig de
Guèmol

N

WALKING ROUTES BETWEEN THE RIVERS FLUVIÀ AND TER

1 THE LAKE OF BANYOLES

▲ Old "pesquera"

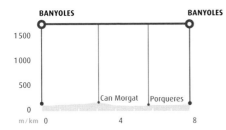

Methods
**Walking,
Nordic walking**

Distance
7-8 km

Duration
2-3 h

Gradients
+50 m / -50 m

The complete tour of the perimeter of the most well-known lake in Catalonian allows us to discover a unique ecosystem among bankside woods. The formation of this space is intimately linked to tectonic phenomena, with underground springs that infiltrate the calcareous terrain of the area, equidistant between the Pyrenees to the west, the plain of Empordà to the east, the river Flubià to the north and the Ter to the south.

ROUTE

We leave from the old centre of **Banyoles** (170 m), a town that was founded in 812, when some Benedictine monks founded a **monastery** dedicated to St Stephen. The same monks began the construction of canals for agricultural use, which today total six, around a marvellous lake that measures 2.1 km in length, is 750 metres wide and 6.6 kilometres diameter. At the end of the 19th century, on the bank of the lake closest to the town, the local residents built twenty beautiful fishing platforms in romantic style –called *pesqueras, fisheries*–, which ended up as leisure and free time areas and which today have different uses. In 1992, the lake of Banyoles hosted the rowing sports in the Barcelona Olympic Games, which converted both the lake itself and the modern installations of the **Club Natació Banyoles** into an international reference. Alongside these installations we find the fantastic **Park of La Draga**, where it is a great pleasure starting the walk on the path that borders the lake. It also features the precinct of a **Neolithic settlement** that dates from around 5300 BC. In any case, it is right here where we can decide on a variant of the route if we go to a part behind the La Draga Sports Centre, where the **Puig de Sant Martirià** (242 m) rises, with the remains of an old convent and the best viewpoint to take in a bird's eye view of the lake. To find the beginning of the path, which climbs the top of this hill, you have to go the end of Carrer Sant Martirià, a route signposted with the marks of the GR-1 path. It then continues via a local path to the **district of Lió**, to connect with the main path that goes around the lake at its northern tip.

The outline of the main path, heading north from the Park of La Draga, takes us to an attractive **wooden cabin** fitted out as a viewpoint, and then to a pretty **jetty** that is used as the finishing area of the regatta field. From here we embark on the tour around the extreme north of the lake, passing by the **Amaradors meadow**, which has a bird-watching observatory in order to observe the original ecosystem. We then head south, enjoying the section that conserves the best **bankside woods** of the lake. We must walk parallel to a county road, but always on the good surface of the marked path, which has different connections to a series of excellent **viewpoints**. We thus reach the sensational **church of Santa Maria de Porqueres** (185 m), from the 12th century, raised alongside the remains of an old Iberian settlement. All around extends a harmonious area of cultivated fields and hills covered with diverse woods, with many marked routes to follow on foot or by bicycle. From here we set off on the final part of the tour of the lake around the south end, where there are the majority of *pesqueres*, some of them really beautiful architecturally, and where we find the main Information Office. The last section to complete the full tour until re-joining the Club Natació Banyoles takes us along a poplar **passage of hundred-year-old plane trees** that offers a great diversity of leisure services.

1

▲▼ Autumn in the lake

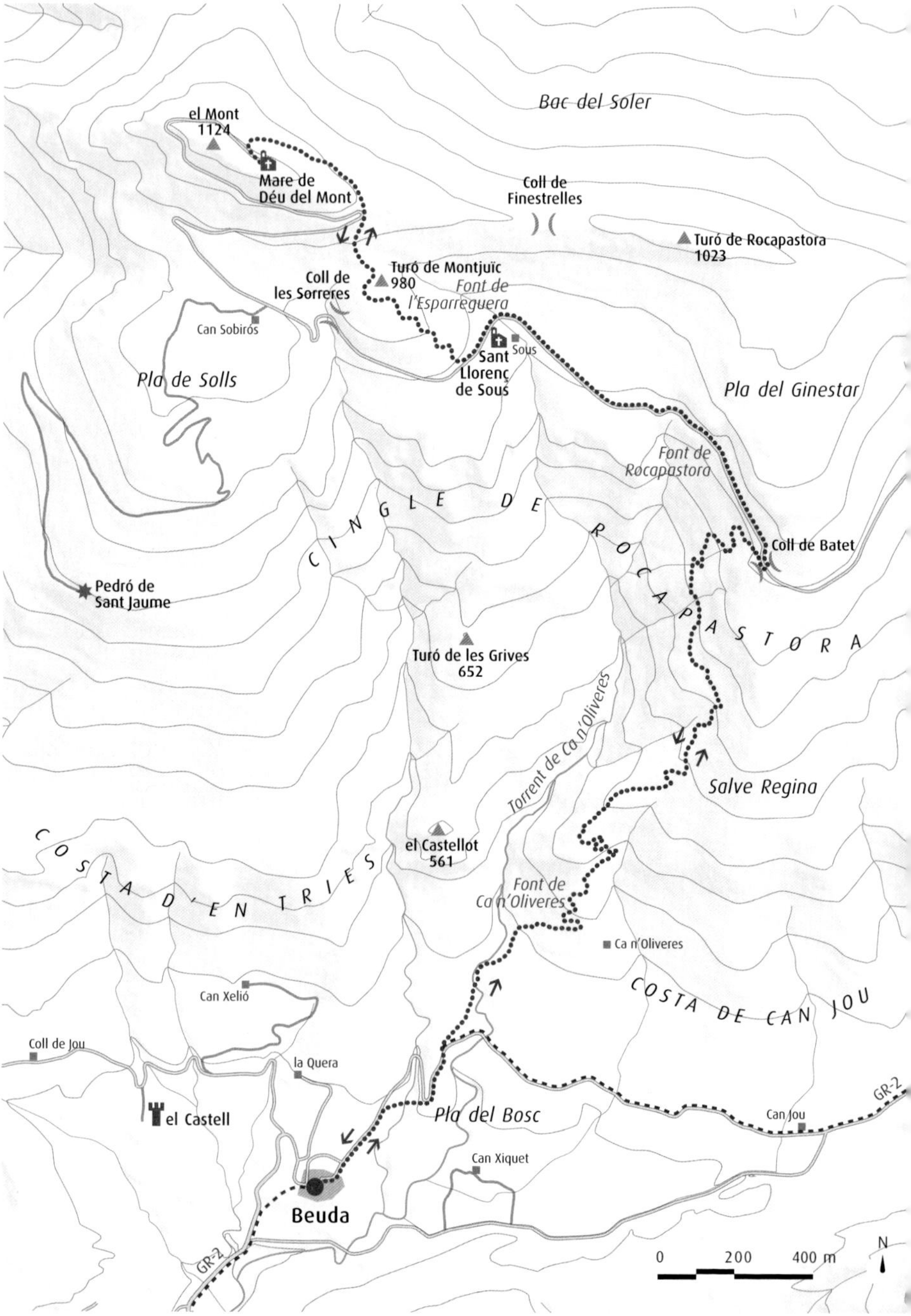

Bac del Soler

el Mont
1124

Mare de
Déu del Mont

Coll de
Finestrelles

Turó de Rocapastora
1023

Coll de
les Sorreres

Turó de Montjuïc
980

Font de
l'Esparreguera

Can Sobirós

Sant
Llorenç
de Sous

Sous

Pla del Ginestar

Pla de Solls

Font de
Rocapastora

C I N G L E   D E   R O C A P A S T O R A

Coll de Batet

Pedró de
Sant Jaume

Turó de les Grives
652

Salve Regina

Torrent de Ca n'Oliveres

el Castellot
561

Font de
Ca n'Oliveres

C O S T A   D ' E N   T R I E S

Ca n'Oliveres

C O S T A   D E   C A N   J O U

Can Xelió

Coll de Jou

la Quera

el Castell

Pla del Bosc

Can Xiquet

Can Jou

GR-2

Beuda

GR-2

0   200   400 m

N

2 THE MOUNTAIN OF THE MONT

▲ Statue of Jacint Verdaguer in the sanctuary of Mont

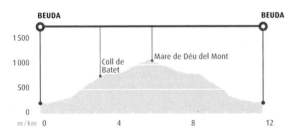

Methods
Walking, trekking

Distance
12 km

Duration
4-5 h

Gradients
+800 m / -800 m

Situated on the limit between Alta Garrotxa and the Plana de l'Empordà, this dominant mountain offers a route with steep gradients of climbs and descents, on which we use the old paths that led to the monastery of Sant Llorenç de Sous and the sanctuary situated at the top, all in a there and back route with departure and arrival in the quiet village of Beuda.

ROUTE

With good access by road to Besalú, the village of **Beuda** (330 m) has an outstanding church of Romanesque origin, beside which we find some path indicators and a couple of restaurants. On the outskirts there is also a beautiful fortified farmhouse of medieval origin, known as the **castle of**

▲ Castle of Beuda

Beuda. We leave on the route of an excellent asphalted track, with the accompaniment of the red and white markers of the GR-2 path, for one kilometre until the **Pla del Bosc** (360 m). We must ignore the secondary path on the left that goes to the crag where the remains of the fortification of Castellot and some popular climbing spots are. We leave the asphalted track and continue towards the village of Maià de Montcal and begin the climb along a forest track, surrounded by thick holm-oak and pine woods. A sign informs us that we are entering the Space of Natural Interest of Alta Garrotxa, just as we leave the course of the track that leads to the entrance of **Mas de Can Oliveres** (410 m).

We then come to other signs that we should pay close attention to, since we have two possibilities: to the right, the main path indicated as a Short Distance path, which passes by the crag of Roca Pastora; to the left, the path that passes by the Puig del Castellot, which has a much more vertical route in a wild setting and which is only appropriate for experienced walkers. Our route there and back uses the path with yellow markers, which firstly crosses a pine wood and then starts on a climb that winds its way up, gradually entering a wood of holm-oaks and oaks. We thus reach a spur of rock known as **Salve Regina** (670 m), from where we get a marvellous view of the setting of the village of Beuda. We finally reach the **Coll de Batet** (810 m), where we come to the road to the sanctuary of Mont, leaving to the right the popular fountain of **Roca Pastora** (820 m) below a spectacular calcareous crag.

We continue upwards on the road for one kilometre until reaching the ruins of **Sant Llorenç de Sous** (870 m), an old Benedictine monastery already documented in 871. An 11th-century church, a cloister and the rest of the rooms complete a complex that, despite being in ruins, still possesses great character as a monument. On the right hand side of the road is the indicator of the path to take and we begin another climb with a steep gradient, always under the cover of trees. From here we must follow a marked path in green and orange, which is winding until reaching the **Collet de les Sorreres** (980 m), and from here until reencountering the road a little higher up. At the beginning of a bend on the same road to the left, we turn right to the last section of the path, well-marked, which enters the shady area of the mountain. We can enjoy a lovely way, the remains of the cobbles revealing to us that it has been used for many centuries, we reach the crest and finally the road below the **sanctuary of the Mare de Déu del Mont** (1,124 m), which has been and still is a destination of great devotion for all the villages of the region, despite the close presence of some large telecommunication antennae. Here we discover the same atmosphere and panorama that Jacint Verdaguer enjoyed in 1884, when he stayed in the old guesthouse to finish the last fragments of his poem *Can-*

igó. Looking northwards, the Catalan national mountain, Canigó, appears magnificent, but the views towards other points are equally outstanding. Perhaps, though, we will not find the best perspective to make out the main silhouettes that define the county of Alt Empordà, from the massif of Les Salines to Cap de Creus, with the Empordà reduced by the gulf of Roses at our feet. The complex of buildings erected between 1311 and 1318 –church and hostel– was reformed in 2002 to continue the accommodation and restaurant service with more comfort. To return to Beuda, we take the same route back.

3 THE VOLCANOES OF LA GARROTXA
(from Les Preses to Santa Pau)

▲ **Hermitage of Santa Margarida**

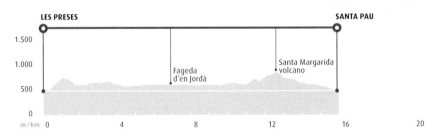

Methods
**Walking,
Nordic walking**

Distance
16 km

Duration
5-6 h

Gradients
+600 m / -570 m

The Natural Park of the Volcanic Zone of La Garrotxa was created in 1982. It includes 11 municipalities, 40 volcanic craters and an infinite number of forest masses of great value. Our route follows from beginning to end the route of the GR-2 path (red and white markings), within the central space of the reserve, between the villages of Les Preses and Santa Pau.

ROUTE
We leave from the village of **Les Preses** (470 m), between the municipal football pitch and the entrance to a campsite. Initially we embark on a steep climb inside a magnificent wood that connects with the entrance paths to the moun-

▲ **Autumn colors in the Serra del Corb**

tain of **Puig Rodó** (936 m), where the popular Xenacs Recreation Area is. Taking care with the signs, we cross the **Coll del Volcà del Racó** (610 m) to pass along the north face of the **Serra del Corb**, where we make a spectacular encirclement amidst beech and holm-oak woods below a crag. We must also cross a series of wild streams. We thus reach the church of **Sant Miquel del Corb** (610 m), of Romanesque origin, from where we continue along a comfortable path to **Mas de l'Antiga** (570 m), and from there the church of **Sant Martí del Corb** (590 m), also of Romanesque origin, in a setting of great beauty alongside an old fountain. We then drop to the farmland of the **Pla de Sant Miquel** (510 m), where we go along the local road for a while, culminating a little further on, at the entrance to some farmhouses. We carry on along a forest track rising gently, ignoring secondary turnings to the left and right. We thus reach the crossroads of **Can Jordà** (575 m), one of the different administrative centres of the Natural Park. To the left, the path, in a little under half a kilometre, leads to the famous spot of the **Fageda d'en Jordà** (550 m), a place where the density off the beech wood that gives it its name is of special interest due to being in the middle of the old outflows of lava that gradually accumulated in the successive eruptive periods of the **Croscat Volcano** (789 m) –the last eruption occurring about 11,500 years ago–, which today is the tallest volcano on the Iberian Peninsula, with a height of 170 metres.

At all times we continue on the GR long-distance path, which in one kilometre comes out at an asphalted track. The route along this track takes us to the installations of the **Cooperativa La Fageda** (570 m), dedicated to dairy produce, and we complete this section of one kilometre when leaving on the right the rural tourism centre of **Mas del Prat de la Plaça** (570 m). From here we tackle a steep climb, along a rather slippery path since it is a very humid area beneath the wood that culminates in the **Collada de Sacot** (670 m), facing the **church of Sant Miquel de Sacot**, of Romanesque origin but rebuilt in the 18th century. We then descend to a harmonious area of farmland at the foot of the Santa Margarida volcano, where we cross another asphalted track and negotiate new slopes along a pleasant path until reaching the **Collada de Bassols** (670 m). Shortly before we will have left on the right a path that leads to the **Serra de Colltort**, from where there are great views across the central area of the Volcanic Zone, while the GR-2 path continues heading east towards the village of Santa Pau. From the Collada de Bassols itself, however, a path leaves that simply cannot be ignored that climbs the south side of the **Santa Margarida volcano** (748 m) to the top, where we find, beside a house, the entrance to the most aesthetically pleasing and known crater in the reserve, 400 metres in diameter and 70 metres deep, with a popular **hermitage** dedicated to Saint Margaret in the centre.

For a while, then, we have left the GR-2 path to one side to enjoy this small excursion across the Santa Margarida Volcano. We must go down the north side, where we come across the amazing **Mas de Caselles** (660 m), one of the many examples of the old traditional life in harmony with nature. Immediately after we come out to a forest track, leaving on the left the road that links Olot and Santa Pau.

We turn right and drop down the track until reaching **Mas de Collelldemir** (580 m), where we link up with the GR-2 path again. To the side we can take in the old deposits of lapilli of the **Roca Negra volcano** (654 m), a spectacular example of volcanic subsoil that was used for industrial purposes during the years before the creation of the Natural Park. The last kilometre and a half to Santa Pau is along an asphalted track, and we should be careful not to miss the point where we must take a narrow path that follows the course of the **stream of Pujolars**, with a steep descent, which leads directly to the village of **Santa Pau** (500 m). The memorable entry through an arcade of this historic county town cannot end in a better place than its emblematic **Plaça Major**, the village square, in a typical network of narrow medieval streets that conserve the original layout, from between the 14th and 15th centuries, with a solid feudal castle in the upper part.

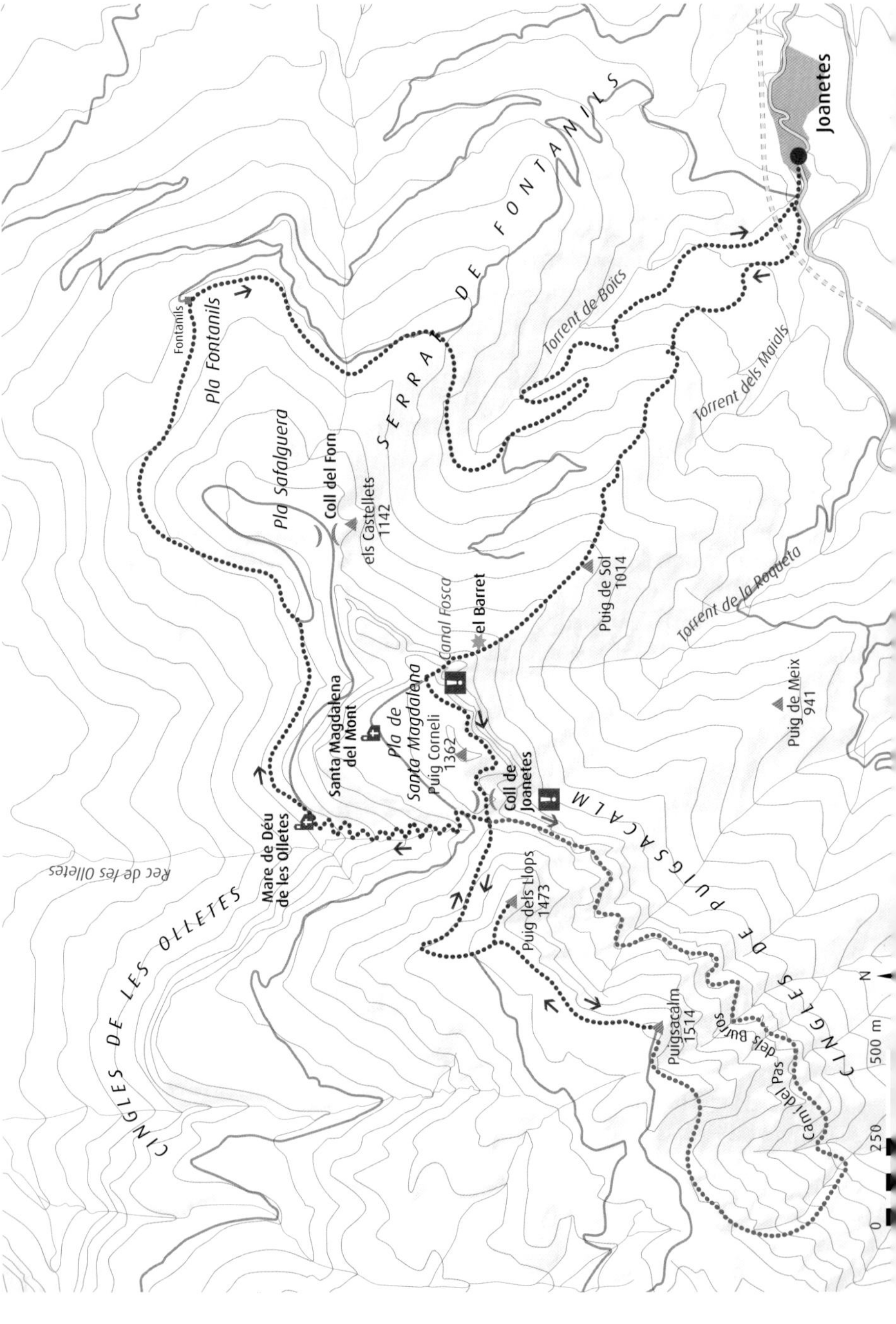

Joanetes

SERRA DE FONTANILS

Torrent de Boïcs

Torrent dels Maials

Torrent de la Roqueta

Fontanils

Pla Fontanils

Pla Safalguera

Coll del Forn

els Castellets 1142

Canal Fosca

el Barret

Puig de Sol 1014

Puig de Meix 941

Santa Magdalena del Mont

Pla de Santa Magdalena

Puig Corneli 1362

Coll de Joanetes

CINGLES DE PUIGSACALM

Mare de Déu de les Olletes

Rec de les Olletes

CINGLES DE LES OLLETES

Puig dels Llops 1473

Puigsacalm 1514

Pas dels Buïsos

Camí del

N

500 m

250

0

WALKING ROUTES BETWEEN THE RIVERS FLUVIÀ AND TER

4 THE MASSIF OF PUIGSACALM

▲ On the path of the "Pas dels Burros"

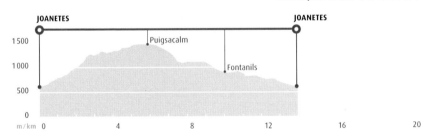

Methods
Walking, trekking

Distance
14-17 km

Duration
5-7 h

Gradients
+1,100 m / -1,100 m

High-level circular route in one of the most spectacular spaces of the Girona lands, which also represents one of the best natural watchtowers. To tackle this route you need trekking experience and be in good form, since we cross wild crags with several chained passes, always under the cover of extraordinary woods.

ROUTE

We set off from the village of **Joanetes** (605 m), above its church of Romanesque origin, in a lovely network of narrow streets with old stone houses, one of the places with the most essence in the large district of the Vall d'en Bas.

We have to find an asphalted street that goes a little higher up and leaves us beside some signposts. We follow the one that points towards Santa Magdalena and El Barret, and we start the walk on this path following the yellow markers, passing a wall shortly after. We gradually gain height passing through an attractive holm-oak wood, until ending up above the large spur of the **Puig del Sol** (1,014 m). Here we can take in the majestic crags and channels that characterise the south slope of the massif of Puigsacalm, and we can even make out the route to follow over a very wild and rocky terrain. We then reach a stone with the inscription "El Barret" and continue on the right, always following the yellow markers of a path with constant zigzags. We thus reach the first iron walkways that help the climb up, and a little higher, the start of what is called the **Canal Fosca** –also called the Channel of the Hooks–, which as its name indicates, has a large line of passing points with steps and iron handrails, of almost 200 metres vertically. The exit of the channel culminates in the meadows of the **Pla de Santa Magdalena** (1,305 m). Here we cross a fence for the cattle and leave the path on the right that goes down to the hermitage of Santa Magdalena del Mont (1,270 m). We continue on the left heading for **Puig Corneli** (1,362 m), crowned by some telecommunication antennae. The path goes between this mountain and the crags that we have just climbed, making a spectacular tour until reaching the **Coll de Joanetes** (1,292 m).

At the Coll de Joanetes we come to a sign that offers us two options to climb to the peak of Puigsacalm. On the right we have the more direct route, which passes through Puig dels Llops, and on the left, the longer route and the one that requires more Trekking experience, by the **Pas dels Burros** (Pass of the Donkeys). If we follow the sensational route of the Pass of the Donkeys, we must be very careful to look for the yellow markers, among crags, beech woods and ravines, with constant climbs and descents. The final climb along a rocky projection and a sensational beech wood leaves us on the popular path that comes from the Collada de Bracons, from where it is just a question of a gentle climb to the grass ramp that culminates in the peak of **Puigsacalm** (1,514 m). From here to the **Puig dels Llops** (1,473 m) and the path down to the hermitage of Santa Magdalena, we alternate between a series of

▲ View of Puigsacalm from the Pla de Santa Magdalena

▲ **On the Puig dels Llops**

meadows and woods where once again we must pay attention in order to find the way-marks, and above all on the final section over rocky projections. This path comes out on the forest track that leads to the hermit-age of Santa Magdalena, a track that we must cross following the marker that shows the continuation of the path with yellow markers towards the chapel of the Mare de Déu de les Olletes and the village of Sant Privat d'en Bas. We thus embark on a sec-tion of amazing descents along an old cob-bled path, with lots of winding turns, fitted between new crags and ravines, in the shade of a very dense wood. On reaching the spot of the **Mare de Déu de les Olletes** (1,030 m) we discover a chapel hidden below a crag in the setting of a fantastic beech wood. The

path then becomes less steep and levels out and we must ignore the continuation of the descent to the village of Sant Privat d'en Bas (crossroads). Following the marker, we begin the return path to Joanetes, also waymarked with yellow markers, a path that takes a long turn to cross the **Serra de Fontanilles** and which ends by linking up with another old path that leads to several farmhouses, cur-rently abandoned. In the final part we come once again to the wood of holm-oaks and oaks that surrounds the village of Joanetes.

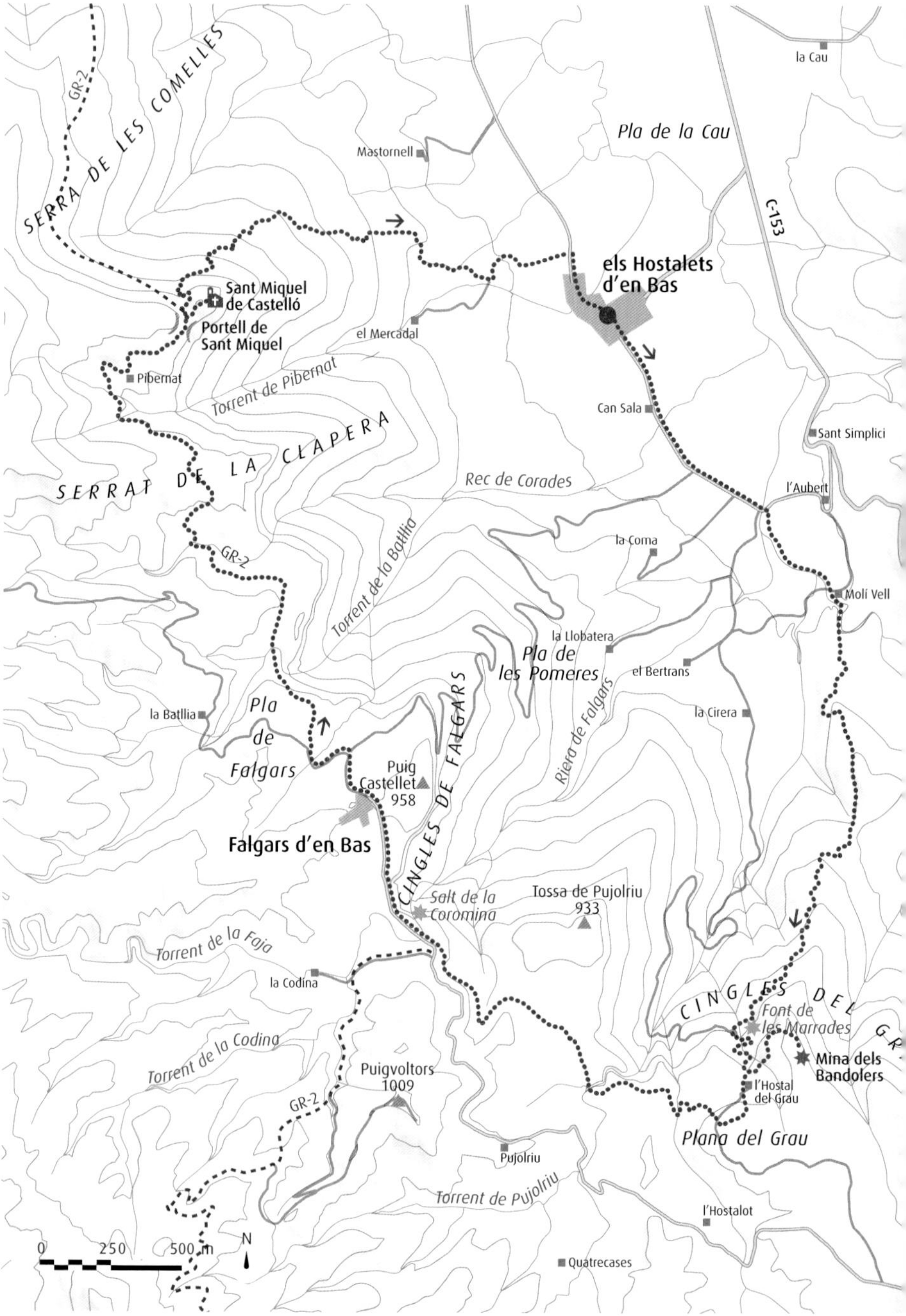

GR-2

SERRA DE LES COMELLES

la Cau

Pla de la Cau

Mastornell

C-153

els Hostalets
d'en Bas

Sant Miquel
de Castelló

Portell de
Sant Miquel

el Mercadal

Can Sala

Sant Simplici

Pibernat

l'Aubert

Torrent de Pibernat

SERRAT DE LA CLAPERA

Rec de Corades

Molí Vell

GR-2

Torrent de la Bаѕllia

la Coma

Pla de
les Pomeres

la Llobatera

Riera de Falgars

el Bertrans

la Cirera

la Batllia

Pla
de
Falgars

Puig
Castellet
958

CINGLES DE FALGARS

Falgars d'en Bas

Salt de la
Coromina

Tossa de Pujolriu
933

Torrent de la Foja

CINGLES DEL GR

Font de
les Marrades

la Codina

Mina dels
Bandolers

Torrent de la Codina

Puigvoltors
1009

l'Hostal
del Grau

GR-2

Plana del Grau

Pujolriu

Torrent de Pujolriu

l'Hostalot

0   250   500 m

N

Quatrecases

5 THE CRAGS OF HOSTALETS D'EN BAS

5

▲ Crossing the stream of Pujolriu

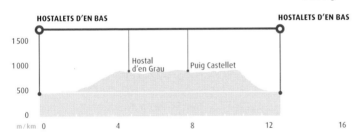

Methods
**Walking,
Nordic walking**

Distance
13 km

Duration
4-5 h

Gradients
+650 m / -650 m

At the foot of the massif of Collsacabra, the pretty village of Hostalets d'en Bas originated as a logistic base of the *Camí ral* (Royal way) between Vic and Olot, created in the 18th century. Other paths across the crags of this exceptional massif complete an excellent network of marked paths that allow us to form a wonderful circular route full of unforgettable spots.

ROUTE

We leave from the church of **Hostalets d'en Bas** (490 m), taking Carrer de Vic heading south, where we come to an indicator of the Saint James Way to Cantonigròs and Vic.

▲ General panorama with Falgars d'en Bas in the foreground

We then go along a quiet local road between cultivated fields for one kilometre. When we reach a bend, we must take the marked path on the right that crosses a field towards the old **Mas del Molí Vell** (500 m), beside a bridge that crosses a small stream. The origin of this mill dates back to the Middle Ages, but it was at the end of the 18th century, with the construction of the Royal Way between Vic and Olot, when the place was used as a meeting point for pedlars who made the journey on mules between the two towns. It is right here where we begin the climb of this sensational way to the peaks of the **massif of Collsacabra**, with some initial metres on a dirt track until reaching the connection with the original way on the right. During the first kilometre, the path is well covered by a dense holm-oak wood, and

is winding all the way. We gradually begin to see the slabs of original stone and the protection structures of the 18th century, and we can enjoy a natural and historic setting where time stands still. We thus reach the **Font de les Marrades** (830 m), inside a beech wood at the foot of the walls of the **Cingle del Grau**. A little further up on the left is the path that in 5 minutes leads to the **Mina dels Bandolers** (880), a spectacular corridor of calcareous rock. On returning to the *Camí ral*, we complete the final part of the zigzags that culminate in the **Hostal del Grau** (890 m), another historic settlement totally linked to the major activity of travellers and goods that came through here from the late 18th to the mid-20th century.

On reaching a crossroads with a sign, we stop following the *Camí ral* to take another signposted path, always with yellow markers, towards Hostalets d'en Bas via Falgars.

In the first section we drop beneath a dense beech wood to cross the **stream of l'Hostalot** (870 m), and from here we continue until the **stream of Pujolriu** (850 m), where we come out at some beautiful pastureland, passing on our left the large **Mas de Pujolriu** (900 m). We then cross the fields with the guidance of the yellow markers, on a maze-like path, and finally we climb to the asphalted track that leads to Falgars d'en Bas over the **Cingle de la Coromina** (910 m), enjoying below us the spectacular **waterfall of the Salt de la Coromina**, which drops 150 metres vertically. Half a kilometre further on we come to **Falgars d'en Bas** (950 m), a small rural village on a plateau, which features a large rural tourism guesthouse and its church dedicated to Saint Peter. From here we continue along a comfortable dirt track signposted by the GR-2 path (yellow and white marks) leaving to the right a track and a path that lead directly to Hostalets d'en Bas, which in case of need would leave us with an hour's walk.

To complete the route in the best way possible, our way follows the wide track over the line of crags of the massif of Collsacabra, with small climbs and descents crossing bucolic meadows, until reaching the **Mas de Pibernat** (910 m), which has an old fountain beside it, where we once again check a new signpost. A little further on we reach the surprising pass of the **Portell de Sant Miquel** (930 m), which stands out for a corridor of rock at the foot of the watchtower where the **hermitage-castle of Sant Miquel de Castelló** (955 m) stands. This enclave is documented from the 10th century, with a small walkers' refuge, where we can take in the last crag of the massif of Collsacabra and the whole **Vall d'en Bas** at our feet. Once again at the Portell de Sant Miquel, we follow the last indicator and connect with the path to Hostalets d'en Bas, with the yellow markers as guides, through a large wood of oaks and holm-oaks. In the initial part we advance over an old cobbled path that has a steep slope and sharp bends. The path gradually becomes more comfortable, although we must take care on the humid and slippery areas. Once in the low part of the mountain, we come out to an area of scattered farmhouses, and further down the road that leads to Hostalets d'en Bas from the north.

▲ Sant Miquel de Castelló

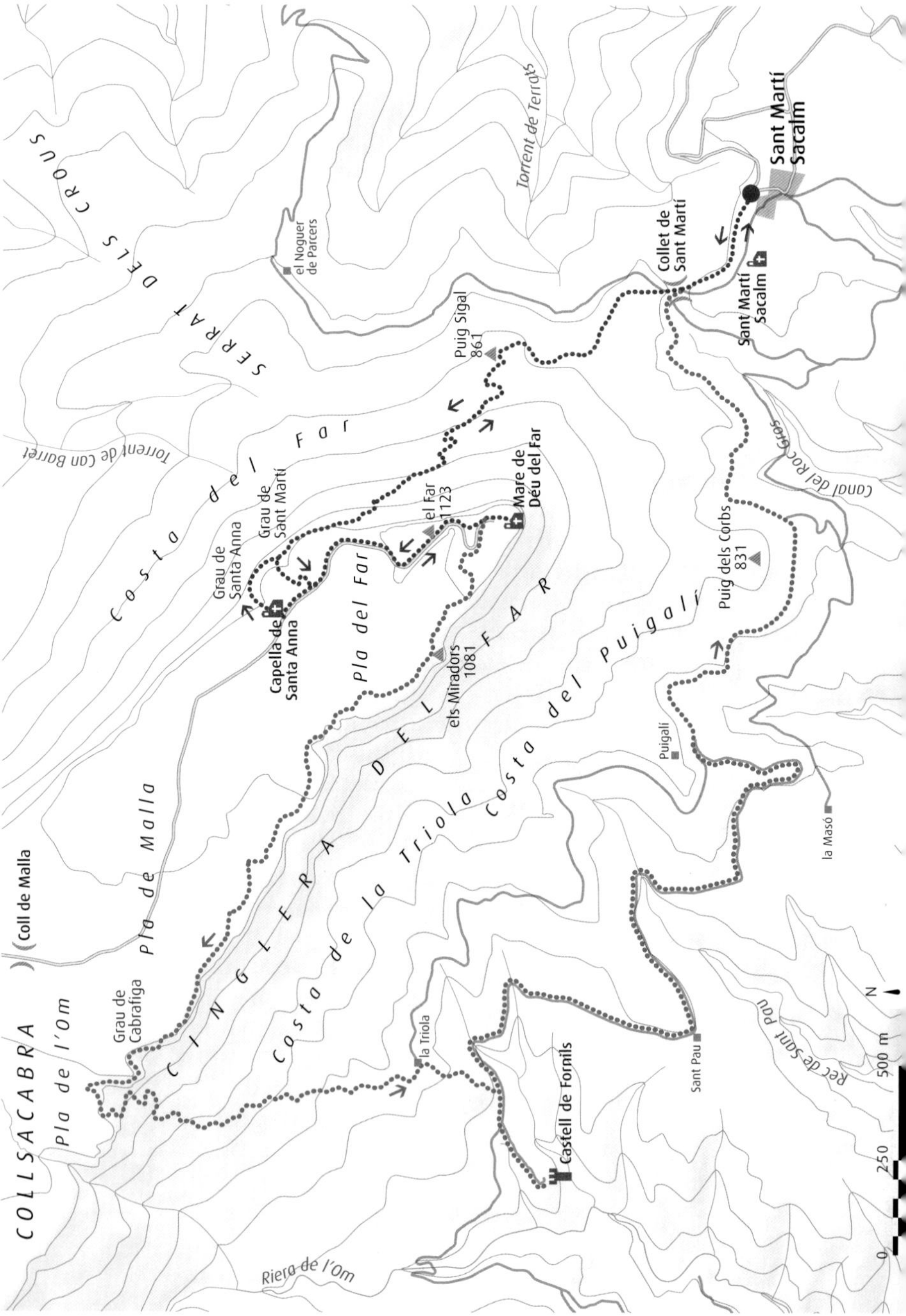

Sant Martí Sacalm

SERRAT DELS CROUS

el Noguer de Parcers

Torrent de Terrats

Collet de Sant Martí

Sant Martí Sacalm

Puig Sigal 861

Costa del Far

Torrent de Can Barret

Grau de Sant Martí

Grau de Santa Anna

el Far 1123

Mare de Déu del Far

Canal del Roc Gros

Capella de Santa Anna

Pla del Far

Puig dels Corbs 831

els Miradors 1081

CINGLERA DEL FAR

Costa del Puigalí

Pla de Malla

Puigalí

la Masó

COLLSACABRA

Pla de l'Om

Grau de Cabrafiga

Costa de la Triola

la Triola

Sant Pau

Rec de Sant Pou

(Coll de Malla

N

500 m

Castell de Fornils

250

Riera de l'Om

0

6 THE CINGLERA DEL FAR

▲ On the Collet de Sant Martí

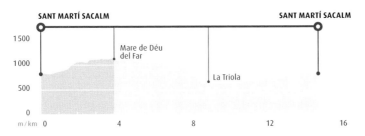

Methods
Walking, trekking

Distance
8 km (route there and back)

Duration
2-3 h

Gradients
+350 m / -350 m

The extreme southeast of the massif of Collsacabra has a spearhead that projects like a veritable petrified lighthouse, and exceptional crag of 3 kilometres in length with two sides that rise above the Vall de Susqueda to the south and the Vall d'Hostoles to the north. The trip has the option of either a shorter there and back route or a circular one for more experienced trekkers.

ROUTE
The solitary village of **Sant Martí Sacalm** (820 m) is best reached by road from the village of Amer, after a climb full of bends that leaves us at the foot of the majestic Cinglera

▲ On the Cinglera del Far path of the Grau de Cabrafiga

del Far. From this small rural village which dates back to the 12th century, situated at the northernmost end of the county of La Selva, we can appreciate a sensation of grandness and environmental purity like few other places. Before starting off, we should find some signposts and take the Short-Distance that follows the way of the old *Camí ral* between Sant Benet and the Sanctuary of El Far (yellow and white markers) and which will take us past the chapel of Santa Anna. Shortly after we come to the **Collet de Sant Martí** (850 m), a crossroads in the centre of a beautiful meadow, from where we begin a gentle climb to the Cinclera del Far through a fantastic holm-oak wood. We then enter a mixed wood of great richness and start climbing a steeper slope, until linking up with a marvellous cobbled path that takes us

back in time. Some way further on we come to a signpost to climb to the top of the Cinglera, either via the **Grau de Sant Martí** (short route), or a little further on via the **Grau de Santa Anna** (long route). The short route is steeper and more spectacular –recommended to climb up–, whereas the long route is gentler and leaves us alongside the **chapel of Santa Anna** (1,070 m) –recommendable to come down. In any case, we come out on the road that we must go along for one kilometre before reaching the **Sanctuary of El Far** (1,123 m), an authentic eagle's nest, with origins in the 13th century, which has a popular accommodation and restaurant service.

6

FROM THE SANCTUARY OF EL FAR TO SANT MARTÍ SACALM VIA THE *CINGLERA*   ► V

Distance
14 - 15 km
(circular route via the Cinglera del Far)

Duration
5 - 7 h

Gradients
+650 m / -650 m

This second part of the route, which enables us to make a circular route, is only recommendable for experienced trekkers. We have to go back a little along the road and find an electrified gate for the cattle on the left. We must go through it to drop gently through a dense wood, taking a path marked with white that takes us to the precipices of the **Cinglera del Far**. Once at the first viewpoint over an impressive crag, we alternate between sections of wood and others close to the walls of the crag, always with the white marker guides. After a really thrilling walk, we reach a fence, from which extends a large area of fields with some farmhouses on the right. Here we have to pay great attention, since below us appears the higher entrance of the **Grau de Cabrafiga** (970 m), from where we begin a very steep drop, following the red markers. This drop culminates in the interior of a beautiful holm-oak wood, until reaching a wide, stony path, where we must ignore some turnings to the left. Our route always goes straight down along the main path to the **Mas de La Triola** (670 m), from where we have the option of visiting the remains of the **castle of Fornils** (585 m), located a little further down. From the meadows of La Triola we begin the return to Sant Martí Sacalm along a comfortable dirt track, passing through **Can Sant Pau** (650 m), where we discover an old farmhouse with a church. Further on we leave on the left the remains of **Mas Puiggalí** (750 m), and finally we reencounter the Collet de Sant Martí and the route from the beginning of the trip.

▲ On the Cinglera del Far

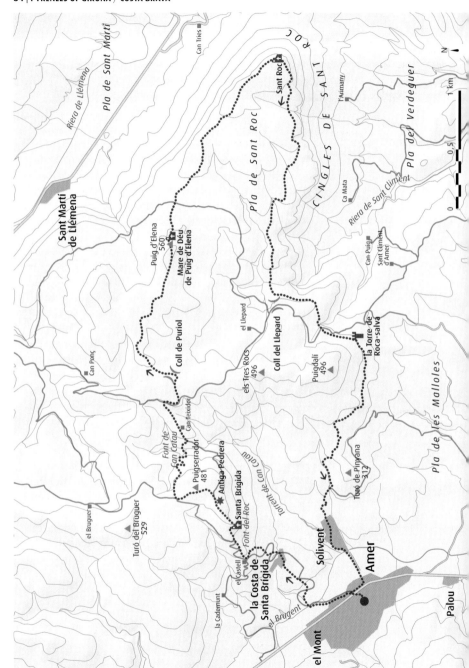

7 THE HERMITAGES OF AMER

▲ In the hermitage of Sant Roc

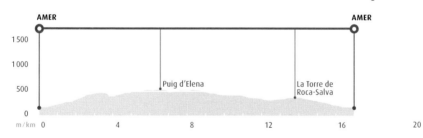

Methods
**Walking,
Nordic walking**

Distance
17 km

Duration
5 - 7 h

Gradients
+700 m / -700 m

To the northeast of the town of Amer extends an attractive area of crags and hills, with three old hermitages standing on very strategic points. In any case, only the first of the three hermitages belongs to the municipality of Amer. The other two are in Sant Esteve de Llémena, all within a wild and ancient territory, full of areas to look for fossils.

ROUTE

We leave from the old centre of **Amer** (190 m), beside its emblematic arcaded square, and we head towards the other end of the town to cross the main road until reaching the banks of the **river** Brugent, which we cross via a bridge. Beside us is the municipal football pitch and the beginning of the cemented track to the hermitage of Santa Brígida. From here we follow the yellow markers of a short-distance path with a steep slope, which for a few moments passes through a pretty zone of fields until coming to the same track as before alongside a picturesque farmhouse-restaurant. From this point on, the signposted path to Santa Brígida follows a course across a spur of rock. We must cross the track one more time before coming to the remains of **Mas del Castell** (340 m). The covering of holm-oaks and a path cut into the rock embellish this way until the upper part of the spectacular calcareous crag on which the **hermitage of Santa Brígida** (445) is placed, overlooking a

fantastic panoramic view. This hermitage was built in the 11th century and rebuilt in the 17th century, and its etymological origin confirms the link with the Celtic goddess Brigid. In the lower part are some popular climbing routes, but to continue along the marked path we must go back a little and climb to an old **stone quarry** (480 m). We then take an easy path until reaching a fork, where we follow the sign that marks the way to the fountain of Can Catau. In this way we stop following the yellow markers of the short-distance path to follow only the markers of the *Ruta de les Ermites* (Route of the Hermitages). We embark on a descent below the wood with many zigzags until the **fountain and stream of Can Catau** (360 m), from

▲ In the spot of Santa Brígida

where we climb again along a route of the same characteristics to the viewpoint beside the ruins of **Mas dels Fusos** (430 m).

Further on we cross the asphalted track that leads to the nucleus of La Barroca on passing the **Coll de Puliol** (485 m). We continue climbing along a wide path between fields and woods to reach the bucolic spot of the **hermitage of Santa Lena** (560 m), built in the 13th century. Here we once again take in a great panoramic view before a steep descent along a slippery path. On the final part of this path we come out in some fields and reach a junction the paths of the **Coll de Sant Roc** (480 m). Following the signs to the hermitage of Sant Roc, we begin a long section of climbing path heading southeast, over a very rocky zone and through a dense wood. We always follow the wider path and with white markers, until reaching the sensational watchtower of the **hermitage of Sant Roc** (602), situated at the top of a calcareous crag. Below us, to the north, we take in the harmonious **Vall de Llémena**, with the mountain of Rocacorba crowned by some large telecommunications antennae. More distant, towards the east, stands out the whole extension of reliefs that mark the **Vall del Ter** as far as the Illes Medes. From here we begin the return trip to Amer along the upper part of the long line of the **Cingles de Sant Roc**, gradually dropping with the guide of the white markers. In the first part, the path runs over irregular terrain that leads us to a **viewpoint** (567 m) above a crag. We then cross an area where we will walk over a veritable carpet of small fossils, called

nummulites, typical of some structures of calcareous rock.

The continuous descent leads us to the **stream of Sant Climent** (370 m), which we cross over some pretty stepping stones to once again climb up another slope through the wood. Be careful at the crossings and forks, and we must always follow the signs to the tower of Rocasalva, crossing a stream before coming out at the asphalted track below Mas El Llepard. On crossing this track, we start off on a wider path that will take us above the **tower of Rocasalva** (320 m), a fortified farmhouse of medieval origin, also with an etymological origin that points to Celtic roots. We then make the final climb to the right to go over a hill populated by a pretty pine wood. The last section of the route has a maze-like trajectory where we will have to take great care in following the white markers among tracks and paths, with access to different farmhouses. In any case, the walk is very pleasant and alternates between fields and woods in a well-conserved rural setting. This is the way to the higher part of the **Solivent urbanisation** (240 m), from where we just need to drop down along a road that crosses the river Brugent via a bridge and takes us back to the village of Amer.

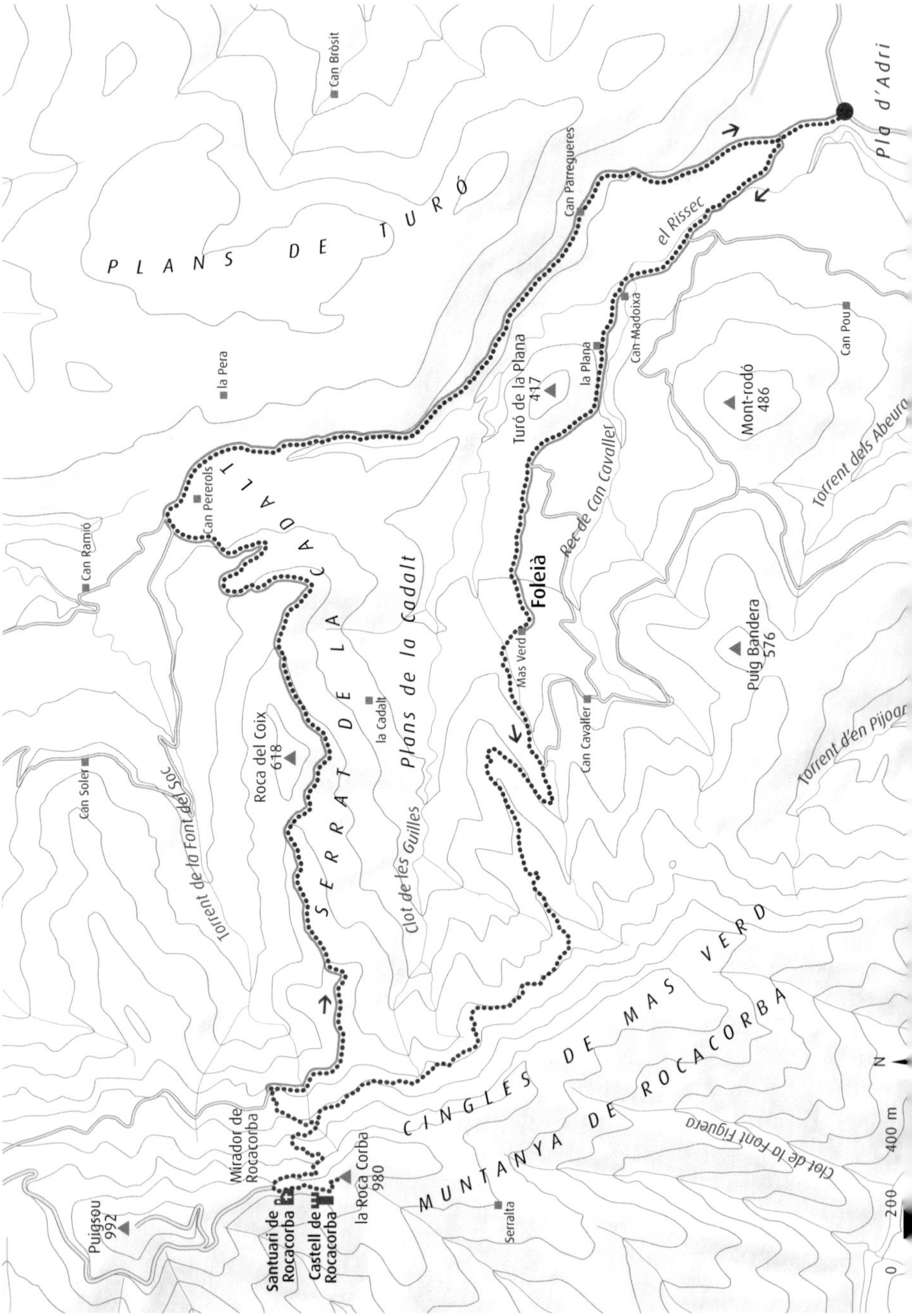
Pla d'Adri
Can Brósit
PLANS DE TURÓ
Can Parregueres
el Rissec
la Pera
Can Madoixa
Can Pou
la Plana
Turó de la Plana
417
Mont-rodó
486
Can Pererols
SERRAT DE LA CADALT
Rec de Can Cavalles
Can Ramió
Foleià
Plans de la Cadalt
Mas Verd
Puig Bandera
576
la Cadalt
Roca del Coix
618
Can Cavaller
Can Soler
Torrent de la Font del Soc
Clot de les Guilles
CINGLES DE MAS VERD
MUNTANYA DE ROCACORBA
Mirador de Rocacorba
Clot de la Font Figuera
la Roca Corba
980
Puigsou
992
Santuari de Rocacorba
Castell de Rocacorba
Serralta
N
0
200
400 m

WALKING ROUTES BETWEEN THE RIVERS FLUVIÀ AND TER

8 THE MOUNTAIN OF ROCACORBA

8

▲

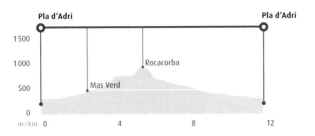

Methods
Walking,
Nordic walking

Distance
12 km

Duration
4 - 5 h

Gradients
+700 m / -700 m

Close to the city of Girona, this mountain represents a major natural watchtower between the Pyrenees and the Vall del Ter. The main reference is the medieval sanctuary located on the upper part, on top of a spectacular crag. The route we suggest enables us to enjoy the great rural setting along a lovely path that climbs up through a wood.

ROUTE

From afar, the dominant mountain of Rocacorba stands out for some large telecommunication antennae on its main peak. The small and quiet village of **Canet d'Adri** (250 m), 15 kilometres by road to the north of Girona, is the gateway, although we can continue for 1.5 kilometres more to set off from the church of Sant Vicenç. The asphalted road ends on the **Pla d'Adri** (320 m), an area of farmland where we find the crossroads with several farmhouses and the signpost that informs us of the start of the forest track to the nucleus of Biert, on the left. This is where we start from and return to on our route and begin walking along this track. After a few metres we reach a second crossing, where we must follow the sign that marks the beginning of the *Camí de Rocacorba*, to the left, along a branch of track that drops gently to the bed of the **stream of Rissec** (310 m). On crossing this stream we begin to climb along the same forest track, always following the white and yellow marks of the short-distance path that leads to the sanctuary of Rocacorba. A little further on we pass on our left the pretty farmhouse of **Can Madoixa** (335 m), and then, on the right, **Mas de La Plana** (345 m), with an old stone washhouse beside the path. After crossing a wood we come out to an area of farmland. Here we discover the fantastic rural nucleus of **Foleià** (410 m), made up of a series of old stone houses, rehabilitated as rural tourism accommodation. Having reached the last of these houses, we come to the beginning of the climb to Rocacorba, with a sign on a holm-oak tree. We thus embark on a path that goes through a marvellous wood, with an outstanding presence of ashes, maples, hazelnuts, oaks and holm-oaks, all accompanied by a wild undergrowth and many forest streams.

▲ **Beginning of the route between old farmhouses**

Our path rapidly gains height, due to series of zigzags, until reaching the top of a hillock, always in the dense wood. The gradual climb alternates along the upper part of the streams, with narrow and slippery parts in which you must go with care. On the right we pass at all times the main streams, which we can identify partially through some gaps in the wood. At a given moment we enter into the rockiest and steepest part, just below a large crag where the sanctuary of Rocacorba is placed. On our right we come to a **signpost** (800 m) that shows the descent to Biert, where we will have to return after having visited the sanctuary. We complete the last section along the route of an old cobbled path, with short zigzags, that culminates at the **foot of the crag of the sanctuary of Rocacorba** (930 m). From this point we have to climb some steps to reach the **upper part of the crag** (980 m), going through the door of the sanctuary. This spot was originally a fortification, already mentioned in the 11th century. Between the 14th and 15th centuries the old castle was transformed into a sanctuary, but some strong earth-quakes destroyed it. It was not until the 18th century when the current building was constructed, which occupies a strategic position over an extensive territory.

If we want to climb up to the peak of **Puigsou** (992 m), occupied by the telecommunication antennae that overlook the mountain, we have a path on the right of the vehicle track, above an attractive rocky spur. Once again on the signpost to go up, the proposal to go towards Biert and Canet d'Adri via the Collet de Pererols represents a longer route, mainly along forest tracks. At the beginning, however, we still move along a path of wild terrain, with quite a few zigzags, until coming out onto the first section of **track** (700 m). Once here, we follow the markers and signs to Biert on a stony path that drops via a series of hills, with a final part of zigzags and steep gradients. We thus reach the **Collet de Pererols** (430 m), a cross-roads with a large water tank beside it. On the left we leave the turning to the nucleus of Biert and head down on the right, thus taking the long track to Canet d'Adri, 3 kilometres away. On the final part we pass by **Mas de Can Parregueres** (350 m), which has a historic fountain beside it and from where it is just a question of following the way while taking in the landscape over which the route has passed.

▲ Sanctuary of Rocacorba

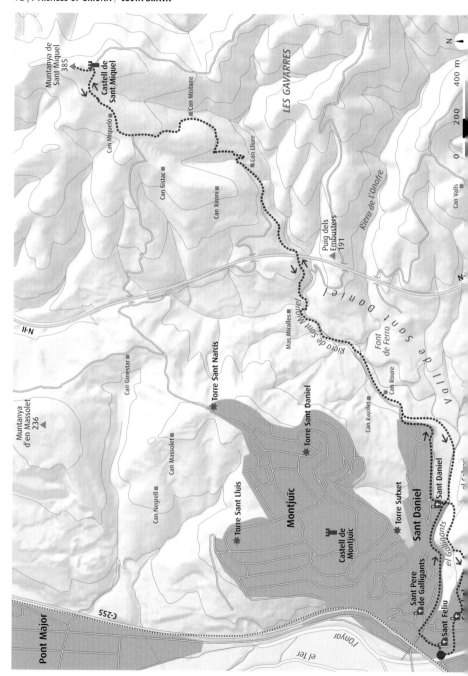

9

THE VALLEY OF SANT DANIEL AND THE CASTLE OF SANT MIQUEL

9

▲ **City walls of Girona**

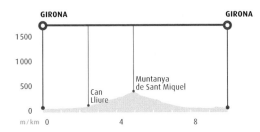

Methods
**Walking,
Nordic walking**

Distance
10 km

Duration
3 - 4 h

Gradients
+400 m / -400 m

On the outskirts of the city of Girona, on the side that connects with the massif of Les Gavarres, we come across a marvellous area where we can make the most of Mediterranean nature. The route across the valley of Sant Daniel (in Catalan, Vall de Sant Daniel) to the hill where the historic castle of Sant Miquel stands, offers a very gratifying trip, with the option of doing some variants to complement it.

ROUTE

The monumental **historic centre of Girona** (70 m) is the beginning and end of this there and back route, since the Vall de Sant Daniel is just on the back part of the old city walls.

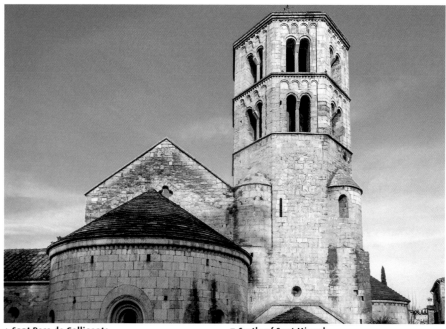

▲ Sant Pere de Galligants ▼ Castle of Sant Miquel

9

From the **river Onyar**, passing by the **church of Sant Feliu**, we should look for the sign that marks the way to the Vall de Sant Daniel from the **monastery of Sant Pere de Galligants** (75 m). From this fantastic building in the purest Catalan Romanesque style, which has been reconverted into one of the centres of the Archaeological Museum of Catalonia, we follow the road for half a kilometre, with the **river Galligants** on the right. We then reach the wall of the **monastery of Sant Daniel** (80 m), also in Romanesque style and unique in Catalonia, which is still home to a community of Benedictine nuns. From here we continue along the left, going around the wall of the monastery, following the signs and markers of the short-distance path that will guide us to the castle of Sant Miquel. After passing a cemetery that we leave on the right, we enter into the actual Vall de Sant Daniel, in the setting of the **Natural Space of the Massif of Les Gavarres**. From here to the castle high up we enjoy a very pleasant way through a large wood. In this initial part we leave on the right the way to the fountain of Ferro, where an interesting path passes that climbs to several viewpoints. We head on up the mountain alongside the **Stream of Miralles** and then we cross this watercourse over the **Pont d'en Miralles** or *bridge of Miralles* (110 m). Shortly after we go below the Girona ring-road, the point where the downhill part is the steepest, with a very pretty section of path that ends linking up with a wide forest track. We immediately go around the pretty

farmhouse of **Can Lliure** (210 m), where the track has a sharp bend.

Below we leave the **stream of Sant Miquel** that collects a large part of the water of the regions, paying attention to the markers of our path, which from Can Lliure makes its way across rocky terrain, with a marked gradient, that saves us from taking the track and thus climbing more directly. After crossing the track a little higher up and climbing a steep section, we reach the ruins of **Cal Mistaire** (290 m). Now inside a very leafy wood we then come to the path that leads to the **Font Martina** (305 m), from where we set off on the final climb, passing by the remains of **Can Micaló** (340 m). We finally reach an attractive plain, equipped as a **picnic area** (380 m), with the old tower of the **castle of Sant Miquel** (395 m) a little further on. The origin of this fortification in ruins dates back to the Middle Ages, and includes, beside the tower, a moat, walls and a hermitage. From the top of the tower there is an excellent view across the Ter valley, with the backdrop of the Pyrenees. The return along the same way requires care not to slip on the steep parts. Once at the crossroads of paths at the monastery of Sant Daniel, it is well worth climbing up to the remains of the **Gironella Tower** (140 m), from where we can get to the old city walls of Girona to complete the route spectacularly.

10

THE VALLEY OF ARBÚCIES AND THE CASTLE OF MONTSORIU

▲ Oak woods in the initial part of the route

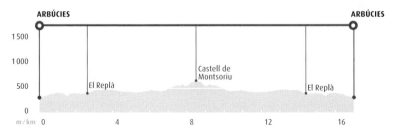

Methods
Walking,
Nordic walking

Distance
17 km

Duration
5-7 h

Gradients
+600 m / -600 m

At the foot of the massif of Montseny there are a great many corners that house natural spots of great beauty and which are also excellent exponents of the well-conserved Mediterranean ecosystem. The climb to the majestic castle of Montsoriu, as well as the visit to the town of Arbúcies, offer a perfect complement to this there and back route.

ROUTE

Our route follows the whole short-distance path between Arbúcies and the castle of Montsoriu (white and yellow marks), the same path we will have to take to come back. The town of **Arbúcies** (310 m) has several neighbourhoods on either side

▲ Old centre of Arbúcies

of a fantastic stream that has historically guaranteed one of the best supplies of water in Catalonia, with lots of fountains and wells. The start and finishing point of the route is the old centre of the town, behind the Plaça de la Vila. From here, our route coincides with the GR-83 path for the first 2 kilometres, between the massif of Canigó and the town of Mataró. We take Carrer Vern and Carrer Maül to set off on the first climb of the day through some attractive terraced orchards, until reaching a **viewpoint** (360 m) over the town. Taking care with the markers, we follow an old path that drops to the **stream of Sot de les Ànimes** (340 m) and climbs again to the cross of the **Costa d'en Malla** (360 m). We then go through a pine wood and oak wood to drop towards the **stream of Sot Cremat** (320 m), where we find vegetation typical of sub-humid Mediterranean ecosystems. From here we reach a fork where we bid farewell to the GR-83 path and continue on the left following the path sign between Arbúcies and Montsoriu. Just here we now enter into the **Natural Park of Montseny**. We are on a pleasant way through the spot of the **Prats del Morer** (370 m), until coming out to a forest track in the direction of **Mas del Replà** (380 m), which we pass a little lower down. We must continue on this track for quite a while, making slight climbs and descents to cross different streams, with some secondary turnings where we should be careful with the signs.

Further on the way we cross the **stream of Sot de Can Pendó** (400 m) where we find several paths in a wild space, with an old fountain by the side. From here we begin to drop towards the Turó de Montsoriu, beneath a dense forest covering, along a series of very winding tracks and ways. We finally reach the **Coll de Castellar** (500 m), where we come to a crossroads with signs, with two options to climb to the castle of Montsoriu. To the left, making a long tour on a track, and to the right, on the same marked path we have been following for the whole trip so far, and which offers a much more attractive climb through a pine wood, with short zigzags. We thus reach the **castle of Montsoriu** (634 m), which crowns the mountain of the same name, built between the 12th and 14th centuries and considered the best example of Gothic military architecture in Catalonia. Notwithstanding, the spot had already been inhabited in the Iberian era, in the 4th to 2nd centuries BC, and it is one of the best watchtowers in the lands of Girona. The visit to the fortress offers a tour of the walls, towers and interior corridors which invite us to take a trip through time and enjoy excellent views from one side to another. We return to Arbúcies along the same route which we now know, but this time the other way.

▲ Castle of Montsoriu

Walking routes on the COSTA BRAVA

After the city of Barcelona, the Costa Brava is the most important tourist brand in Catalonia and without doubt one of the most important in Europe. The succession of natural spaces we come across all along this coast, from the frontier with France to the mouth of the river Tordera, represents a veritable paradise for doing all kinds of open-air activities. Between sea and mountain, the tripper has tracks and paths across spots of incomparable beauty. The nexus that joins all these routes is the Long-Distance Mediterranean path, the GR-92, which runs along the Catalan coast end to end and which on the Costa Brava provides exceptional sections thanks to the existence of what are called the *Camins de ronda*. These paths have their origins from centuries ago, when they were used to watch over the coast and to reach points of difficult access. In modern times, some sections have been broken due to the construction of chalets, but in other parts they have been very well rehabilitated for public use. With 220 kilometres of route, the Costa Brava has achieved recognition in recent years as a reference destination for trekking, precisely because of the value of its routes in harmony with the landscape.

Our choice of routes begins in the far north, where the Pyrenean mountain range plunges into the Mediterranean, giving form to a section of coast unique in the world, made up of rocks of plutonic origin, sculpted with great force by the action of wind and sea. The Natural Park of Cap de Creus is the figure that recognises all the values of this untamed territory, both in terms of landscape and history, at the service of the best model of active tourism, which a little further south contrasts with the width of the gulf of Roses and the second largest humid zone of Catalonia: the Natural Park of the Aiguamolls de l'Empordà, a symbol of the fragility of the natural ecosystems in relation to human activity. Further on we come to the massif of Montgrí, the massif of Begur and the massif of L'Ardenya, with a series of marvellous routes where the trekker enjoys incomparable sensations via cliffs, woods and beaches in the wildest state, but also with the clear presence of most historical human settlements from the Roman period to today.

◄ **Coastal path between Llafranc and Tamariu.**

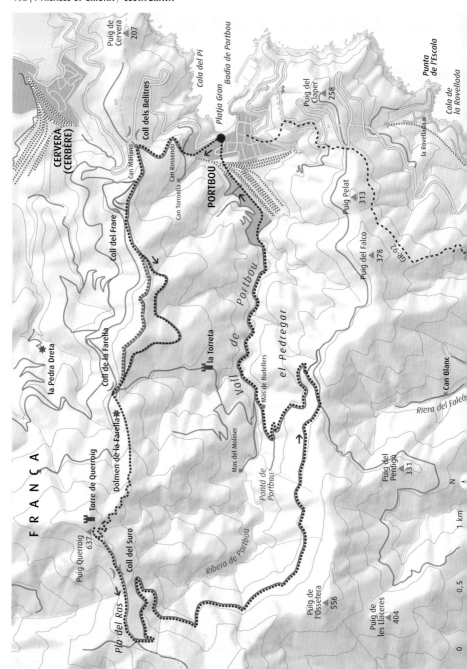

1 THE VALLEY OF PORTBOU

▲ Contemplating the bay of Portbou

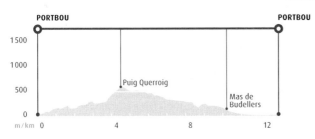

Methods
Walking,
Nordic walking

Distance
13 km

Duration
4-5 h

Gradients
+700 m / -700 m

This is a circular route that goes around the valley of Portbou (in Catalan, the Vall de Portbou), the last valley of the Pyrenees, on the frontier with France. The walk enables us to enjoy the mountains of the massif of L'Albera over the Mediterranean, with the climb up to the heights of Querroig, a mountain crowned by an old fortress and an astonishing geodesic side, with an exceptional view.

ROUTE

We leave from the beach, the **Playa Gran de Portbou**, finding some steps that cross the N-260 road. We then go alongside the local school and climb up Carrer de Sant Jordi to the end, climbing a series of steep cement ramps, always following the yellow markers to the **Coll dels Belitres** (165 m). Once here we come to the French border, the road that goes to the town of Cerbère (Cervera) and a small Memorial of the Exile, in homage to the half a million people who crossed the Pyrenees fleeing from the troops of Franco during the Civil War in the first half of 1939. We head west and follow a forest track, above the Vall de Portbou, with good views over the **bay of Portbou** and its historic trans-border railway station. We totally ignore the branch track that follows the line of the border on the French side and which we meet up with again having reached the pass of the **Coll de la Farella** (309 m). From this point, we connect up with a lovely path, across reliefs of rocks and a surprising holm-oak wood, which in its lower part we discover the small **megalithic dolmen of La Farella**. The steep climb, however, requires concentration and effort at all times. We thus reach the peak of **Puig de Querroig** (637 m), where recent excavations and cleaning work have managed to recondition the remains of a fortress documented as far back as 981. After taking in a privileged panorama to both sides of the Pyrenees, we continue the path over the frontier crest, which gives us a sensational view of the **Natural Park of L'Albera**, covered with wild mountains and very diverse ecosystems that confirm its singular geographic position.

The descent from the Puig de Querroig to the **Coll de Rumpissar** (538 m) –also called Coll del Suro–, shows us the connection with what is called the Walter Benjamin Route, the German Jewish philosopher who crossed this Pyrenean pass with the help of the French Resistance, escaping from the Nazis in 1940, although he died on the same day in the town of Portbou in unusual circumstances. Our way reaches a little further on the **Pla del Ras** (555 m), from where a forest track starts that goes through the **Vall de Portbou** by its south side, and which we should follow for some kilometres. Half way along this track, we must find a sign that marks the descent to Portbou within the valley, with a steep slope initially until coming out at some former farmland, and then we come to **Mas de Budellers**, a farmhouse surrounded by exotic vegetation. On the left we ignore the branch of the track that leads to the small **reservoir of Portbou**, which we have been looking at for a large part of the route from the high part of the valley. We cover the last kilometres on the asphalt of a track that at its end crosses the monumental **Portbou train station** through a long tunnel, and which comes out in the town centre.

▲ General panorama of Portbou

▼ The old castle of Puig de Querroig

2 WALKING ROUTES BETWEEN THE RIVERS FLUVIÀ AND TER
SANT PERE DE RODES

▲ The coastal path between Port de la Selva and Llançà

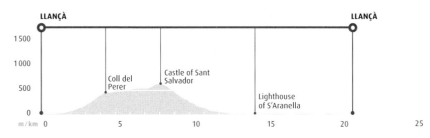

Methods
Walking,
Nordic walking

Distance
21 km

Duration
7-8 h

Gradients
+850 m / -850 m

It is a circular route in the western end of the Natural Park of Cap de Creus, with a first part along the old ways to the mythical monastery of Sant Pere de Rodes, one of the most important medieval monuments in Europe. The return to the beginning along the fantastic coastal path between the towns of Port de la Selva and Llançà is a wonderful climax.

ROUTE
We leave from the **Plaça Major of Llançà**, surrounded by historical buildings that confirm the antiquity of its old centre, one kilometre inland from the port district. To start with, we follow at all times the red and white markers of the

GR-11 path to Sant Pere de Rodes. We must look for the regulatory signs in an urban area of new streets that contrasts with the pretty rural setting that surrounds the town. The first steps along the pleasant path that climbs the **En Prim stream** enables us to warm up before approaching a steep climb to the pas of the **Coll del Perer** (360 m), taking in the old dry stone walls that for so many centuries made agriculture possible all over the Cap de Creus peninsula. Also, from the Coll del Perer itself we get an excellent perspective of the **mountain of Verdera** and all the route we have before us, in which stands out, over a large balcony, the monastery of Sant Pere de Rodes. We set off again, with a new slope to overcome a hillock, from where we link up with the route of a forest track climbing gently which comes out on the road between Vilajuïga and Port de la Selva. Just before coming out on the road we pass, next to the way, the well-conserved **dolmen of the Pallera**, one of the many megalithic monuments spread around the area, dated between 300 and 1500 before Christ. On crossing the road (car park), we immediately come to the steps that take us to the stunning **church of Santa Helena** (535 m), with a spectacular arcade on the side and the archaeological remains of the village when several hundred people lived here during the age of splendour of **Sant Pere de Rodes** (520 m), an exceptional monument that we can see ahead of us with a comfortable way to reach it.

We thus reach a legendary monastic complex, founded in 878 but enlarged in later years, with an age of splendour between the 13th and 14th centuries. It is undoubtedly a not-to-be-missed visit, which requires more than an hour to tour the different rooms without rushing. Of note is the church with Carolingian and Caliphal designs, as well as the two large towers of the Romanesque fortification. The path down starts right by the entrance door for 15 minutes to the highest point of the Verdera mountain, occupied by the **castle of Sant Salvador** (670 m), a visit we recommend because it offers one of the most amazing views of Catalan lands, since with a bird's-eye view we can take in the whole space that extends from the point of Cap de Creus to the massif of Canigó, passing by the gulf of Roses. Once again in Sant Pere de Rodes, we start the return trip to Llança, taking great care to find the marked path that leads to the little village of La Vall

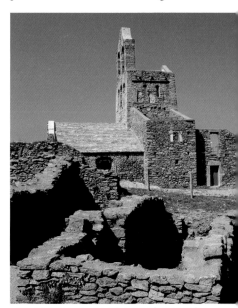

▲ **Church and ancient settlement of Santa Helena**

▲ Sant Pere de Rodes with Port de la Selva on the horizon

de Santa Creu. Firstly we must cross the road and then take a fantastic cobbled way that still shows a large part of the original route from the medieval era. The houses in **La Vall de Santa Creu** (130 m) today form a space trapped in time, surrounded by holm-oaks, oaks and chestnut trees among streets carved in living stone, where some 200 people once lived (although today there are no more than a dozen). Fountains, wells, mills, orchards and farmhouses complete the set, which we can continue discovering along the marked way towards the coast.

On coming out at the road between Port de la Selva and Llançà, we walk a few metres to the left before coming to the entrance of the **Port de la Vall campsite**, which we must go through in its entirety to reach the beach of the same name, the point where we link up with **coastal path** over the reliefs of the coastline, a route marked with the signs of the GR-92 path. Once here we head towards Llançà, noting at the beginning passing by the **Punta de s'Arenella**, with the presence of a lighthouse built in 1910. Further on we go past a series of coves and low cliffs, with constant ups and downs, which make the walk fun, despite having to go past a large number of chalets. At all times the beauty of the coast and the cover of some pine woods compensate for the final effort, which ends in the popular **Port de Llançà**. To return to the starting point, we must go back a kilometre along the avenues of the town centre.

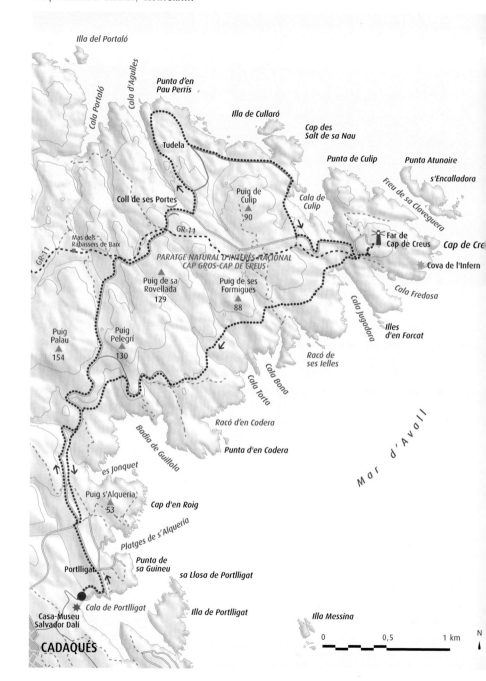

3 CAP DE CREUS

▲ Cadaqués

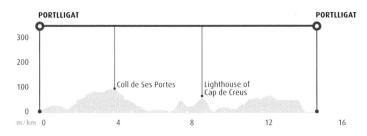

Methods
**Walking,
Nordic walking**

Distance
15 km

Duration
5-6 h

Gradients
+450 m / -450 m

A circular route focused on the eastern end of the Natural Park of Cap de Creus, which is also the eastern end of the Iberian Peninsula, with the beauty of the village of Cadaqués as a complement. The walk through a spectacular geology and unique in the world allows us to discover exceptional spots that inspired Salvador Dalí.

ROUTE

Our starting point is in **Portlligat** (car park), beside the **Dalí House-Museum**, which is a compilation of all the work of the brilliant painter from Empordà, as well as its direct link with an ideal of Mediterranean paradise that was maintained intact until the end of the 20th century. We take the marked path that leads us to the road between Cadaqués and the Cap de Creus lighthouse, where we walk along the asphalt for 3.5 kilometres, ignoring all the signposted ways that appear on the left and right. Having reached the **Coll de ses Portes** (105 m), the road drops sharply and leaves us at the entrance to **Tudela** on the left (car park), a space rehabilitated in the best way possible and which today allows us to take a first-class naturalist route. We leave the road here and enter into this spot, which between 1961 and 2011 was occupied by an urbanisation of chalets, today wiped off the map to show all the geological and scenic splendour of the area, with its rock formations of volcanic origins directly related to the folds of the Pyrenean range and some very harsh environmental conditions.

The thematic route that uses the old way that connected the whole urbanisation takes us from the viewpoints over the dramatic **Cala d'Agulles** to the **jetty of Cala Culip**. In this latter spot we must follow the signs that lead to an old **fishermen's hut**, from where a path leads that climbs a wild ravine and which returns us to the asphalt of the road to the Cap de Creus lighthouse, which appears just in front of us. We ignore throughout this section the markings of the GR-11 path, since it is more practical to stay on the route of the road, with good views of the spectacular natural landscape surrounding us.

We climb to the highest point of the hill crowned by the buildings of the **Cap de**

▲ On the coastal path

Creus lighthouse (82 m) by means of the historic cobbled path that comes from **Cala Fredosa**, an old natural jetty until the road was built in modern times. Although the current buildings (restaurant, guesthouse, tourist information office and lighthouse) date back to 1853, the spot was already used in Roman times to make a light signal as a guide for sailors to pass this dangerous point. Here we can take different paths that are optional for us, such as going down to the **point of Cap de Creus** or go over a bridge of natural rock that shapes the monumental **Cova de l'infern** o *cove of hell*. To get back on the return route to Cadaqués we must drop down along the path to the road, just over a bridge that in the form of an isthmus divides the **bay of Culip** on the right and **Cala Jugadora** on the left.

By means of a rocky slope we drop towards Cala Jugadora, marked by yellowish tones, and in this way we begin the walk along the old **coastal path** between the Cap de Creus lighthouse and Cadaqués, which at all times has a cobbled route along with an impressive botanical representation of Mediterranean species. The irregular terrain and a succession of tight streams that come out in the sea make progress rather demanding, with continuous ups and downs. In any case, going over a series of stone bridges or between ancient dry stone walls make the experience quite unforgettable. A final drop with a steep gradient leaves us on a dirt track that leads to several chalets and the beaches of the beautiful **bay of Guillola**. We should take great care with the signposting to Cadaqués when starting out on the way between dry stone walls and terraces with ol-

ive groves. On coming out again on the road, we go a few metres downhill until coming to, on the left, a sign that indicates a final section of path along the **Des Jonquet stream**, covered by dense vegetation with a final climb. Having reached one of the crossroads that lead to Portlligat, we recommend taking the wide cemented street that goes to the **coves of S'Alqueria**, and from here to the beach of Portlligat. From behind the Dalí House-Museum leaves the old way to the town centre of **Cadaqués**, where we can complete the day with a visit to its attractive **old centre** and the coastal path of 3 kilometres to the **Calanans lighthouse**, two proposals in one of the prettiest fishing villages in all the Mediterranean.

▲ **Dalinian formation in Tudela**

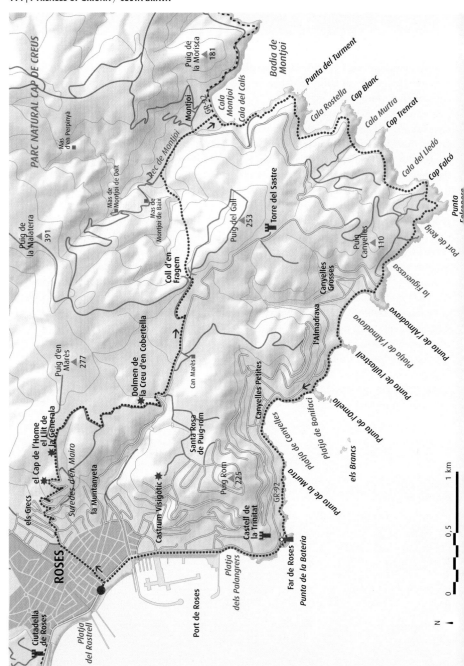

PARC NATURAL CAP DE CREUS

Puig de la Morisca 181

Mas d'en Perpinyà

Puig de la Malaterra 391

Badia de Montjoi

Punta del Turment

Cala Rostella

Cap Blanc

Cala Montjoi

Cala del Calis

Cala Murtra

Cap Trencat

Montjoi

GR-92

Bec de Montjoi

Mas de Montjoi de Dalt

Mas de Montjoi de Baix

Cala del Lledó

Cap Falcó

Coll d'en Fragem

Puig del Gall 253

Torre del Sastre

Punta Falconera

Port de Reig

Puig Canyelles 110

la Figueirossa

Canyelles Grosses

Puig d'en Marès 277

Can Marès

Dolmen de la Creu d'en Cobertella

l'Almadrava

Punta de l'Almadrava

Platja de l'Almadrava

Punta de l'Ullastrell

Santa Rosa de Puig-rom

Canyelles Petites

el Cap de l'Home el Llit de la Generala

els Grecs

Suredes d'en Mairo

la Muntanyeta

Castrum Visigòtic

Puig Rom 225

Punta de l'Omello

platja de Canyelles

platja de Bonifaci

Punta de la murta

els Brancs

ROSES

Castell de la Trinitat

GR-92

Far de Roses

Punta de la Bateria

Ciutadella de Roses

Platja del Rastrell

Port de Roses

Platja dels Palangres

N

0   0,5   1 km

4

AROUND ROSES

4

▲ On the coastal path between the beach of Almadrava and Roses

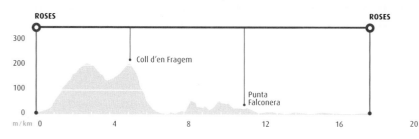

Methods
**Walking,
Nordic walking**

Distance
18 km

Duration
6-7 h

Gradients
+550 m / -550 m

A circular route around the municipality of Roses, which focuses on a large number of historic and natural elements, with a marked contrast between the inland and coastal landscape. While on the outward trip we visit one of the best megalithic monumental complexes in Catalonia, on the return we enjoy all the beauty of a coastline blessed by the gods.

ROUTE

We leave from the **promenade of Roses**, the attractive Avinguda de Rhode, which recall the founding of the town by the Greek colonists in 776 BC. Located on the corner of Carrer Francesc Macià, we follow it straight up until reach-

▲ Bay of Montjoi

ing Avinguda Pau Casals and connect with Carrer de Grecs. We then begin to climb along the winding road of Carrer Pitàgores, which offers us a fine view over the urban centre of Roses and its historic bay. Having reached the final bend in this street, before it ends, we find on the left a flat space where there is the well-conserved **dolmen of Cap de l'Home** or *dolmen of the man's head* (150 m), the first point on what is called the Megalithic Route of Roses, signposted with wooden posts and coloured arrows. A little higher up is the pretty **dolmen of the Llit de la Generala** (170 m), from which we must follow the route that marks the way to the dolmen of the Creu d'en Cobertella, the

largest of them all and which also marks the way of our route. After leaving a series of **menhirs** alongside a winding path, we discover the impressive **dolmen of the Creu d'en Cobertella** (170 m), considered the largest in all Catalonia, measuring 2.5 metres in height, 3 metres wide and 6 metres long. A perfectly cobbled path drops directly to the road that joins Roses with Cala Montjoi, which is our objective. We walk on asphalt for one kilometre. We have the option of approaching the interesting remains of the old **Visigoth *castrum*** or fort from the 7th century over the watchtower of **Puig Rom** (225 m), which dominates the whole bay of Roses, with a path that also leaves from the road between Roses and Cala Montjoi on the right.

Once we have completed the asphalted section, on our left we find the start of a dirt track that climbs to the hills of the Pla de les Gates, Puig Rodó and Puig Alt, which we follow climbing gradually for half a kilometre until reaching a marked bend. We come to the **Coll de Fragem** (205 m), a panoramic viewpoint over the unknown **Vall de Montjoi**, with an old fortified farmhouse in the centre. From here we take a path on the right, signposted by yellow marks, which drops steeply. On reaching the low part, we come to some large oak woods and some bucolic cultivated fields, and link up with a wide way parallel to the **Montjoi stream,** (restaurants and holiday centre). This is where the road ends from Roses and where the long forest track begins to the coves of Jóncols and Cadaqués, which we do not take. Above the sand of the small **bay of Montjoi**, we can take in the last mountains of the Pyrenees before they enter the sea, noting the magnificent promontory of **Cap Norfeu** (175 m), crowned by the remains of an old circular watchtower built in 1598 and destroyed in 1643 by the French armada. From here we follow completely the route of red and white markers of the GR-92 path to Roses, on a walk of continuous ups and downs, between cliffs and pine woods, which requires care in some irregular points.

Having reached the **point of the Turment**, we discover a corner of great beauty, followed by a short climb to reach **Cala Ros-tella**, solitary and concealed. We then reach **Cala Murtra** (nudist area), which has an unspoilt pebble beach. Passing through this spot obliges us to once again climb to come out into a dense pine wood over very craggy cliffs. This section leads us to the **Falconera point**, with spectacular views to both sides, where we discover some large military bunkers from the mid-20th century. We then go around the **small cove of Port Reig** from above and the **point of Figuerassa**, the last passing points outside the extensive urbanised space that characterises the current town of Roses and which exemplifies very well the setting of the **beach of La Almadrava**. From this lovely beach of crystalline waters we begin the final section of the coastal path, perfectly conditioned between chalets and restaurants, that links up with the **beach of Canyelles**, the **lighthouse of Roses**, from 1864, with the remains of the **castle of the Trinitat**, from 1543, and finally the fishing **port of Roses**, a royal port since 1304. Once again on the Avingude de Rhode, it is worth going along the whole avenue visiting the historic **Ciutadella de Roses**, built in the times of the emperor Charles V, where the remains of the old Greek, Roman and medieval city are found.

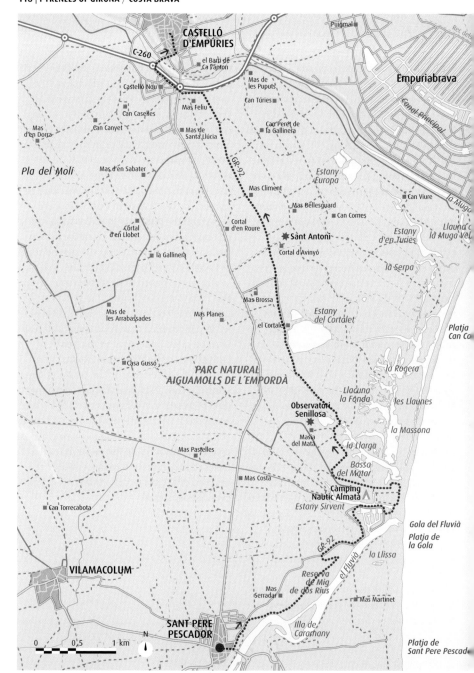

5 AIGUAMOLLS DE L'EMPORDÀ

▲ Beach of Can Comes

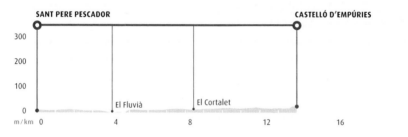

SANT PERE PESCADOR   CASTELLÓ D'EMPÚRIES

El Fluvià   El Cortalet

m/km 0   4   8   12   16   20

Methods
**Walking,
Nordic walking**

Distance
14 km

Duration
5-6 h

Gradients
+100 m / -100 m

This is a straight route from Sant Pere Pescador, along the attractive course of the river Fluvià with an end in the historic town of Castelló d'Empuries. The route crosses the central sector of the Natural Park of the Aiguamolls de l'Empordà, the second largest humid zone in Catalonia, with hundreds of catalogued species. We recommend the use of the regular bus route to link up with the two towns.

ROUTE

We begin the walk in the quiet village of **Sant Pere Pesca-dor** (5 m), at the junction of Carrer Provença and Carrer Joncar and the dirt track that goes to the **Mig de Dos Rius**

▲ Common teal

Reserve (signpost), which is where we must follow the route of the GR-92 path throughout the route (red and white markers). On reaching a car park on the right, we come to the start of the ecological path called *Camí de les Llúdrigues* (Way of the Otters), that runs alongside the **river Fluvià**. Here we discover the **island of Caramany** (Integral Reserve), created in 1979 as a result of the opening of a new canal on the left bank of the river to avoid erosion. Beneath a lovely coppice, we can note the attraction of the river ecosystems, where there is great biodiversity, being the ideal habitat for many species of birds, mammals, fish, reptiles, amphibians and insects. As we progress, we come to a narrower stretch and which for some periods of the year is full of water, which can make it difficult to pass. On crossing a zone of reedbeds and a field of fruit trees, we leave the asphalted track from Sant Pere Pescador (track from Joncar), that we follow until reaching its final point at the **jetty of La Llissa**. The mouth of the river – the **Gola del Fluvià**– appears a little further on, although we are forced to go around the

whole perimeter of what was once an old urbanisation project with canals. Shortly before coming to the river again, we discover the surprising **drawbridge** that crosses the entrance canal to the **Almatà nautical campsite** and which in fact we must use to go over a dense reedbed, with an interesting panorama. Following the signs that mark the GR-92 route, we cross some metres over the sand of the **beach of Can Comes**, which borders the sea space of the **Natural Park of the Aiguamolls de l'Empordà**, a spot of incomparable beauty.

The route around the outside of the campsite then presents us with the fantastic **Route of the Massona**, which ends in the visitors reception centre established in the farmhouse of Cortalet, our next objective. This route is the most important in the park, since it approaches the largest extension with category of Integral Reserve, with ten **birdwatching observatories** to spend some time discovering some of the 300 species of birds that have been catalogued, of which 100 inhabit the spot all year round, such as storks and ducks of all types. The series of observation points is concentrated above all around the main sector, called **Les Llaunes**, where five large coastal lagoons are interconnected. We should also mention that the trace of wild mammals is also clearly present, among which feature the boar, fox or genet as regular species, as well as the otter and buck deer as reintroduced species. Without the need to mention each observatory, it is well worth pointing out the turning towards the **farmhouse of the Matà**

5

–an optional there and back path–, identifiable for the silhouette of large silos where rice was stored, with an outstanding observatory installed in the top part in order to take in the whole extension of the Aiguamolls de l'Empordà between the Pyrenees and the Mediterranean (Senillosa Observatory).

After restarting the route along the main path, we carry on to complete the other observatories. Once in the **farmhouse of Cortalet**, it is very gratifying to spend some time among the observatories of the large lake of the same name. From here we just need to follow the sign that marks the route to Castelló d'Empúries, which consists of 5 kilometres on dirt track between farm-land. We reach the destination after avoiding the main road between Roses and Figueres, enjoying the way over the **river Muga** via a bridge. It is worth mentioning the location, a little further ahead, of an **old bridge** (Pont Vell) of seven arches, which is well worth seeing by using a pretty path alongside the river. From this point we complete the trip with a climb to the old centre of **Castelló d'Empúries** (15 m), with its typically medieval narrow streets and a first-class **Gothic church**. Around this town there are some other interesting areas belonging to the Natural Park of the Aiguamolls de l'Empordà, with good routes to enjoy all its attractions.

▲ **Birds, the main stars in the Aiguamolls de l'Empordà**

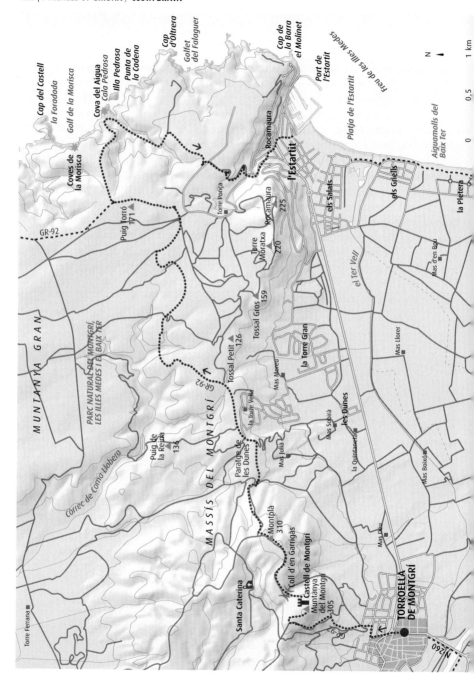

6

THE MASSIF OF MONTGRÍ

6

▲ Close to Cala Pedrosa, with the Roca Foradada in the background

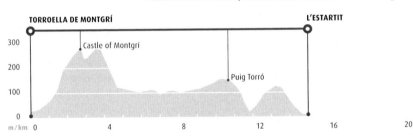

Methods
Walking, trekking

Distance
15 km

Duration
5-7 h

Gradients
+850 m / -850 m

This is a straight route between Torroella de Montgrí and L'Estartit (bus service), from the mountain where an emblematic medieval castle stands, to a totally wild irregular coastline. Even though the central part of the route is easy, both the initial part and the finish require great care and physical dexterity, due to irregular nature of the terrain and the steep gradients.

ROUTE

We set the starting point in the town centre of **Torroella de Montgrí** (5 m), just by the roundabout where Passeig de Catalunya meets with the road that leads to the port of

▲ Castle of Montgrí

L'Estartit (6 kilometres away as the crow flies). Worth noting is the old centre of Torroella, with remains of the **medieval wall** from the 13th and 14th centuries that closes the urban layout designed with the model of the classical Roman encampments, considered the best example of this type in Empordà. For the first two-thirds of the route we have to follow the red and white markers of the GR–92 path to the town of L'Escala. We thus take the way that crosses a lovely décor of fields of olive groves to climb to the central mountain that characterises the silhouette of the massif of Montgrí, crowned by the structure of a large square-shaped castle. It is worth pointing out that the whole route is over a calcareous terrain that is very rough and not easy at some points, as

we can see during the climb to the castle of Montgrí, where half way up we come to a series of small stone **chapels** related to old processions to the hermitage of Santa Caterina, which is hidden on the other side of the massif. A little higher up, we pass the **Coll de la Creu** (185 m) and go along a section of sharp bends over large fractures of rock, until reaching the entrance to the **castle of Montgrí** (305 m). This imposing fortification was built between 1294 and 1301, under the mandate of the Catalan monarchs, but it was never finished. We can enter it via some interior stairs, to enjoy a great 360° panoramic view. To continue along the GR–92 path we should be very careful on the difficult steep descent to reach the pass of the **Coll d'en Garrigàs** (215 m),

6

which separates the mountain of the castle and that of Montplà.

Having crowned **Montplà** (310 m), we pass alongside the path of a forest fire control cabin, as well as a path that drops to the wide **Coll de Puig-roig** (240 m). We always follow the way of the GR-92, setting off on a new rather difficult and stony section, which requires care when flanking the north side of the mountain below some large walls of rock, and later on a steep descent that enters a very dense wood. We thus reach the **spot of Les Dunes** (130 m), where we find a picnic area with a fountain. A sign tells us of the origin of some dunes which in the early 20th century had to be stopped with the planting of pine trees. Today these dunes have become totally fossilised and the pine woods are spread along the whole massif. For a short time we go along an asphalted track that leads to the **urbanisation of the Torre Vella**. The marked path leaves the track to the left and goes behind the last chalets that make up the perimeter of this urbanisation. We begin to go along the central space of the massif of Montgrí, a vast mass of forest in which alternate stone pines, Aleppo pines and cluster pines. We always keep to the route of the GR-92, with short climbs and descents, paying attention at several forks and crossroads.

When we go along the wide forest track that links the towns of L'Estartit and L'Escala, we should change direction completely, heading north if we want to follow the proposed route. Otherwise, we have the option of ending the route at this point (path indicator). Just after going over the plateau of **Puig Torró** (171 m), we come to another sign, in this case indicating the way to the unspoilt coves of Ferriol and Pedrosa, and therefore we stop following the GR-92 path here. From this point we follow the green and white marks of the Local Path to the sea. A little lower down, we go right heading for Cala Pedrosa (sign), starting a steep and stony descent that takes us to a spectacular viewpoint over the **cliffs of the coast of Montgrí** and which offers a marvellous view of the **Roca Foradada** (Holed Rock), a gigantic arch of natural rock that allows boats to pass under. We then discover the wild **Cala Pedrosa**, well concealed between islets and points. Our path to L'Estartit now enters a fantastic holm-oak wood along a ravine, with a demanding climb to reach a crossroads of forest tracks.

At this point we take on the right, heading south, the track inland towards L'Estartit, a plethoric and unforgettable finale in a town founded in the 18th century as a fishermen's district of Torroella de Montgrí and today an internationally known tourist resort.

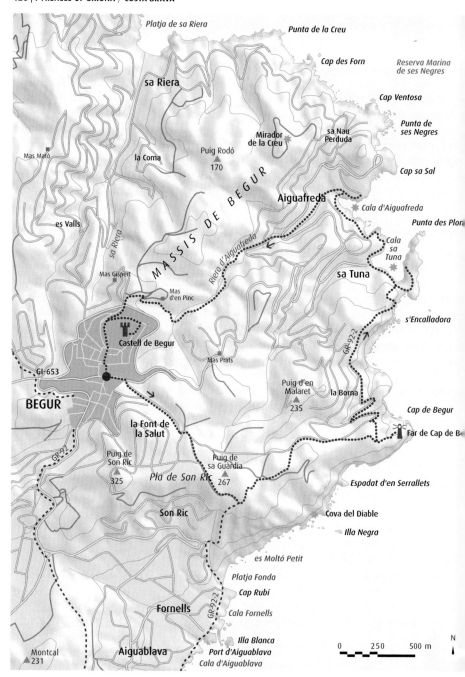

Platja de sa Riera
Punta de la Creu
Cap des Forn
Reserva Marina
de ses Negres
sa Riera
Cap Ventosa
Punta de
ses Negres
Mirador
de la Creu
sa Nau
Perduda
Puig Rodó
170
la Coma
Cap sa Sal
Mas Mató
MASSIS DE BEGUR
Aiguafreda
Cala d'Aiguafreda
Punta des Plon
es Valls
sa Riera
Riera d'Aiguafreda
Cala
sa
Tuna
Mas Gispert
sa Tuna
Mas
d'en Pinc
Castell de Begur
s'Encalladora
GI-653
Mas Prats
GR-92-2
BEGUR
Puig d'en
Malaret
235
la Borna
Cap de Begur
la Font de
la Salut
Far de Cap de B
GR-92
Puig de
Son Ric
325
Puig de
sa Guàrdia
267
Pla de Son Ric
Espadat d'en Serrallets
Son Ric
Cova del Diable
Illa Negra
es Moltó Petit
Platja Fonda
Cap Rubí
Fornells
GR-92-2
Cala Fornells
Illa Blanca
Montcal
231
Aiguablava
Port d'Aiguablava
Cala d'Aiguablava

0   250   500 m

N

7 THE CAP DE BEGUR

▲ Panorama of Begur

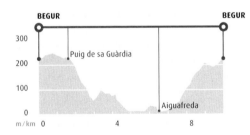

Methods
Walking,
Nordic walking

Distance
10 km

Duration
3 - 4 h

Gradients
+450 m / -450 m

This is a circular route around the municipality of Begur alongside its central seafront, with an easy approach to the point of the cape, where we come to an old lighthouse on cliffs to the magical coves of Sa Tuna and Aiguafreda. The return to Begur is through a small biological reserve, completing a route of great beauty and contrasts.

ROUTE
We leave from the old centre of **Begur** (210 m), a unique town for both the position it occupies atop a mountain over the Costa Brava and its long history and heritage, which is well worth investigating at the end of the walk. To find the

proposed route, you must look for the start of the Camí del Semàfor, which climbs gently to the **Pla de Son Ric**, where several residential chalets are spread out among vegetation of Mediterranean woods. We should pay attention to the diverse forks on this asphalted street, seeking on the right a street that connects with one of the variants of the GR-92 path, from the bay of Aiguablava. Just on passing **Puig de Sa Guàrdia** (267 m), looking towards the sea, a sign appears and the characteristic red and white marks, with a wonderful path that looks out over the **bay of Aiguablava** from high up. Further on we come to the asphalted street of the Camí del Semàfor again heading towards the Cap de Begur and we turn right when we come to another fork that leads to an urbanisation of chalets. The marked path takes us to the point of the **Cap de Begur** and we have to go there and back to complete the visit. The path then takes the form of bends and turns in descent inside a dense wood, until coming out in the low part of the same urbanisation. Once here, we continue along an asphalted road until reaching some steps, on the right, that help us reach some impressive **cliffs** covered by a lovely pine wood. We should be very careful to follow the signs correctly, as well as not tripping on this abrupt and stony terrain. On leaving the small area of flat land full of thickets outside the wood, we come to a large **stone pillar,** from where there is another marvellous view, in this case over the cove of Sa Tuna.

We go down with great care due to the steep gradient over the last clifftop, with a spectacular perspective of the Cap de Begur. We immediately come to a perfectly conditioned coastal path with wooden railings, just above the wild reliefs of the point of **Es Plom**. The pleasant walk beneath a canopy of pine trees leads us directly to the **cove of Sa Tuna**, an old Mediterranean paradise reconverted into a holiday village. You have to go to the other side of the cove to find the continuation of the coastal path to Aiguafreda, lots of fun with a series of ups and down with steps and walkways. We thus reach the peaceful jetty of the **cove of Aiguafreda**, overlooked by the outline of a large hotel on the promontory of the **Cap Sa Sal**, a destination for diving fans, on being the entrance point to the **Marine Reserve of Ses Negres**, which extends along this section of coastline. From here we return towards Begur following the route of a Local Path (green and white marks). We go down

▲ **On the way to Sa Tuna**

▲ The Cap de Begur from the path to Sa Tuna

Carrer de Aiguafreda and Carrer Garbí (junction), until coming to a series of signs that tell us of the route to reach Es Quinze and Mas de'n Pinc. Following the signs, we go on a lovely path that enters a large holm-oak wood that covers the **stream of Aiguafreda**, where miraculously the original Mediterranean ecosystem has been maintained. Some steps and a small botanical route along what is called **Es Quinze** precede the walk past the historic **Mas d'en Pinc**, where we discover one of the eleven surveillance towers that the village of Begur once had during its age of splendour, in the 16th century. A little further on, we cross the ring-road of Begur and climb up Carrer Sant Ramon to visit the remains of the **castle of Begur** (264 m), documented since 1019. Below us we have the last extensive panorama of the walk, which allows us to take in nearly all the lands of Empordà. The descent from the castle to the **old centre** of the town reveals a pretty network of streets of medieval origin with watchtowers, as well as the large **19th-century mansions** of a large number of families who made their fortunes in the former American colonies.

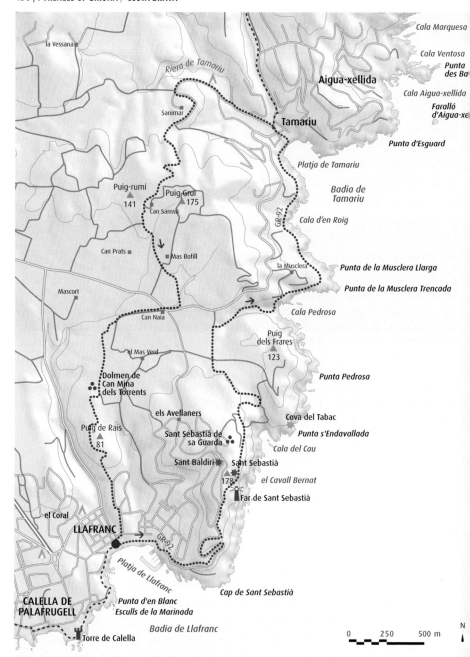

la Vessana

Cala Marquesa

Cala Ventosa

Punta des Ba

Riera de Tamariu

Aigua-xellida

Cala Aigua-xellida

Sanimar

Faralló d'Aigua-xe

Tamariu

Punta d'Esguard

Platja de Tamariu

Puig-rumí
141

Puig Grui
175

Can Samsó

Badia de Tamariu

GR-92

Cala d'en Roig

Can Prats

Mas Bofill

la Musclera

Punta de la Musclera Llarga

Punta de la Musclera Trencada

Mascort

Can Naia

Cala Pedrosa

Puig dels Frares
123

el Mas Verd

Punta Pedrosa

Dolmen de Can Mina dels Torrents

els Avellaners

Cova del Tabac

Punta s'Endavallada

Puig de Rais
81

Sant Sebastià de sa Guarda

Cala del Cau

Sant Baldiri

Sant Sebastià

el Cavall Bernat

178

Far de Sant Sebastià

el Coral

LLAFRANC

GR-92

CALELLA DE PALAFRUGELL

Platja de Llafranc

Punta d'en Blanc
Esculls de la Marinada

Cap de Sant Sebastià

Badia de Llafranc

Torre de Calella

0   250   500 m

N

8 THE CAP DE SANT SEBASTIÀ 8

▲ Tamariu

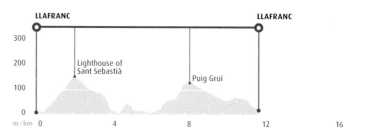

Methods
**Walking,
Nordic walking**

Distance
12 km

Duration
4-5 h

Gradients
+450 m / -450 m

This is a circular route, with the outwards path parallel to the coast following the GR-92 path between Llafranc and Tamariu (red and white marks), in which we alternate sensational views over high cliffs and the discovery of wild corners.
The return through thick woods enables us to compare the magnificent coastal scenery with the typical rural scenery of the lands of Empordà.

ROUTE
We start off from the **Passeig Cypsela in Llafranc**, beneath the lovely canopy of pine trees facing the local beach and the blue Mediterranean waters. At the end of this avenue, at the

entrance to the village's **sports port**, we should pay attention to the sign of the GR-92, which marks our route up some steps that helps us gain height quickly.

Once in the Passeig de Pau Casals, we continue along the road upwards, with some zigzags to climb the impressive cliffs of the **Cap de Sant Sebastià**, although the succession of chalets and cover of the pine trees do not give us many views. Only on reaching the entrance to the **lighthouse of Sant Sebastià**, built in 1857, do we get the first major panorama of the day: the Costa Brava to the south and the lands of Empurdà inland. From here we take some steps to link up with the path that goes round a popular **hermitage-hostel from the 18th century**, today reconverted into a luxury. We immediately come to the dominant **watchtower** from 1445, placed at the highest point of the **Puig de Sant Sebastià** (178 m). A little further on

we come to the excellent archaeological space of an **Iberian settlement** from the 4th century BC. Below us, the height of the cliffs is really impressive. We should pay attention on the next section of the path, which requires care due to the verticality of a series of rocky steps that we must go down. The path then turns inland to cross a thick pine wood until coming out onto a rural track. We must find between two estates the following marker to Tamariu, from where we begin a steep descent, parallel to the wild stream that comes out in the amazing **Cala Pedrosa**, totally covered with large stones, in which there is an old fisherman's hut in the shadow of the marvellous cliff of **Puig dels Frares** (123 m).

From Cala Pedrosa we take an interesting coastal path between rock steps and wooden handrails that enable us to cross the aesthetically pleasing reliefs of the **point of La Musclera**. We immediately come to an easy section through a pine wood until coming to the next stretch of path alongside the outline of the coast. The perimeter of several chalets marks our way, but at a given moment the marks of the GR-92 oblige us to drop directly along a very rocky zone to come to the pretty jetty of the **Cala d'en Roig**. We continue along a section of coastal path that leads directly to the sand of the fantastic beach of **Tamariu**, the smallest of the three old fishermen's districts of the municipal district of Palafrugell. If we have a little time to spare, we can go, behind an urbanisation of chalets, along the coastal path to the **Cala de Aigua-xelida**, which has a very spectacu-

▲ Path between the lighthouse of Sant Sebastià and Cala Pedrosa

▲ On the way between Cala Pedrosa and Tamariu

lar route. From Tamariu, to return to Lla-franc, we use a Short-Distance path (yellow and white marks), which in this case leads us inland passing the entrance to a campsite (Carrer de Costa Rica).

After completing a climb over a wide stretch of asphalt, we reach a junction and follow the marks of the path to the end of the urbanisation of chalets that surrounds Tamariu. We suddenly find ourselves in a thick Mediterranean wood, among oaks, holm-oaks and pine trees. Here we connect with a section of path that rises steeply until close to the peak of **Puig Gruí** (165 m). On coming out on a forest track, we begin a gentle descent that stops on the road between Tamariu and Palafrugell. Being attentive to the signposting, we walk for a few metres on this asphalted road and immediately take an easy path between estates and farmland. Further on we leave to one side the path to the interesting **dolmen of Can Mina dels Torrents**, dated around 2000 BC. Just here we begin the final descent to Llafranc, with a final section through an urbanisation of chalets until the rear part of the **church of Santa Rosa**. In this part of the village it is highly recommendable to go and see the archaeological remains of an old **Roman wine press** (Carrer del Coral), created in the 1st century BC, which tells us of the important Roman presence on the Costa Brava for five hundred years.

9 FROM SANT FELIU DE GUÍXOLS TO PALAMÓS

▲ On the coastal path between Platja d'Aro and Calonge

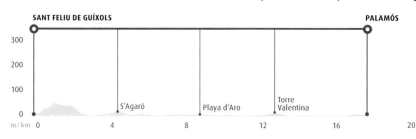

Methods
**Walking,
Nordic walking**

Distance
18 km

Duration
6 - 7 h

Gradients
+350 m / -350 m

One-way walk through a heavily humanised and tourist area, although we go very close to the coastline due to a succession of very attractive coastal paths. On the route of the GR-92 path we cross a large number of coves and cliffs covered by pine woods, with constant ups and downs. A regular bus line links all the towns and villages.

ROUTE

We start the walk at the **port of Sant Feliu de Guíxols**, walking along the wharves where the green route, the Vía Verde, ends, from Girona. Here we see a sign that goes to **Cala Jonca**, which we find hidden among large cliffs and the breakwater that closes the port. Some long steps take us out as far as a **viewpoint**, where we connect with the GR-92 path (red and white marks), which we follow until the end of the route. Here is where we start the first section of the coastal path, climbing a little until the fantastic **viewpoint of the Molí de les Forques** (80 m), where the road between Sant Feliu and Sant Pol passes by. From here we go down some more steps, under the cover of pine and oak woods, leaving on the right the entrance to the **Cala del Molí**. This cove has a spectacular circuit equipped for climbers, but our path passes by and continues until reaching the **Cala de L'Ametller**, where we enjoy its crystalline waters in a very beautiful setting. The scene

becomes even more glorious on getting to the **cliffs of Molar and Cap de Mort**, full of little corners of true fantasy, here featuring the **viewpoint of Les Mestresses** (70 m). Also of note in this section are the corners of **Cala En Oliu** and **Cala del Peix**, which we can see from above. The way between more rock steps and passages as well as a few more metres of the road between Sant Feliu and Sant Pol, and finally we go through a sensational **tunnel**. The delightful **Cala Maset** and the spot of **La Caleta** close this unforgettable coastal path, before coming out on the long **beach of Sant Pol**, which has several tourist establishments alongside an attractive promenade of wooden planks. At the opposite end of this avenue we find some old

▲ Cala de la Roca del Paller

9

bathing changing rooms and the start of the coastal path of S'Agaró.

The **coastal path of S'Agaró**, 2 kilometres in length, is an exemplary work made between the 1920s and 1930s, as a response to the installation, over the **mountain of S'Agaró,** of a series of chalets and luxury hotels aimed at the wealthiest members of society. Here we can enjoy a large number of viewpoints and corners of great beauty that culminate in the sands of the large **beach of Sa Conca**, all surrounded by pine woods. From here, the GR-92 path goes round the **sports port of Platja d'Aro** and takes us to a bridge that crosses the **river Ridaura**. From this point, we drop to the beginning of the esplanade of Platja d'Aro, the busiest tourist centre on the route. Having gone to the end of the **esplanade of Platja d'Aro**, we start the longest section of coastal paths on the route of nearly 4 kilometres, which begins at the emblematic monolithic rock of **Cavall Bernat**, 7 metres high. Close to this point, in an urban area, is the perimeter of an ancient **Roman villa**, easily identifiable due to the archaeological excavations. However, before entering the coastal paths, we have to cross the busy **beach of La Rovira**.

We then go along a surprising succession of tunnels excavated from the rock, through which the path progresses to connect with the **coves of Sa Cova and Pi**, both with steps under the cover of pine trees. A little further on we reach the attractive **Cala de Belladona**, protected by an islet, and after **Cap Roig**, and aesthetically pleasing promontory of clay and granite, with some pine trees, that separates the two coves of fine sand which we have to cross. Immediately after, we go below the walls of a large hotel via a long metallic walkway, from where the path goes up to reach the **beaches of Ses Torretes and Can Cristus**, which we must cross all the way. From the last beach, we go through a pretty tunnel that leads to the small **Cala del Forn**, surrounded by an attractive reedbed. The next part of the walk, between steps and ramps, culminates by going along the unspoilt enclaves of **Cala Els Esculls**, **Cala de la Roca del Paller** and the **Cap de Roques Planes**. Finally, the coastal path rises a final time to enable us a view of the **bay of Palamós** at our feet. Just above, we discover the slender **Torre dels Perpinyà**, a modern reproduction of one of the many watchtowers that extended all along the Costa Brava from the Middle Ages. Shortly after we complete the coastal path by reaching the historic **Torre Valentina**, this one the original, built at the end of the 16th century and today in the shadow of a large tourist complex. From here we cover the last kilometres on the esplanades that join the pretty **beaches of Sant Antoni de Calonge** and the large **port of Palamós**. It is an urban route of 4 kilometres to comfortably end the walk.

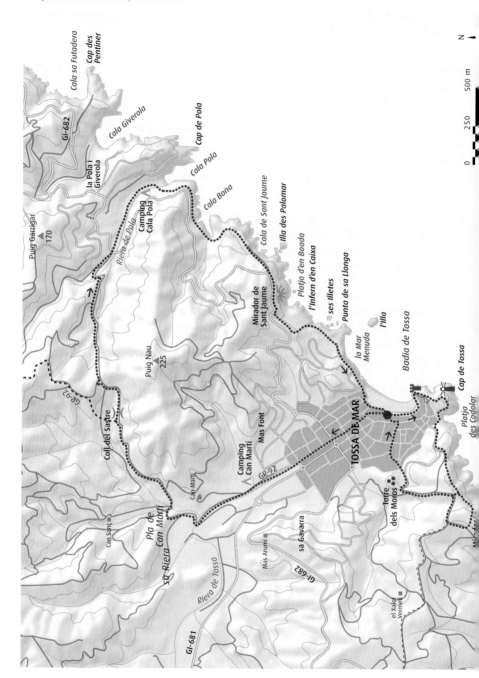

Cala sa Futadera
Cap des Pentiner
Cala Giverola
GI-682
la Pola i Giverola
Puig Garrigàr
170
Cap de Pola
Cala Pola
Riera de Pola
Camping Cala Pola
Cala Bona
Cala de Sant Jaume
Illa des Palomar
Mirador de Sant Jaume
Platja d'en Boada
l'Infern d'en Caixa
ses Illetes
Punta de sa Llonga
l'Illa
la Mar Menuda
Badia de Tossa
GR-92
Coll del Sastre
Puig Nau
225
Mas Font
Camping Can Martí
GR-92
Can Martí
TOSSA DE MAR
Cap de Tossa
Platja des Codolar
Torre dels Moros
Pla de Can Martí
sa Riera
Can Sánç
Mas Arumí
GI-682
sa Gavarra
Riera de Tossa
GI-681
el Xalet Vermell

N
0   250   500 m

10 AROUND TOSSA DE MAR 10

▲ Cala Pola

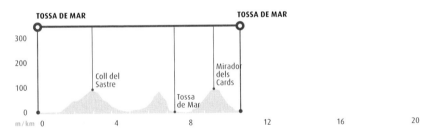

Methods
**Walking,
Nordic walking**

Distance
10 km

Duration
3 - 4 h

Gradients
+450 m / -450 m

This is a circular route across the coastal buttresses of the massif of L'Ardenya, which comprises an exceptional fusion between sea and mountain, with a vast extension of oak and pine woods over wild cliffs. The marvellous old citadel of Tossa de Mar and its environs also offer a fantastic tour to complete the trip.

ROUTE

We leave from the town centre of **Tossa de Mar**, following the course of the Rambla Pau Casals to the end. On passing a campsite to one side, the avenue becomes a dirt track that continues alongside the **stream of Tossa**. On the other ap-

▲ Cap de Tossa

pears the municipal sports area, the moment when we enter the **Parc de Sa Riera**, a very pretty and exuberant forested spot due to the presence of water throughout the year, where a microclimate has favoured the conservation of very large trees. On reaching the **Pla de Sant Martí** (crossroads of paths and tracks), we follow the sign of the GR-92 path and head right, upwards, towards the hermitage of Sant Grau and the Puig de Cadiretes. After crowning the **Coll del Sastre** (125 m), we come to a new sign, that directs us to the right towards Cala Giverola and Cala Pola. We quickly and directly complete a descent to a large car parking area, accessible from the coast road between Tossa de Mar and Sant Feliu de Guíxols. We ignore the climb up to the road and continue downwards, following the course of the **stream of Pola**, which takes us below the

road, with access to a campsite that we cross completely. We thus reach the fantastic **Cala Pola**, within a setting of cliffs and woods that represent the taster of the return coastal path to Tossa de Mar. It is a path that goes over the reliefs of the coast, with constant ups and downs, that requires care on some very craggy points. The signs we must follow on this section are green markers and several signposts. In any case, watching how the majesty of the **massif of L'Ardenya** falls into the Mediterranean Sea in such a stunning way is undoubtedly a real privilege, thanks to a route recently recovered for great walking trips.

After a steep and quite difficult descent we discover the magical **Cala Bona**, a spot where the crystalline waters, the walls of rock and the greenness of the woods have created an unforgettable decor. We continue the walk over some massive cliffs of over 100 metres in height, guarded by several islets below. At a given moment, the signposted path takes us up to a privileged **viewpoint** alongside the coast road, which provides us with an excellent general panorama of Tossa de Mar, from where we should pay attention to find the continuation of the coastal path. Once again we have a steep descent ahead through a dense wood, with a maze-like path but always well-signposted, until coming out into an urbanisation of chalets. Walking through the asphalted streets of Tossa takes us to the pretty **esplanade**, which links the town's different beaches. Not to be missed under any circumstances is a visit to the monumental **Vila Vella**, which appears at the southern end of the **Platja Gran** beach. A recommendable tour involves climbing alongside the **walls** via a series of ramps and linking up with the paths that

lead to the highest point of **Cap de Tossa**, crowned by a lighthouse, where there is a pretty forested park. On the way down we go through the narrow cobbled streets of the only fortified villa of the Catalan coast –established between the 12th and 16th centuries–, and also one of the few conserved in Europe at sea level. The culmination of the route proposed comprises taking the coastal path that climbs behind the walls via some long steps to the viewpoint of the **Punta des Cards** (105 m), located above the most impressive and inaccessible cliffs. To return to the town centre of Tossa, we can repeat the same journey passing by the Vila Vella or by using another signposted way inland from the Punta des Cards as well.

▲ The "Vila Vella" of Tossa

CYCLING
routes

The lands of Girona can boast the best networks in Europe for cycling routes. Their history began some twenty years ago, with the works on the route of the old narrow-gauge railway lines to turn them into cycle-touring routes: what are called the **Vies Verdes** or Green Ways, which today let you pedal between the Pyrenees and the Costa Brava for 150 kilometres. In 2013 a system of routes were opened, complementary to the Vies Verdes, that closes a large circuit of cycle-touring between the centre of the Costa Brava and the south of France, and which is called the **Pirinexus Network**. Simultaneously other local cycle-touring routes were consolidated in the counties of La Selva, Gironès, Baix Empordà, Alt Empordà and Pla de l'Estany, which in this way allows for multiple alternatives over more than 300 kilometres of signposted ways. Moreover, we have the cycling routes for mountain bikes or MBT, with different centres spread around all Girona's counties and thus increasing the total figure to above 600 kilometres.

In our guide we have focused mainly on cycle touring, but using a mountain bike, since it adapts to the needs of most people as well as making it easier to possibly link up routes. We therefore take the Vies Verdes as our base, which mainly have compacted earth tracks, on which we recommend the bicycle as ideal for enjoying active tourism and discovering a region of broad horizons. Therefore, two-thirds of the suggested routes will have a direct relationship with the concept of cycle touring, while the other third of the routes are oriented towards a sportier user or bicycles with greater potential. While half of the routes have a start and finish in the same town, the other half require return transport, either by train between Barcelona and the French border, or using specific bus routes that allow you to take bicycles, for which you will need a special bike bag.

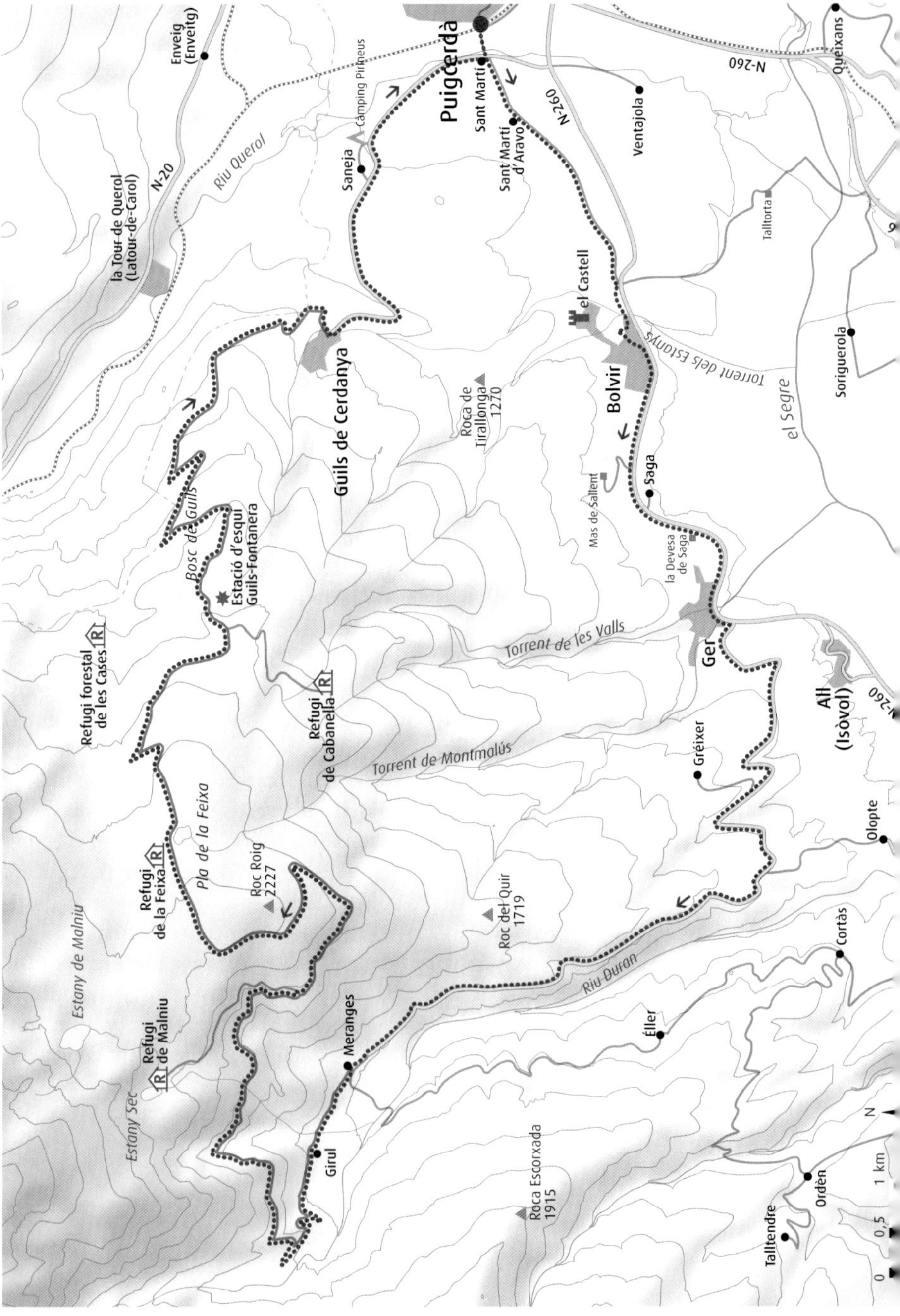
Puigcerdà
Sant Martí
Sant Martí d'Aravo
N-260
Ventajola
Queixans
Enveig (Enveitg)
Camping Pirineus
Saneja
Riu Querol
N-20
la Tour-de-Querol (Latour-de-Carol)
Talltorta
el Castell
Bolvir
Torrent dels Estanys
el Segre
Sorigueerola
Guils de Cerdanya
Roca de Tirallonga 1270
Saga
Mas de Sallent
la Devesa de Saga
Bosc de Guils
Estació d'esquí Guils-Fontanera
Refugi forestal de les Cases
Refugi de Cabanella
Torrent de les Valls
Ger
All (Isòvol)
Gréixer
Torrent de Montmalús
Pla de la Feixa
Refugi de la Feixa
Roc Roig 2227
Roc del Quir 1719
Olopte
Cortàs
Riu Duran
Estany de Malniu
Refugi de Malniu
Meranges
Éller
Estany Sec
Girul
Roca Escorxada 1915
Talltendre
Ordèn
N
0 0.5 1 km

1 AROUND PUIGCERDÀ

▲ **Herd of horses between Ger and Meranges**

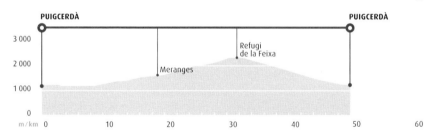

PUIGCERDÀ — PUIGCERDÀ

Refugi de la Feixa

Meranges

Distance
50 km

Gradients
+1,200 m / -1,200 m

Located in the heart of the county of La Cerdanya, we propose a very spectacular route, which climbs up to heights of over 2,000 metres, always using comfortable roads, asphalted tracks and dirt tracks. The route also includes beautiful mountain villages, rural spots with great character and the attractions of the town of Puigcerdà.

ROUTE

The capital of La Cerdanya, **Puigcerdà** (1,200 m), is placed on a large hill at the end of the **valley of the river Querol**, a space of glacial origins that has marked the border with France since the signing of the Treaty of the Pyrenees in

1659. It was founded in 1178, although from those times only a robust **bell tower** remains, and is one of the local emblematic buildings. The other point of interest is a delightful **lake**, which is documented in 1260 and from the late 19th century was rehabilitated as a park for the well-off. To find the starting and finishing point of the route, you should go to the low part of the town, beside the historic trans-frontier **train station**. We leave from here, parallel to the railway line heading towards France, cross the track over a level crossing and we carry on over the **bridge of Sant Martí d'Aravó** (1,160 m), over the river Querol. On the right we leave the road that leads to the village of Guils de Cerdanya, which is where we return to complete the route. For now we carry on straight ahead along a country road to the village of **Bolvir** (1,150 m), a very old human settlement that dates back to the Bronze Age, with remains of an Iberian fortress from be-

tween the 3rd and 1st centuries BC. Here we come to the main road between Puigcerdà and Seu d'Urgell, which we go along for 3 kilometres, until coming to the first turning for the village of **Ger** (1,135 m), beside its cemetery. This village also dates back to very remote times and has a structure of a typical Catalan mountain village, with solid stone houses and slate roofs. Following the signs, we continue along the county road that leads to the village of Meranges, with a route of bends and gentle slopes that make the first climb of the route very pleasant. We thus reach **Meranges** (1,540 m) after 17 kilometres since starting off in Puigcerdà, always enjoying a fantastic rural setting.

Meranges is a pretty and popular spot due to its structure of mountain village with medieval origins, where the main activity of the region is still maintained: cattle and horse breeding. From here we continue along the asphalted track that leads to the refuge of Malniu, and which has a winding route that enables us to take in excellent views. After 6 kilometres, the asphalt ends and turns into a dirt track, still wide and with moderate gradients. We then reach a **fork of tracks** (2,000 m), leaving as optional the continuation of the climb towards the **refuge of Malniu** (2,140 m), 2.5 kilometres away, a highly recommended visit to spend a while in the pure high mountain, among lakes, woods and meadows. The forest track towards Guils de Cerdanya climbs a little more, until reaching the **Pla de la Feixa** (2,210 m), through extensive black pine woods. A little further on we come to the

▲ The lake of Puigcerdà

1

▲ Livestock in the village of Ger

historic **refuge of La Feixa** (2,160 m), of free use, situated in the middle of a large clearing with good views. Further down we come to well-placed fountain, from where we start the final descent to Puigcerdà. With forty kilometres pedalling behind us, we reach the **cross-country skiing resort of Guils-Fontanera** (1,905 m), around which we can note an increase in forest vegetation, and as well as black pines there is a fine representation of birches and sorb trees, very attractive woods during the autumn. From here you just have to glide down a mountain road for 7 steep kilometres, leaving us in the lower part of the village of **Guils de Cerdanya** (1,385 m), the last village on the route, with an outstanding Romanesque church. We complete the return to Puigcerdà along the easy county road that links the two places, passing by the country house of **Sant Vicenç de Saneja** (1,220 m), a good end to savour the landscapist and cultural essence of the large **valley of La Cerdanya**.

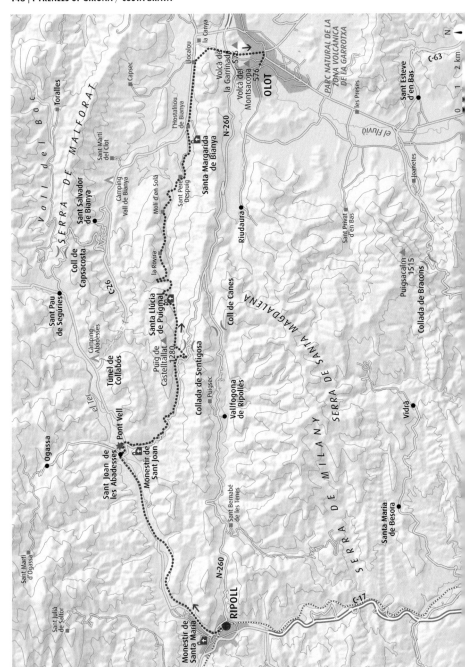

2

FROM RIPOLL TO OLOT ALONG THE GREEN WAY

▲ Monastery of Santa Maria de Ripoll

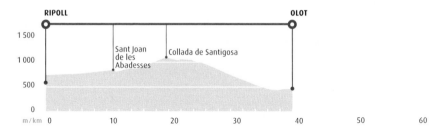

Distance
40 km

Gradients
+500 m / -750 m

We connect two Pyrenean capitals, with the first section along the *Ruta del Ferro*, or Iron Way, which forms part of Girona's cycle-touring network and is related to the former train line of some old mines. On the central part of the route we enjoy the full beauty of the Girona Pyrenees, due to a very solitary section that links up two Vies Verdes.

ROUTE

We leave from the centre of **Ripoll** (690 m), the historic capital of the Girona Pyrenees, with its **monastery of Santa María**, one of the most emblematic in Catalonia. The Ruta del Ferro leaves from the other side of the **river Ter**, with a

▲ Autumn close to Santa Llúcia de Puigmal

totally asphalted way and a gentle climb, always going up the attractive banks of Girona's longest river. After ten calm kilometres, the arrival at **Sant Joan de les
Abadesses** (780 m) is in its old train station.
From here, the Ruta del Ferro continues a
little more until Ogassa, where the old coal
mines are, mined from the early 19th century until 1967. To continue our route, you
have to go down to the bridge on the main
road, which takes us across the river Ter
again, and then through the old centre of
Sant Joan, alongside the fantastic **monastery** of Romanesque origin that gives the
village its name. On the other side of the
village we start the climb on the road to
Olot, via the **Collada de Santigosa**
(1,064 m), which represents 7 kilometres of
climbing on a winding road, with very little
traffic and some shade from the forest. On
reaching the mountain pass, we find on the

left a sign that marks the start of the forest
track to **Santa Llúcia de Puigmal** (850 m),
3.5 kilometres away, a very pretty spot with
a popular hermitage and a fountain. We
find ourselves on the high part of where valleys join, which at the same time joins different climatic atmospheres, as can be seen
from the mixture of pines, beech, oak and
holm-oak woods: a small natural paradise
with great chromatic contrasts according to
the time of the year. From this spot, we continue going down the main track, where we
pass by some fantastic **gorges with waterfalls**. We should then be careful when
reaching some forks, always keeping to the
clearest track, in gradual descent, passing
by a farmhouse in ruins with a fountain, a
small stream and a wall that marks the entrance to the county of La Garrotxa.

After 4.5 kilometres from Santa Llúcia de
Puigmal, we reach the **Mas de La Rovira**

(690 m), also in ruins, on a lovely meadow with a strategic panoramic view over the extensive municipality of **La Vall de Bianya**, from where we make a sharp descent of 2.5 kilometres with some bends. This descent ends in an asphalted track, and a few metres ahead appears the large **Mas del Molí d'en Solà** (460 m), currently a country guesthouse. After another 2 kilometres along the same track we reach the village of **Sant Pere Despuig** (420 m), which has a Romanesque church on a small hill. From here we continue along a quiet local road for 2.5 kilometres, to the village of **L'Hostalnou de Bianya** (370 m), where we connect with a cycling track of 3 kilometres, to the left of the main road, which leads to the village of **Llocalou** (traffic lights). Once here, we cross the road to continue on the cycle track, with another

2.5 kilometres parallel to the **stream of Ridaura**, until coming to the entrances and industrial estates of the lively city of **Olot** (440 m). We can make the end of the route more interesting if we take a cemented track that passes between the **Garrinada volcano** (576 m), on the left, and the **Montsacopa volcano** (538 m), on the right, until Carrer Sant Bernat, which introduces us to the old centre of the city. Around Olot extends the **Natural Park of the Volcanic Zone of La Garrotxa**, which with forty volcanic cones covered with woods, has many routes, being considered the best reserve of these characteristics on the Iberian Peninsula.

▲ The "Via Verda" by Santa Llúcia de Puigmal

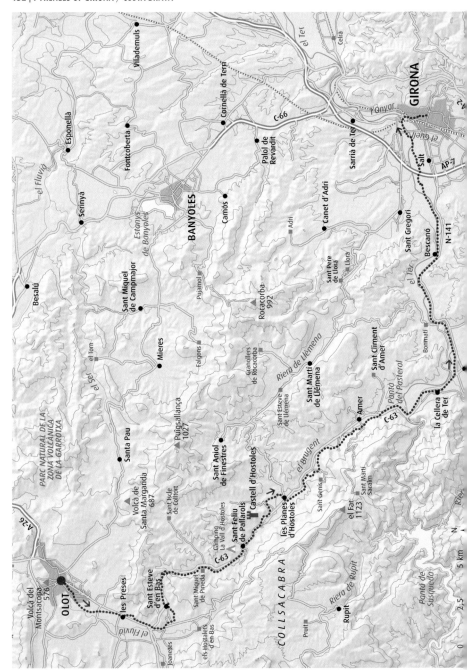

3

FROM OLOT TO GIRONA ALONG THE GREEN WAY

▲ Park of La Devesa in Girona in late autumn

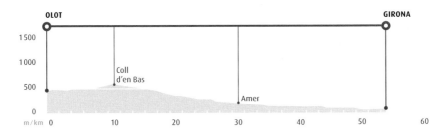

Distance
55 km

Gradients
+250 m / -620 m

Known popularly as the *Ruta del Carrilet*, it is the star route of the Vies Verdes network in the lands of Girona. The reason lies in the route itself over an old train line, through harmonious landscapes, that ran between 1911 and 1969. Its reconversion into a cycle route has been not only a success but also a model to follow.

ROUTE

From the end of the Passeig de Barcelona, in **Olot** (440 m), we find what is called the *Pont de Ferro*, or Iron Bridge, which crosses the **river Fluvià**, close to which begins the green way to Girona. It is a fantastic start through tunnels, woods, fields and old railway stations. During the first 10 kilometres we have to cross lots of junctions, especially between the villages of **Les Preses** (470 m) and **Sant Esteve d'en Bas** (490 m). On this section we can appreciate the great harmony and beauty that extends throughout the length and breadth of the municipality of **La Vall d'en Bas**, a space with different villages spread at the feet of the majestic mountains of the **massif of Puigsacalm** and the **massif of Collsacabra**. Once past the pretty village of Sant Esteve, with its Romanesque church, we begin the climb along a section of old road that crosses the **Coll d'en Bas** (620 m). In total it is less than 2 kilometres of asphalt, between the climb and the descent alongside **La Vall d'Hostoles**, where the next passing point is the church of **Sant Miquel de Pineda** (520 m). We have the main road on our left at all times, the route along the way of **Sant Feliu de Pallerols** (470 m) being a real pleasure. It is just here where we pass through a surprising tunnel that comes out on the way,

and from here to an area of chalets, to finish with a lovely section among riverside vegetation over the **river Brugent**. Just on the 20-kilometre mark, we go under the main road using a 100-metre long tunnel and at the exit the hill on which stands the historic **castle of Hostoles** (584 m). We then go through the entrance to the **hermitage of Àngel**, with a good general view of La Vall d'Hostoles and the large **mountain of Far** on the horizon.

On crossing the river Brugent by a bridge, we enter the village of **Les Planes d'Hostoles** (350 m), just beside its old train station. Once again we must pass to the other side of the main road, after 23 kilometres' cycling. We leave this village behind along a spectacular section of the old train line, excavated through a rocky area, which also has a walkway. We thus enter the county of La Selva, and a little further on we pass on the right a sign that announces a visit on foot to the hermitage of **Sant Genís Sacosta**. From this point we have a section of 2.5 kilometres that will make us negotiate four walkways and which culminates in the spot of **Font Picant**. We immediately enter the village of **Amer** (190 m), with 30 kilometres of the route completed. Amer features the area around the old train station, but above all its old centre with a delightful arcaded **square**. To continue ahead, we pass again several junction and should pay great attention when crossing the main road again, just at the point where the green way goes below a large bridge and the **weir of El Pasteral** (180 m), an infrastructure that, to-

▲ Plaça Major of Amer

▲ Girona

gether with the large reservoirs of Sau and Susqueda, control the flow of the river Ter. A very spectacular variant consists of climbing along the road for 10 kilometres to the **weir of Susqueda** (380 m) and from here cross the **massif of Les Guilleries** on a forest track for 7 kilometres, until the village of Osor, from where there is still 9 kilometres more along a county road to the town of Anglès. Here it links up again with the green way to Girona. For this variant, much more demanding, you should add 20 kilometres to the route total and 450 metres more of uphill and downhill gradients.

Continuing our route, from the village of **La Cellera de Ter** (170 m), we go through pretty farmland and the other towns and villages before entering Girona. First **Anglès** (160 m), with its medieval centre; then **Bonmatí** (150 m), where we go along a pretty section of the river Ter, and finally **Bescanó** (100 m), which we pass on the other side of the road. Once here, we will have covered 45 kilometres of route and a little further on we come to the division of the green way into two very different sections. If we go straight on, it is a more direct route to the centre of the town of Salt, but if we turn to the left, we will have more time to enjoy the banks of the **river Ter**. We suggest the latter, in fact, a route that goes into fantastic riverside woods and brings us to a canoeing school and then the **Parc del Ter**. This pretty final section, through the quietest part of the municipality of **Salt** (80 m), also means we can take several agricultural tracks through a zone of orchards, until reaching the city of **Girona** (70 m). We arrive at the capital of the Girona region via its most emblematic green space: the **Parc de la Devesa**, with its exceptional plane tree wood of some 150 years standing.

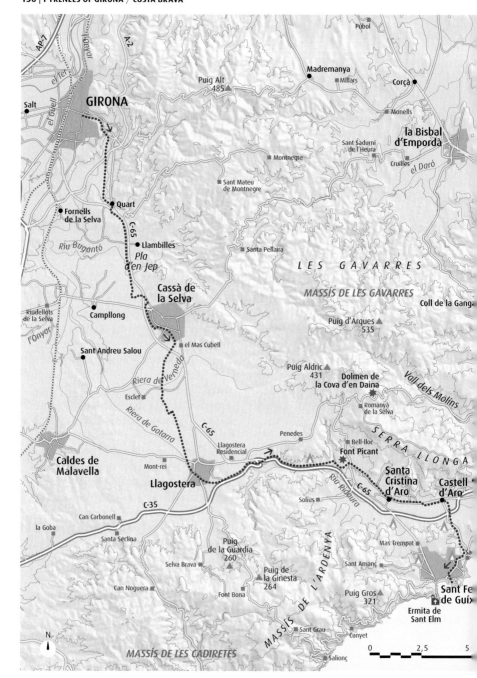

FROM GIRONA TO SANT FELIU DE GUÍXOLS ALONG THE GREEN WAY

4

▲ Beach of Sant Pol in Sant Feliu de Guíxols

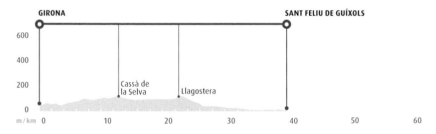

Distance
40 km

Gradients
+150 m / -220 m

This is the second part of the popular *Ruta del Carrilet*, in this case in a transitional space between the Pyrenees of Girona and the heart of the Costa Brava. The old train line found a more extensive scenery here, as well as greater comfort in advancing through a large area of farmland until the corridor of La Vall d'Aro, a destination that has a large number of cycling routes.

ROUTE
We leave from the sensational **old centre of Girona** (70 m), between the river Onyar and the Plaça de Catalunya, following the signs of the cycle-touring lane that leads to the Plaça

dels Països Catalans, a point where we connect with the green way heading to Sant Feliu de Guíxols. For the first few kilometres through the district of La Creueta, we have to go through numerous junctions and forks. This is the way to the old train station of **Quart** (140 m), a quiet village surrounded by an attractive setting of low mountains at the foot of the **massif of Les Gavarres**. The route then leads us directly to the old station of **Llambilles** (150 m), leaving the village a little higher up, just when we have covered the first 10 kilometres. The route to the next village is 5 kilometres more through farmland. **Cassà de la Selva** (140 m) is noted for its connection with forestry work, mainly the exploitation of cork, due to its central position in relation to the large woods of the massif of Les Gavarres. In the outskirts is **Parc Art**, which concentrates numerous works of contemporary art in the open air.

After stopping off at the old train station of Cassà, which is also a cultural centre, we start the longest stretch along this an extensive area of farmland for 8 kilometres, until the town of **Llagostera** (160 m), whose silhouette stands out due to its raised position, with its church of Sant Feliu on the highest part of an old centre where the remains of the old medieval city wall are conserved. Inevitably, the green way takes us to the old train station of Llagostera, and from here continue until we are over the main road from Barcelona, which a little further on ends up connecting with the road from Girona. On this section we enjoy a series of descents that take us to the **Vall d'Aro**, a natural corridor between the massif of Les Gavarres and the **massif of L'Ardenya.**

The route along the Vall d'Aro is very enjoyable, featuring the passing through several pine woods and the presence of pretty

▲ **Old railway station of Santa Cristina d'Aro**

▲ The "Via Verda" in Castell d'Aro

farmhouses converted into restaurants. During the route we pass over the **stream of Salenys** on a pretty bridge, where we also come to a turning to Romanyà de la Selva, on the left. A little further ahead, now at the point of completing thirty kilometres, we pass beside the popular restaurant of **La Font Picant**, attached to an old train station. We soon come to the old train station of **Santa Cristina d'Aro** (30 m), although it is interesting to make a visit of the old village of **Solius** along a local road indicated from the junction of La Font Picant. The village of **Castell d'Aro** (40 m) immediately appears, where it is an absolute must to climb up from the old station to the medieval complex around the church of Santa Maria and the **castle of Benidormiens**. From Castell d'Aro we drop to the **river Ridaura**, which we cross via a sus-

pension bridge, and then the green way leads us to cross the different roads that lead into **Sant Feliu de Guíxols**, with a final descent to its emblematic Passeig de Mar. Once here, we can complete the day with the visit to its millenary **monastery**, or climb to the wonderful viewpoint of the **hermitage** of **Sant Elm**, which, according to tradition, was the point from where this coastline was given the name of "Costa Brava" in 1908.

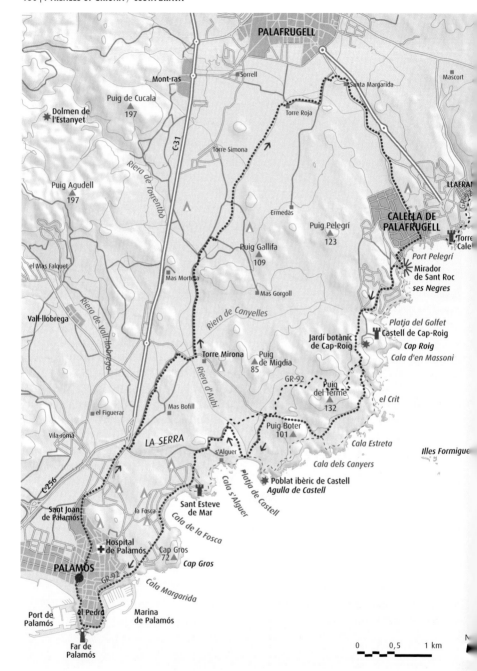

PALAFRUGELL

Mont-ras

Sorrell

Mascort

Santa Margarida

Puig de Cucala
197

Torre Roja

Dolmen de
l'Estanyet

LLAFRA

Torre Simona

C-31

Riera de Torrentbó

Ermedas

CALELLA DE
PALAFRUGELL

Puig Agudell
197

Puig Pelegrí
123

Torre
Cale

Puig Gallifa
109

Port Pelegrí

Mirador
de Sant Roc
ses Negres

el Mas Falquet

Mas Mortera

Mas Gorgoll

Vall-llobrega

Riera de Canyelles

Riera de Vall-llobrega

Platja del Golfet
Castell de Cap-Roig

Jardí botànic
de Cap-Roig

Cap Roig
Cala d'en Massoni

Torre Mirona

Puig
de Migdia
85

GR-92

Riera d'Aubi

Puig
del Terme
132

el Crit

Mas Bofill

el Figuerar

LA SERRA

Puig Boter
101

Cala Estreta

Vila-roma

s'Alguer

Illes Formigue

Cala dels Canyers

C-256

Cala s'Alguer

Platja de Castell

Poblat ibèric de Castell
Agulla de Castell

Sant Joan
de Palamós

la Fosca

Sant Esteve
de Mar

Hospital
de Palamós

Cala de la Fosca

Cap Gros
72

Cap Gros

PALAMÓS

GR-92

Cala Margarida

Port de
Palamós

el Pedró

Marina
de Palamós

Far de
Palamós

0   0,5   1 km

CYCLING ROUTES

5 AROUND PALAMÓS

▲ The "Via Verda" between Mont-ras and Palafrugell

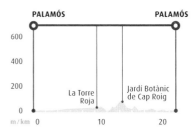

Distance
23 km

Gradients
+250 m / -250 m

On the outward journey the planned circuit goes along the attractive *Ruta del Tren Petit* (Route of the Small Train), the name that recalls the old railway line that went between Palamós, La Bisbal d'Empordà and Girona between 1887 and 1956. For the return we cross the Natural Area of Castell-Cap Roig, which houses one of the last unspoilt corners of the Costa Brava, with some demanding climbs through the Mediterranean woods.

ROUTE
We leave from the **port of Palamós** heading towards Palafrugell via a series of avenues that lead us to the County

▲ **Rural track between Palamós and Palafrugell**

Hospital, from where we connect with a cy-cle lane to a petrol station. Just here is where the Ruta del Tren Petit begins, which crosses a fantastic setting of fields and scattered old farmhouses. We should pay attention to the signs, since we pass many junctions and di-visions along the way. The first one on the left takes us to the village of Vall-llobrega, the second on the right, to the beach of Cas-tell, where we will pass on the return trip. For now we continue always in the direction of Mont-ras and Palafrugell, taking as a ref-erence point the course of the **stream of Aubi**, which at a given moment we cross by a pretty walkway. Further on we cross the lovely fields of the district of **Torre Simona**, now inside the municipality of Mont-ras,

with a long line of reedbeds that accompany the way to the final division along the route. On the left we leave the branch that goes to the village of **Mont-ras**, with its church clearly visible. We turn right and once again cross the stream of Aubi on the side of the old **Mas de la Torre Roja**, until coming out at a cement track that marks the final point of the Ruta del Tren Petit. Towards the right, this track leads to the rural village of **Ermedàs**, but we turn left and come out onto the old road between Palafrugell and Calella de Palafrugell. Once here we pedal towards Calella on this quiet road, which initially takes us around the wall with watchtowers of the beautiful **Mas de Santa Margarida**. After a short climb through an oak wood, we begin the direct descent that takes to the old centre of **Calella de Palafrugell**, with half the route now completed. If we want to take in the fantastic outlines of the coast and continue ahead with our route, we recommend climbing up above the **beach of Port Pelegrí** to the **viewpoint of Sant Roc** (hotel), and from here to the Avinguda de la Costa Brava.

You need to make a full-blooded effort to finish the full climb of the Avinguda de la Costa Brava to the Botanical Garden of Cap Roig. The climb ends at a crossroads of paths, beside a farmhouse that is also one of the entrances to the **Natural Area of Castell-Cap Roig**. Following the sign before us, we go along the forest track to the beach of Castell and Palamós, a route marked initially by the GR-92 path. The track borders the romantic **Botanical Garden of Cap Roig**, which is an optional visit. We must deal with a sharp climb to crown the **Coll de Cap Roig** (120 m), from where we get a full view of the Mediterranean. Here we begin a drop that firstly passes a junction, with a turning to the left that goes to the solitary **Cala del Crit**. Our route continues at all times on the main track. We must take great care with the steep gradient, which is tempting to career down at top speed, and which ends passing some estates and the access track to the marvellous **Cala Estreta**. A little further on we pass the entrance to the **Punta dels Canyers** and set off on another steep climb, always keeping to the forest track. The final descent leaves us at the point where the asphalted road ends that leads to the **beach of**

Castell. In this case it is well worth reaching the sands of this exceptional beach, which houses the remains of an **Iberian settlement** from the 6th century BC over a promontory that closes the bay of the same name. To continue along the route, we go across the sands to the point where the old coastal path starts to Palamós, where we once again find the marks of the GR-92 path, that lead us to the neighbouring **Cala S'Alguer**, where it is not possible to pass by bicycle.

From the beach of Castell we have to take the marked way that climbs the course of the stream of Aubi, through a thick wood, to the **stone bridge** (end of one of the branches of the Ruta del Tren Petit). From here we continue along the signposted cycle lane towards Palamós along the beach of La Fosca, a section where we enjoy lovely scenery amidst fields and woods, until reaching the outside of a campsite. Once over the entrance road to a residential urbanisation, we drop down to the **beach of La Fosca**, within the setting overlooked by the large promontory **Cap Gros**. At the other end of the beach we find the beginning of the road to the town centre of Palamós, which obliges us to climb to reach **Cala Margarida** and the **sports port of Palamós**. A final suggestion is to climb to the **Punta del Molí**, where the **lighthouse of Palamós** stands, with the large wharves from where we started the route on the other side, and the whole of the **bay of Palamós** at our feet.

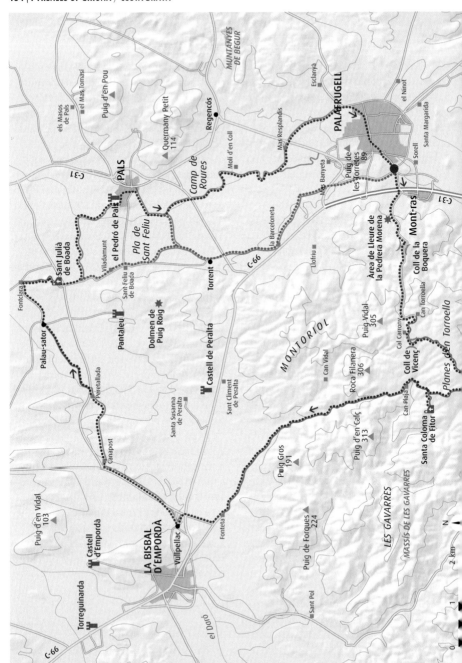

6 AROUND PALAFRUGELL 6

▲ Arrival at Santa Coloma de Fitor

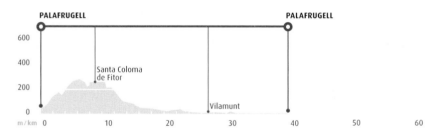

Distance
40 km

Gradients
+500 m / -500 m

This is a circular route that encompasses a rich historical heritage, firstly through the extensive woods of the massif of Les Gavarres, with a difficult section to deal with in Fitor. After enjoying the long descent to end by La Bisbal d'Empordà, the return to Palafrugell enables us to visit spectacular villages, such as Peratallada and Pals, within a fantastic rural setting.

ROUTE
Our starting point is the roundabout that joins the Avingu-da de Espanya and the Avinguda de la Generalitat de **Pala-frugell** (50 m), next to the Tourist Office, in the direction of the turning to the neighbouring village of Mont-ras. At the

▲ Santa Coloma de Fitor

second roundabout that connects with the dual carriageway between Palamós and Palafrugell, we climb up an asphalted ramp, alongside a supermarket, that leads us to **Mont-ras** (50 m), though on the right we pass its small old centre to continue straight on the way of the *Camí de Fitor* (signposted with markers). A little further on we leave on the right the area of the old **Morena Quarry**, conditioned as a leisure area, with a lake. We then start to climb along the long dirt track that leads to Fitor and other destinations of the **massif of Les Gavarres**. We thus reach the **Coll de la Boqueta** (175 m), where different signposted ways meet and we set off on a gentle descent until passing a stream. The track suddenly becomes cemented with a steep ramp to climb that requires a great physical effort. On ending the cemented section we come out beside the estate of **Mas Torroella** (240 m), which we go round with a new climb, leaving to the right the **Mas de Can Carrony** (260 m). A little further on, we reach the wide **Coll de Vicenç** (265 m), where many signposted ways meet up. We must continue on the left, in the direction of Fitor, along the main track suitable for all types of vehicles, disregarding the Short-Distance marked path from Montras which we do use on the return for a short section further ahead. For a while we enjoy a route of slight ascent on a good section of track that crosses the extensive woods of the **Planes d'en Torroella**, where we must ignore the secondary path branches, until reaching the crossroads of the **Pla del Descàrrec** (310 m).

Following a new sign, we begin a descent with some bends, until the wonderful spot of **Santa Coloma de Fitor** (245 m), a Romanesque church with origins in the 10th century, located in the middle of some fields surrounded by the best Mediterranean woods of holm-oaks, oaks and pine trees. Up to here we have done twelve kilometres of our route, but to continue we must go back half a kilometre to a bend on the same track, where the path leaves on the left signposted as Short-Distance to Mont-ras, the same path we left before on the Coll de Vicenç. We continue on this path, with a descent where further down we have to dismount and go on foot along a part of the way that is very broken up, until crossing the **stream of Fitor** (185 m). We then climb to the pass of the pretty farmhouse of **Can Plaja** (210 m), leaving the Short-Distance path on the right. Our route continues straight ahead along the way, which makes a pleasant tour through some fields until the junction of **Camp de la Cadena** (230 m). From here we link up with the main track, which drops through dense woods until the village of Fonteta, with 6 kilometres of route to enjoy all the forest beauty of the massif of Les Gavarres. Once in **Fonteta** (50 m), we discover an interesting group of houses dating from the 16th and 17th centuries, although the origins of the village date back to the 10th century as part of the old *Cami ral*, or royal way, which went from La Bisbal d'Empordà to the coast, passing by the church of Fitor.

From Fonteta, we follow the local road that crosses the main road between Palafrugell and La Bisbal, to the neighbouring village of **Vulpellac** (50 m), where we can appreciate a compact and pretty collection of stone houses around a 14th-century castle-palace. Now with half the route completed, from Vulpellac we follow one of the cycle routes of the Baix Empordà network. The first section, parallel to the road, goes towards Ullastret until **Canapost** (45 m), another tiny village of medieval origin, which features its 12th-century Romanesque church. From Canapost, we link up with one of the variants of the GR-92 path (red and white marks), through a pleasant section of path under the cover of woods, that takes us to **Peratallada** (35 m), a village that boasts one of the best medieval complexes in Catalonia. Peratallada is noted for its walls, with its moat carved out of the living rock, an elegant castle-palace and an unforgettable arcaded square. You have to look for the continuation of the marked route at the other end of the village, in this case along an agricultural path that goes straight to **Palau-sator** (25 m), another village of medieval origin with a closely-knit complex of stone houses around a large Watchtower, which has an arcade at the base. A pleasant cemented path joins Palau-sator with the houses of **Fontclara** (20 m). Here we link up with the way to the small church of **Sant Julià de Boada** (25 m) from the 10th century, from where we must follow a section of cycle route that coincides with the **Pirinexus network**.

From Sant Julià de Boada we follow the signs to the town of Pals, paying attention on passing crossroads and forks through a

▲ Sant Julià de Boada

▲ "Via Verda" betwen Pals and Palafrugell

harmonious patchwork of farmland. We thus clock up thirty kilometres of our route, just at the foot of the monumental **Pedró de Pals** (55 m), which stands out due to its high position in the middle of an exceptional scenic setting, with a popular 13th-century watchtower on the high part. Its church of Sant Pere, from the 15th century, and network of narrow streets between solid medieval walls captivate all visitors who come here. The continuation of the cycle route takes us along a series of ways among amazing reedbeds, and we have to be alert at all times at the crossroads and forks that we come to, always following the signs to Regencós and Palafrugell. On crossing the road between Pals and Torrent, we set off on

the last section through more fields and woods, until coming out to the road to Palafrugell from Regencós. From here on we follow the route marked to the other side. We cover the final kilometres through the centre of Palafrugell, where it is well worth spending a while in its old centre, especially to visit the **Cork Museum**, which possesses an exemplary exhibition about the historic cork industry. Beside this museum stands the **tower of Can Mario**, a spectacular water tank built in 1905, which also speaks to us of past times and which can be visited to enjoy the best panoramic view across Palafrugell and its environs.

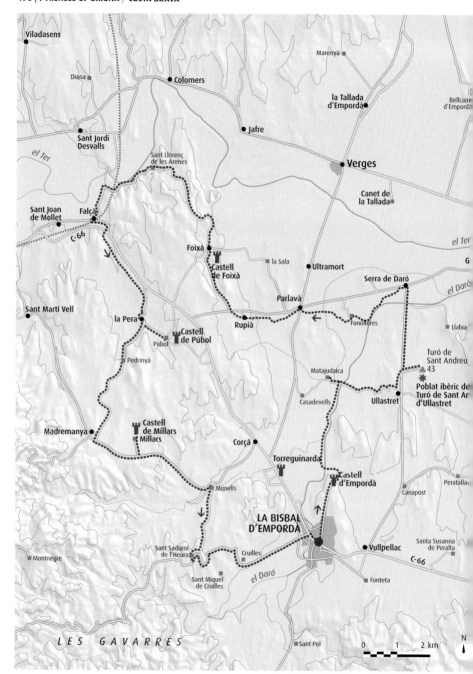

7 AROUND LA BISBAL D'EMPORDÀ

▲ Bridge of Gualta

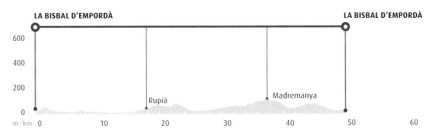

Distance
50 km

Gradients
+400 m / -400 m

The Baix Empordà provides many cycle routes through harmonious rural landscapes. With this suggestion we combine the valley of the river Daró, a section along the river Ter, and the norther perimeter of the massif of Les Gavarres. Using mainly local asphalted ways, this enables us to visit a large number of villages that boast an exceptional historical heritage.

ROUTE

The starting and arrival point is the centre of **La Bisbal d'Empordà** (40 m), the historical capital of Baix Empordà, which has a magnificent old centre of medieval origin. The first section of the cycle-touring route starts beside the **river Daró**, and we have to cross over to its right bank to follow the signs to **Castell d'Empordà** (70 m), even though we have a more direct road to climb to the top of this small village, which is concentrated around a fantastic castle rehabilitated as a hotel-restaurant. We return down again and go along the left bank of the river Daró to follow the cycle route to the outskirts of the village of **Matajudaica** (40 m), which we pass on the left over a small hill. Here we link up with a local road on the right to approach **Ullastret** (50 m), a very well conserved village with an outstanding old centre surrounded by walls. On the outskirts, in the direction of the village of Serra de Daró, is the entrance to the old **Iberian city of Ullastret**, which occupies a strategic position on the **Turó de Sant Andreu** (60 m) and which, dated between the 6th and 2nd centuries BC, is considered the best fortified archaeological precinct of the Iberian period. Having reached this point, we have covered 10 kilometres of the route, and from here we have an unmarked rural path that comes out on the local road between Gualta, Llabià and Serra de Daró. If we want to take a more direct route, we need to go onto the road and cover the 2.5 kilometres to the village of **Serra de Daró** (15 m). In any case, when crossing the river Daró again, we have to meet up again with the cycle route that takes us to the tiny village of **Fonolleres** (15 m), and from here to **Parlavà** (40 m), where we should pay attention at the junction of roads that surrounds the village, which also has a network of typically medieval streets in its old centre.

From Parlavà, we end the signposted route to the neighbouring village of **Rupià** (70 m), with an interesting old centre that conceals an elegant castle-palace linked to the old feudal domains of the bishops of Girona. After some twenty kilometres of cycling, we once again head north and have two sections to reach the village of Foixà. If we want to follow the cycle route taking a longer and quieter trip within an amazing rural setting, we must follow the signs to the village of **La Sala** (40 m), and from here to the pretty houses of **Foixà** (90 m). However, if we want more direct route and visit beforehand the enclave where the **castle of Foixà** stands, from Rupià we need to take a comfortable county road with excellent views. Once in Foixà we follow at all times the signs to Sant Llorenç, along a lovely road that initially climbs among hills and then gifts us with a fantastic descent to the church of **Sant Llorenç de les Arenes** (50 m). We then enjoy a lovely section that goes along the **river Ter**, with a pleasant covering of riverside woods. At a given moment we pass beneath the railway line between Flaçà and Figueres, leaving on the right a detour that drops to the course of the Ter, with a spectacular cement pass. To continue on our route, we have to go by road to the village of **Flaçà** (40 m), known for its large train station, and we must go over a level crossing.

After 30 kilometres of pedalling, we should pay attention in Flaçà to connect with Carrer del Camí de la Pera and cross the main

▲ Ullastret   ▼ Madremanya

▲ The river Ter in the area of Flaçà ▾ Monells

road between Girona and La Bisbal. We thus start a new section of cycle route, which among pretty fields and woods takes us to the village of **La Pera** (80 m), easily identifiable due to its attractive and dominant appearance. One kilometre from here is the **castle of Púbol** (100 m) –restored as the residence of Gala, Salvador Dalí's wife–, which definitely deserves a visit. Back in La Pera, we go along the county road that leads to Madremanya, firstly passing the small treasure of the **church of Sant Andreu de Pedrinyà** (110 m), of Romanesque origin. The gradual climb along the road culminates in the village of **Madremanya** (180 m), where we discover a marvellous centre of medieval origin at the foot of the **massif of Les Gavarres**. Here the etymological study tells us of its origin as *Mater Magna*, a Latin expression related to the richness and strength of the land. Having now covered 40 kilometres, we return towards La Bisbal along a road that goes through Monells, a very popular route for cyclists climbing up to or coming down from the sanctuary of Los Ángeles. A little further on we pass on the left the interesting **castle of Millars** (120 m) –also called Millàs–, which has a church, and where a large heraldic shield confirms its old feudal origins.

The arrival at **Monells** (50 m) passes before its church, from where we must continue a little further along the same road and cross the **river Rissec**, before entering the **old centre**, which conserves one of the best arcaded squares in Catalonia, among fantastic narrow streets of medieval origin. From here we have several options to complete the route. The first consists of going to the village of **Sant Sadurní de l'Heura** (110 m), and from here Cruïlles, going through **Sant Miquel de Cruïlles** (80 m), a route of 3.5 kilometres. The second is to go directly from Monells to the village of Cruïlles, a route of 2.5 kilometres. In both cases we enjoy comfortable pedalling through farmland, always keeping as a reference point the bell towers of the different churches. Once in **Cruïlles** (60 m) we discover the last fortified village on the route, with remains of walls and a sensational circular watchtower at the top of the village. For the final section to La Bisbal d'Empordà, we can use the county road directly for 2.5 kilometres, or choose a way along the left bank of the river Daró for 3 kilometres.

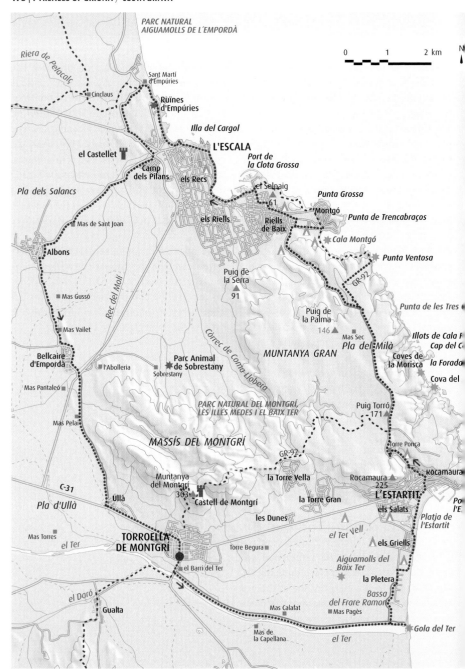

PARC NATURAL
AIGUAMOLLS DE L'EMPORDÀ

0   1   2 km   N

Riera de Pelacalç

Sant Martí
d'Empúries

Cinclaus

Ruïnes
d'Empúries

Illa del Cargol

L'ESCALA

el Castellet

Camp
dels Pilans   els Recs

Port de
la Clota Grossa

et Salnaig
61

Punta Grossa

Pla dels Salancs

Mas de Sant Joan

els Riells

Riells
de Baix

Montgó

Punta de Trencabraços

Albons

Cala Montgó

Punta Ventosa

Mas Gussó

Puig de
la Serra
91

GR-92

Punta de les Tres

Rec del Molí

Puig de
la Palma
146   Mas Sec

Pla del Milà

Illots de Cala F
Cap del C

Mas Vailet

Còrrec de Coma Llobera

MUNTANYA GRAN

Coves de
la Morisca   la Forado

Bellcaire
d'Empordà

l'Abolleria
Sobrestany

Parc Animal
de Sobrestany

Cova del

Mas Pantaleó

PARC NATURAL DEL MONTGRÍ,
LES ILLES MEDES I EL BAIX TER

Puig Torró
171

Mas Pelai

MASSÍS DEL MONTGRÍ

GR-92

Torre Ponça

C-31

Ullà

Muntanya
del Montgrí
303

Castell de Montgrí

la Torre Vella

la Torre Gran

Rocamaura
225

L'ESTARTIT

Rocamaura

Pla d'Ullà

les Dunes

els Salats

Po
l'E
Platja de
l'Estartit

Mas Torres

el Ter

TORROELLA
DE MONTGRÍ

Torre Begura

el Ter Vell

els Griells

el Barri del Ter

Aiguamolls del
Baix Ter

la Pletera

el Daró

Gualta

Mas Calafat

Mas Pagès

Bassa
del Frare Ramon

Gola del Ter

Mas de
la Capellana

el Ter

8 AROUND TORROELLA DE MONTGRÍ

▲ The massif of Montgrí seen from the reedbeds of Pals

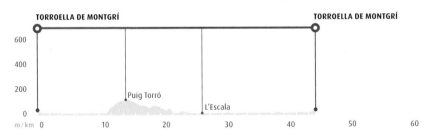

Distance
45 km

Gradients
+300 m / -300 m

Between the space of the Baix Ter and the massif of Montgrí, our route offers a good combination of contrasts, with the option of a short route concentrated on the Pla de Torroella, or a longer one that takes us to the town of L'Escala; two options for two tastes or interests and which in either case allows us to enjoy some of the best scenery of the Costa Brava.

ROUTE

We leave from **Torroella de Montgrí** (5 m), to the left of the bridge over the **river Ter**, from where a local cycle touring route leaves to the mouth of the river. It is a route of 6 kilometres among spectacular reedbeds and fruit orchards, which shortly after leaving passes on the left the variant that passes by the old Mas de la Torre Begura. We continue always along the marked way closer to the river, until what is known as the **Gola del Ter**, the flow of which may fluctuate greatly according to the rainfall or the season. Ahead of us we see the incomparable setting of the **Illes Medes**, enjoying at the same time a pretty tour beside a small coastal lagoon –the **Bassa del Frare Ramon**–, which forms part of the **Natural reserve of Baix Ter**, a space recently constituted in a Natural Park, along with the Illes Medes and the massif of Montgrí. Our route towards L'Estartit passes a campsite, where it connects with the marked way that leads to the abovementioned **Torre Begura**, to end here a short route of 15 kilometres. At this junction is also the access to the **Aiguamolls del Ter Vell**, which by either route is an absolute must to see, since from some observation points we can see what an ecosystem of humid areas can offer us, with a fine sample of flora and fauna. We immediately reach the **esplanade of L'Estartit**, which goes along its large beach. We must cross the whole town centre to find the start of the next section of the route, just by the entrance to the Estartit campsite. At this point we have covered 10 kilometres of route and should go up the street called **Pujada de la Primavera**. Here there are signs to the town of L'Escala, the route forcing us to complete a steep climb of 2 kilometres to reach the **massif of Montgrí**. This unique space of calcareous rock has large pine woods inland on one side, and a wild coast on the other.

We always continue along an asphalted track that turns into a dirt track at the very end of the climb. A little further on we come to a junction where we turn right to head north. We are now on the main track between L'Estartit and L'Escala, which is stony but wide all along the way. We should ignore the secondary turnings to the left and right, until reaching the way to the viewpoint of the **Punta Ventosa** (90 m), which turns right on a branch track after 6.5 kilometres from the Pujada de la Primavera. This viewpoint, which was once a former military zone, is 1.5 kilometres from the main track and it is really well worth taking the small detour and include it in our route, since from here there are some spectacular views over cliffs nearly one hundred metres high, as well as over the marvellous **bay of Cala Montgó**. This is where one of the best sections of the GR-92 path passes, and which goes along the whole Catalan coast. Back on the main track to L'Escala, we begin a fantastic descent with a final asphalted section that comes out in the urbanisations around the abovementioned Cala Montgó (you should add 2 kilometres there and back).

From Cala Montgó to the beaches of Empúries, going over the pass, along the esplanade and through the old quarter of **L'Escala**, we have to cover 5 kilometres to complete 30 of the route. Beside the **beaches of Empúries** leaves a lovely avenue that leads to the medieval village of **Sant Martí d'Empuries**, with the ruins of the legendary **Greco-Roman city** of Empúries half way as an optional visit (you should add another

▲ **On the outskirts of Torroella de Montgrí**

2 kilometres there and back). To return to Torroella de Montgrí from the beaches of Empúries, we link up with a county road that takes us to the village of Albons, following a cycle route that also coincides with a section of the **Pirinexus network**. Once in **Albons** (10 m), we have either a direct road or the cycle touring route, to the neighbouring village of **Bellcaire d'Empordà** (20 m), which features a large medieval fortification in the upper part. From here we cross the main road between L'Escala and Torroella, following the signs to connect up with a local road to the small village of **Ullà** (10 m), at the foot of the highest peaks of the massif of Montgrí. From this village we just have to follow the marked way a couple of kilome-

tres more until reaching the old centre of Torroella de Montgrí, hidden behind its old **medieval walls**.

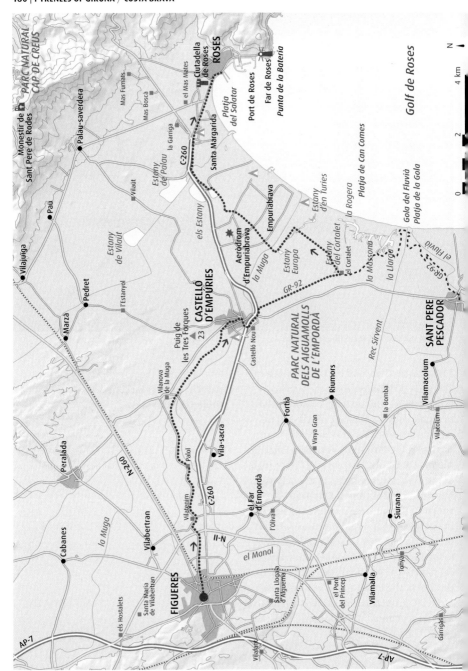

PARC NATURAL
CAP DE CREUS

Monestir de
Sant Pere de Rodes

Palau-saverdera

Vilajuïga

Pau

Pedret

Marzà

Vilaüt

Estany
de Vilaüt

L'Estanyol

els Estany

Estany
de Palau

la Garriga

C-260

Mas Fumats

Mas Bosca

el Mas Mates

Ciutadella
de Roses

ROSES

Santa Margarida

Platja
del Salatar

Port de Roses

Far de Roses

Punta de la Bateria

Golf de Roses

N

0   2   4 km

Empuriabrava

Aeròdrom
d'Empuriabrava

la Muga

Estany
Europa

Estany
del Cortalet

el Cortalet

GR-92

Estany d'en Turies

la Rogera

la Mossona

la Llarga

Platja de Can Comes

Gola del Fluvià
Platja de la Gola

el Fluvià

GR-92

**SANT PERE
PESCADOR**

Vilamacolum

Vilacolum

**CASTELLÓ
D'EMPÚRIES**

Puig de
les Tres Forques

23

Castelló Nou

Vilanova
de la Muga

PARC NATURAL
DELS AIGUAMOLLS
DE L'EMPORDÀ

Rec Sirvent

Riumors

Fortià

Vinya Gran

la Bomba

Palol

Vila-sacra

Peralada

la Muga

N-260

Cabanes

Vilabertran

Santa Maria
de Vilabertran

els Hostalets

Vilatenim

C-260

II-N

el Manol

el Far
d'Empordà

l'Oliva

FIGUERES

Santa Llogaia
d'Àlguema

el Pont
del Princep

Vilamalla

Vilamalla

Siurana

Tor-roja

Garrigàs

Vilaür

AP-7

AP-7

Golf de Roses

9

FROM FIGUERES TO ROSES BY THE AIGUAMOLLS DEL EMPORDÀ

9

▲ Aiguamolls de l'Empordà

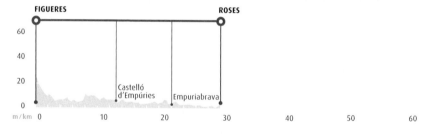

Distance
30 km

Gradients
+100 m / -140 m

The route proposed crosses a large part of the extensive plain of Alt Empordà, using several cycle touring circuits. First we go along the Via Verda of the Muga, until Castelló d'Empúries, and then the *Ruta dels Estanys* (Lakes Route), in the second largest wetlands of Catalonia. Altogether, it is a route of broad horizons to savour the great pleasure of going on bike trips.

ROUTE

Known mainly for the attraction of the **Dalí Museum**, the lively city of **Figueres** (40 m) is an excellent setting for cycle touring. We leave from bedside the train station that links

▲ Castelló d'Empúries

Figueres and Llançà, crossing the railway line via a level crossing and from here take the long Carrer de Vilatenim, which takes us out of the town without traffic problems. After passing beneath the ring-road, we go through the village of **Vilatenim** (25 m) to continue the cycling route at all times to Roses, along a cemented way that also doubles up as a local road. We then pass beside the village of **Palol** (20 m) and finally we come to the right bank of the **river Muga**, with the village of **Vilanova de la Muga** (15 m) on the other side. For about half a kilometre we follow the course of the river until reaching the confluence with the **river Manol**, which is also a crossroads. Here we come to the passing point equipped to cross

the river Muga, which may be problematic on very rainy days. We thus climb a lovely way through riverside vegetation, which after 3 kilometres leads us to **Castelló d'Empúries** (15 m), to complete a total of 10 kilometres from Figueres. This town requires a visit to climb up to its magnificent **Gothic church**, considered the best temple of these characteristics in the whole of the Empordà. Once we have come down from the old centre of Castelló d'Empúries, we approach the river Muga again, just beside the **Pont Vell or *Old Bridge*** of seven spans. At this point we have the option of taking a variant if we link up with the **cycle touring route of the Pirinexus network**, which goes to the towns of Sant Pere Pescador and

L'Escala around the outside of the Natural Park of the Aiguamolls de l'Empordà, through attractive paddy fields and fruit orchards. The total route between Figueres and L'Escala is thirty kilometres.

Our proposal consists of going down to a second bridge located a little further down from the Pont Vell, where we come to the signposting of the GR-92 path (red and white marks), which crosses the entire central space of the natural park. At the beginning we cross the roads that surround Castelló d'Empúries, and then link up with a long dirt track through farmland, to come out on the road that leads to the **Cortalet farmhouse**, the visitors centre. Having reached this point we have cycled 16 kilometres of the route. Several routes start from this popular spot to enjoy some of the best parts of the **Natural Park of the Aiguamolls de l'Empordà**. Before, however, we can stop off at the observatories around the **lake of Cortalet**, which houses a fine representation of birds from among the 300 species that can be seen in the reserve throughout the year. Just behind the Cortalet farmhouse is the bird observatory called Aguait dels Roncaires, and the start of the next section of the cycle touring route to Empuriabrava and Roses. Following the signs we find along a pleasant rural way, we have the option of visiting the **Túries lake**. We thus complete the 3 kilometres to the **Europa lake**, where we find four observatories of birds where we can take another contemplative break. A little further on, we pass a purification plant and immediately meet up again with the river Muga. To cross it we use a spectacular walkway that leads directly to a large urbanisation of canals, which is **Empuriabrava**. We cross the whole urbanisation to the opposite end, having to pay attention to the cycle route among more junctions and forks.

At a given moment we come to an asphalted way the crosses before the **Madral canal**, one of the largest natural canals in the area. We then come to the entrance to the **Santa Margarida** urbanisation, very close to the road between Castelló d'Empúries and Roses. At this point we have completed 25 kilometres of the route and once again we have two options to continue. If we want to end the route at the esplanade of **Roses**, we should continue for 2 kilometres along different streets and roads until finding another section of the GR-92 path, which takes us to the town via the entrance gate of its old citadel, which houses the archaeological remains of the ancient Greek, Roman and medieval cities. But if we are still ready to pedal more kilometres and return to Figueres, from Santa Margarida we can link up with the continuation of the Ruta dels Estanys to Castelló d'Empúries crossing other sections of the Natural Park of the Aiguamolls de l'Empordà. From Castelló d'Empúries we have to repeat the outward journey the other way round, which would complete a full route, with start and finish in Figueres, of a total of 50 kilometres.

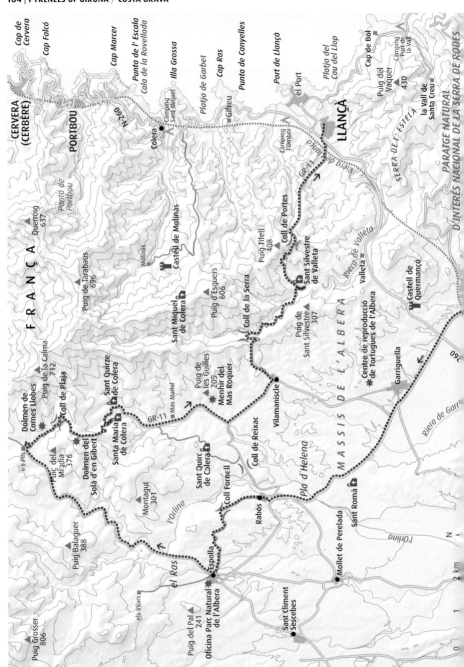

10

FROM VILAJUÏGA TO LLANÇÀ BY THE MASSIF OF L'ALBERA

▲ Spot with "L'Albera cows" in the environs of Mas Pils

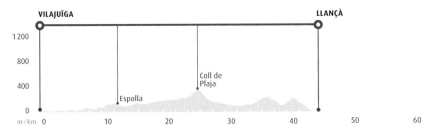

Distance
45 km

Gradients
+750 m / -800 m

The plan for this route involves following the train line between Barcelona and the French border, with stations in Vilajuïga and Llançà. Whereas in the first part of the route we go through small villages at the foot of the massif of L'Albera, in the second part we pedal through solitary valleys that conceal fantastic spots that include some historical monuments of great value.

ROUTE

We leave from **Vilajuïga** (50 m), a village at the foot of the **Rodes range** that has a very attractive setting that features vineyards and olive groves, the remains of the old **castle of**

Quermançó, of medieval origin, as well as a fantastic megalithic route to do on foot, which tours a dozen dolmens dated between the fourth and second millennium BC. The village of Vilajuïga is also known for having one of the best sources of mineral water in Catalonia, commercialised since 1904. With all these references, we set off heading west on the road that goes from the village to **Garriguella** (60 m), 4 kilometres away, where we continue enjoying a privileged rural setting between vineyards and olive groves. On the outskirts of this village is the **Turtle Reproduction Centre of L'Albera**, responsible for the conservation of the Mediterranean turtle. We carry on along a quiet county road to the village of **Rabós** (110 m), easily identifiable due to its dominant church over the course of the **river Orlina**. From here we have the option of taking a partially cemented rural way, which goes from behind the village, or return to the county road that continues more easily for 4 kilometres to the village of Espolla. In either case, we reach **Espolla** (120 m), where we discover a pretty complex of buildings of medieval origin that includes the **Office of the Natural park of L'Albera**. We are just at the foot of this stunning natural space, and from Espolla we have an asphalted track that climbs the whole **valley of the river Orlina** to the Coll de Banyuls, leading us to the heart of the reserve. The route on this track, through fields and Mediterranean woods, is a delight for all the senses, with the presence of old farmhouses, routes to discover diverse megalithic monuments, as well as herds of cows from L'Albera, an autochthonous species of the region, on both sides of the frontier, protected by the European Union.

After 8 kilometres from Espolla we reach **Mas Pils** (250 m), the last settlement of the valley, surrounded by lovely meadows and holm-oak trees. From this point the asphalted track completes the climb to the **Coll de Banyuls** (357 m), an old frontier pass that leads to the French side in 2 kilometres. From de Mas Pils and to the end of the route in Llançà, we continue along the signposted forest tracks with the red and white marks of the trans-Pyrenean GR-11 path. We then cross the river Orlina and set off on the hardest climb of the day, of 2 kilometres, on which we pass the entrance to the **dolmen of Comes Llobes** (280 m). Having reached the pass of the **Coll de Plaja** (390 m), we have the descent of 2 kilometres, where we must be careful of the broken surface on a steep slope. We thus reach the impressive remains of the monastery of **Sant Quirze de Colera** (175 m), one of the most important Catalan monuments of Romanesque origin. Recent reconstruction work has helped recover the dignity of this old Benedictine monastic centre built between the 10th and 12th centuries, which rivalled Sant Pere de Rodes in power. The natural setting in which it is placed invites us to go on some good walking trips and even enjoy good food in the restaurant beside it, fitted out inside an old farmyard.

Once in Sant Quirze de Colera, with 25 kilometres of pedalling behind us, we start a very pleasant section, along the main track, that leads to the villages of Rabós and Vilamaniscle. Just before completing the part of this track, on the left there is a path that, in a few metres, leads us to the **menhir of Mas Roquer** (105 m), a highly recommendable visit. We immediately come to an asphalted track that leads to **Vilamaniscle** (150 m), another typical rural village of Empordà of stone houses, surrounded by vineyards and olive groves. The next forest track leaves from the high part of the village, with another demanding climb to the pass of the **Coll de la Serra** (250 m), from where we can take in the powerful **Puig d'Esquers** (606 m) on the other side of **La Vall de Sant Silvestre**. With 35 kilometres completed, we enter into this stunning valley parallel to the **stream of La Valleta**, and a little further on we discover the pretty church of **Sant Silvestre de Valleta** (140 m), in a bucolic setting

among old crop terraces. From this point we set off on the final ascent which is very steep to the pass of the **Coll de Portes** (259 m), which rewards us with an unforgettable panorama, with the Mediterranean Sea on the horizon, breaking into the coves and bays of the northernmost end of the Costa Brava. A dizzy descent to **Llançà** ends the route. We should pay attention when crossing the main road, with the old centre of the town on the other side. The visit to the Port district and the end in the train station closes the trip, but if we want to return to Vilajuïga along the national road, we should add 10 kilometres and 150 metres of climbing.

▲ Sant Quirze de Colera

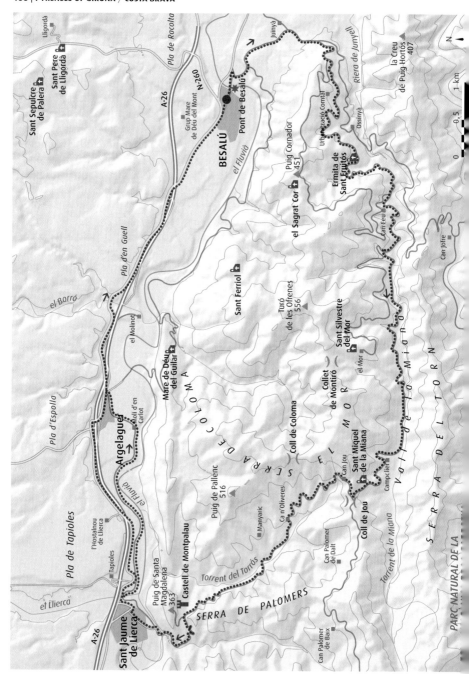

CYCLING ROUTES

11

AROUND BESALÚ

11

▲ **Pont Vell of Besalú**

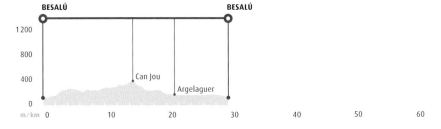

Distance
30 km

Gradients
+500 m / -500 m

This circular route that leaves from and arrives at one of the most important medieval towns in Catalonia proposes a trip that on the outward journey goes along forest tracks through valleys covered by dense woods, while the return trip follows the course of the river Fluvià along a flat area, along a rural way and the route of the former national road.

ROUTE

We leave from **Besalú** (150 m) via the car park with restaurants alongside the monumental **Pont Vell**. At the beginning we follow an asphalted way to Mas Pitre and the Besalú campsite, but after a few metres we leave it on the left to take

▲ **Hermitage of Sant Fruitós**

a way that marks the GR-1 path (red and white markers), although it will be for just 1 kilometre, until coming to an asphalted track to an urbanisation. In half a kilometre, we connect on the right with a forest track that climbs, and 2 kilometres higher up we come to a branch track, also on the right, that leads to the **sanctuary of the Sagrat Cor**, over **Puig Cornador** (451 m), with 3 kilometres of tough climbing. The climb to this sanctuary, from which there is a fantastic view, could be an excellent complement, but you should calculate your supplies of energy well. We continue along the main track to the **hermitage of Sant Fruitós** (290 m), of Romanesque origin and passing point of the GR-2

path. Once here, we have covered 5 kilometres of the route, but the track takes us 100 metres lower that we will have to recover on climbing the entire **valley of La Miana**. In any case, the climb along the main track is gradual and is only steep in the final kilometre to reach the **Coll de Can Jou** (431 m), after 14 kilometres of pedalling. Here we discover an attractive series of farmhouses reconverted into rural tourism accommodation, with the old church of Sant Miquel de la Miana at the end of this area. Starting off again, we begin a pleasant descent of 2.5 kilometres on the opposite side of the **range of El Mor**. We pass by the **Mas de Can Oliveres** (320 m) and cross a wild stream, within a dense wood.

We immediately start a gentle climb to the **Coll del Pla de Can Font** (282 m), situated at the foot of the **Puig de Santa Magdalena de Montpalau** (363 m), where we come to a path that invites us to climb for 10 minutes to the peak, where there are the remains of a hermitage and a castle.

On the other side of the Coll del Pla de Can Font, we pass the entrance to the rural tourism house of El Turrós. Our route continues on the opposite side, on an asphalted track, with a direct descent to a fantastic spot where we come to the **river Fluvià** (180 m), which we cross via a long cement passing point. Just after this passing point, which provides a good example of riverside wood, we have done 20 kilometres of the trip and we enter the village of **Sant Jaume de Llierca** (220 m), passing by an old factory from the 19th century. To visit the old centre of this village we must climb on the left from the old road and then go back down, to a roundabout that connects with the main road between Olot and Girona. Once here, the easiest option to end the route is to continue at all times on the route of the old national road to Besalú. For thse who want to enjoy a pretty country lane, however, we should leave the road at the same roundabout on the right. This way, 3 kilometres among fields and riverside woods, comes out on an asphalted track, 1 kilometre before the village of **Argelaguer** (180 m), which we can reach via the old Carrer de la Muralla and discover its interesting network of narrow streets of medieval origin. From Argelaguer we carry on ahead, now indeed along the old

road parallel to the main road, which makes us go through a number of roundabouts with very little traffic and therefore posing no problem going by bike. We end the trip in the spectacular **old centre of Besalú**, which conserves a large number of buildings from between the 12th and 14th centuries.

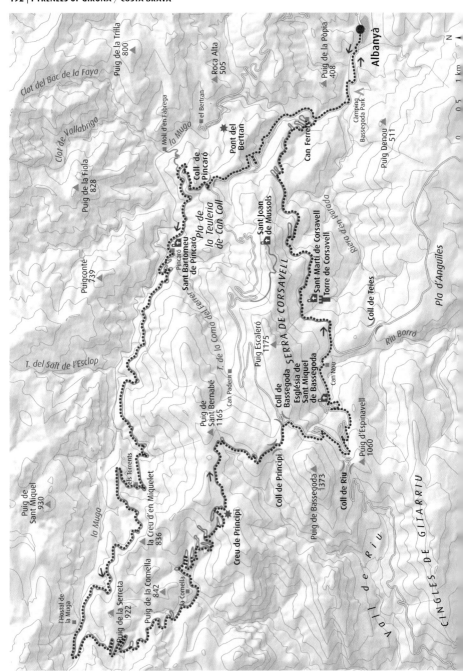

CYCLING ROUTES

12 AROUND ALBANYÀ

12

12

▲ Alternative route between Sant Miquel de Bassegoda and Besalú

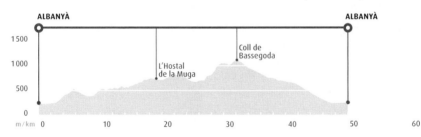

Distance
50 km

Gradients
+1,300 m / -1,300 m

This is the toughest route among our suggestions, since it concentrates a total of over one thousand metres in accumulated climbs, through some of the remotest areas of the Alta Garrotxa. Between the valley of La Muga and the massif of Bassegoda, the sensation of solitude turns the cyclist into a veritable explorer of territories of great environmental and scenic worth.

ROUTE

The small village of **Albanyà** (240 m) is at the end of a road that comes from Figueresin one of the largest municipalities of Catalonia, where nature rules in its wildest state. Just on starting the route along the asphalted track that goes to the Bassegoda campsite, we can take in from a stone bridge the beauty of the **river Muga**, which comes from the mountains of the Alta Garrotxa. A little further on from this campsite, now on a dirt track, we pass on the left the branch of track that comes from the heights of the massif of Bassegoda, by which we will return. For the moment, though, we continue straight on, and start climbing towards the **Coll de Pincaró** (550 m), and shortly before reaching it come to a second fork, where we must take the right, always in the direction of the Hostal de la Muga. On the drop down the other side of the pass, we go alongside the enclave occupied by the church of **Sant Bartomeu de Pincaró** (420 m), of Romanesque origin, with a path that goes from the track. Having covered the first 8 kilometres of the route, we begin a long stretch of climbs, with an occasional descent, that takes us up the **entire valley of La Muga**, with excellent panoramas. Just on 20 kilometres of the route, we pass over the river Muga itself, and then come to the old farmhouse of the **Hostal de la Muga** (720 m), an old frontier pass from where a path leads that, after a few metres, enters the French side of the Pyrenees. Our route continues along the main track and crosses the river Muga again a little higher up. Shortly after, we reach the **Coll del Mas Sobirà** (840 m), from where we take in a great panoramic view of the massif of the Bassegoda, our goal. There is now a steep descent that makes us lose height quickly, leaving on the right a fork that leads to the

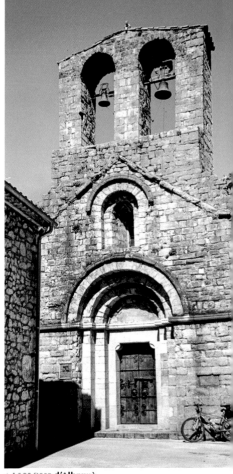

▲ Sant Pere d'Albanyà

church of Sant Julià de Ribelles. 4 kilometres from Mas Sobirà, we cross the **stream of La Comella** (680 m), in a rich forested setting, from where we begin the toughest climb of the route.

Even though the track has a series of zigzags to make the climb easier, facing us is almost 400 metres of climbing in 5 kilometres. The reward comes to us on reaching the pass of the **Creu de Principi** (1,055 m), a wonderful mountain spot with an impressive view over the north face of the **Puig de Bassegoda** (1,373). The track then goes gently for 3 kilometres, through pine woods, to the **Coll de Principi** (1,115 m), the highest point on the route after 34 kilometres, through which a section of the GR-11 trans-Pyrenean path also passes. Shortly after starting the descent from this pass, we leave on the right a branch of the track that can be taken to climb to the Puig de Bassegoda, with a final part across a crag fitted with a line of chains (we should add at least an hour to the total for the route there and back). The drop along the main track crosses the pretty spot of the **Coll de Bassegoda** (1,105 m), a connecting point with the track from the Coll de Pincaró, although we continue straight to begin the dizzying descent beneath the mass of the Puig de Bassegoda, with a cemented initial section.

2 kilometres from the Coll de Bassegoda, we leave on the right the branch of the track that goes to the valley of Sant Aniol to Saternes, with 10 kilometres of great riding. We always head downwards, towards Albanyà. Having done 38 kilometres, we come to the entrance to the church of **Sant Miquel de Bassegoda** (810 m), of Romanesque origin, a former parish church of a large area that throughout the 20th century lost the majority of its population. Beside the church is **Mas de Can Galant**, with an adapted mountain refuge. The track continues beneath this spot, with a section along the **stream of Borró**, until the pretty **Mas de Can Nou** (760 m). We immediately pass on the right the track that leads to the village of Lliurona, which also enables the connection with other tracks to drop down to the valley of the river Fluvià close to Besalú. Having reached this point, we just need to carry on enjoying a great but demanding downhill ride, leaving on the right the entrance to the church of **Sant Martí de Corsavell** (590 m). The final and steepest part of the drop has a cemented section with sharp bends to Mas de **Can Ferrers** (280 m), below which we come again to the track we started on parallel to the river Muga.

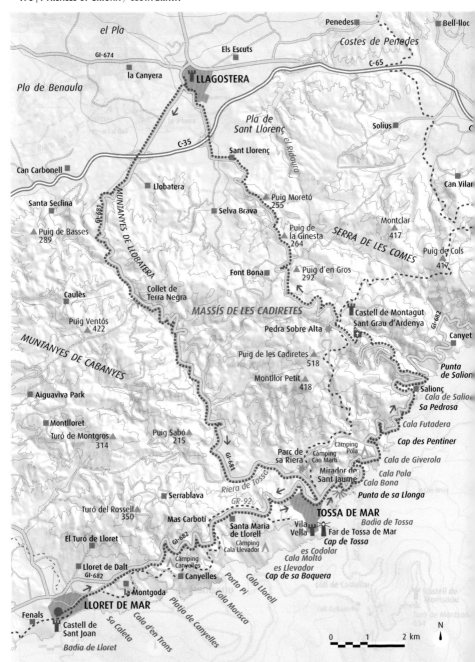

AROUND THE COAST OF LA SELVA

▲ Sant Grau road

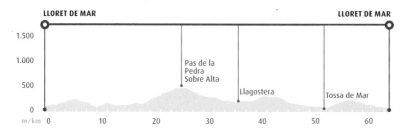

Distance
65 km

Gradients
+1,150 m / -1,150 m

An international sporting and tourist referent, the Selva coastal area provides a spectacular route for road cycling, with an incomparable combination between sea and mountain. Of special note is the ride through the massif of Ardenya-Cadiretes, full of turns, slopes and impressive bird's-eye views.

ROUTE

We leave from the town centre of **Lloret de Mar**, where we start climbing along the road to Tossa de Mar, through a typical Mediterranean wood that becomes a perfect introduction to the natural space that a large part of this route goes through. Between holm-oaks, cork oaks and pine woods, the first 5 kilometres of climbs with a maximum gradient of 8%, ensure you warm up quickly and give you the feeling that the route will be great fun at all times. On either side of the road we pass the entrances to diverse urbanisations until reaching the **pass of Mas Carbotí** (180 m), from where we begin a very direct descent that ends in the centre of **Tossa de Mar**. On the right we pass the **Platja Gran** beach of Tossa and the impressive **Vila Vella**, which we recommend you visit on the way back. Following the signs to Sant Feliu de Guíxols, we restart the route along the mythical section of road that joins two of the most emblematic towns of the Costa Brava. The GI-

682 road runs along the entire coastal section of the **massif of Ardenya-Cadiretes**, something that has made it one of the most beautiful panoramic roads in the world. Moreover, the fact that little traffic passes makes it a perfect route for cycle tourists.

From Tossa de Mar we must face a tough climb to reach the pass of the **viewpoint of Sant Jaume** (100 m), a poplar balcony from where you get an unforgettable great view over marvellous cliffs. The road immediately enters a section of constant bends in order to cross successively the abrupt ravines that come out into the sea. On our route we have to make two descents with their accompanying climbs, which lead to as many as three really beautiful coves. The first, called

▲ **Hermitage of Sant Grau d'Ardenya**

13

▲ The Pedra Sobre Alta

Cala Bona, is totally unspoilt and only accessible on foot; the second, **Cala Pola**, has a splendid **viewpoint** from the road and campsite inland; and the third, **Cala Giverola**, has a top-quality beach at the foot of a large tourist complex specialised in receiving road cyclists, and therefore, to take into account as a resting and service spot.

Passing Cala Giverola we maintain a height of around 100 metres' altitude over the sea, having to go through a short tunnel and immediately leaving on the right the entrance to **Cala Salionç**, which is surrounded by a large urbanisation of apartments. A little further on we reach the junction with the road that leads to the

hermitage of Sant Grau, our next destination after 20 kilometres of pedalling. We thus bid farewell to the coastal road and start the longest climb of the day, of 7 kilometres to reach a fantastic mountain pass with some sections that reach 13% gradient. Several hairpins and the views help us achieve our goal to a great extent, which initially leaves us before the entrance to the **hermitage of Sant Grau d'Ardenya** (380 m). This place appears documented in the 15th century, although the origin of the church is the 17th century. A reform in 1882 gave it interesting neo-Romanesque style. In the mid-20th century a hotel was added, which only opened for ten years. Today the visitor has a pleasant bar-restaurant that is open every day in summer and only the weekends the rest of the year.

From Sant Grau d'Ardenya we should continue climbing along a road that leads to Llagostera in order to cross the **pass of the Pedra Sobre Alta** (480 m). We should pay attention on the left, where two forest tracks meet with a parking space, to find the sign that shows how close the "Pedra Sobre Alta", the high rock on top, is, just 150 metres from the road. This impressive formation of granite made up of large irregular blocks, conceals at the base a small megalithic monument from the Bronze Age, classified as a para-dolmen for the fact that it has a structure of a funerary chamber adapted to the same geological structure.

After stopping off here, we begin the dizzying descent to Llagostera under the cover of an extensive forest , which requires more attention due to the very sharp bends along the way. The final part of the solitary GIP-6821 road comes out at the bucolic farmlands of the **hamlet of Sant Llorenç**, just before crossing a road bridge of the C-35. Shortly after we reach the town of **Llagostera** (160 m), in the part where the Green Way runs between Girona and Sant Feliu de Guíxols. On reaching a crossroads, we pass on the right the old centre of the town, having to take here the main road to Tossa de Mar.

Once on the asphalt of the GI-681 road, now having covered 40 kilometres, we cross the C-35 again and start a gradual climb to reach the **Coll of Terra Negra** (260 m). This is the junction of the old paths that joined the towns of Tossa de Mar, Caldes de Malavella and Santa Coloma de Farners, today a "green way" for walking and mountain biking. We continue on the road, however, and start a very exciting descent that covers the whole length of the **valley of Tossa**, which marks the western limits of the massif of Ardenya-Cadiretes. In this case, the width of the road provides greater safety and allows us to take in an attractive natural setting. On re-encountering Tossa de Mar we pass through the surprising **park of Sa Riera**, which expresses perfectly the natural values of the spot in which the town is hidden.

The **stream of Tossa** is covered here by thick vegetation, with a flow of water all year round before its urban route and its outlet at the foot of the "Vila Vella", the old town.

On returning to Lloret de Mar we repeat the section of coast road but in the other direction.

▲ The Vila Vella of Tossa de Mar

▲ Coastal road where it passes Cala Pola

Sea routes in
KAYAK

The Costa Brava is a geographic space that has experienced heavy pressure from urbanisation due to it being a destination of mass tourism although, paradoxically, it still preserves some sectors, the most inaccessible on foot, that enable the kayaker to experience unforgettable moments; moments that we could not enjoy in any other type of vessel, because only the kayak can pass through narrow passages, can negotiate the way between rocks and islets, enter caves and natural tunnels in the half dark and stop off at a wild cove or at the foot of a high cliff among seabirds. The Mediterranean, however, with its sudden meteorological changes and its own internal dynamic, may become as dangerous as the large oceans. With this in mind, sea kayaking, compared to the bicycle, demands the best weather and travelling conditions, an accessible means all year round as long as we have the appropriate material, but which always requires the best conditions possible.

In any case, taking into account the technique required to do kayaking, without doubt we must ensure that we always learn and progress with a monitor or a person with more expertise. It is also very important to take into account the basic precautions, how to set out on trips with other kayakers, analysing very carefully the weather forecasts, dominate the main safety protocols and use the material properly. In this guide, nevertheless, without forgetting the importance of the sporting component, we understand kayaking as basically a leisure activity, as well as an ideal means of transport to enjoy one of the best coastlines in Europe, an activity that is one of the most respectful and with all the values that define the high category of some of the natural spaces of the Costa Brava. In our case, the eight routes selected coincide will all the sections of the coast where there are mountainous reliefs. We should also be aware of the importance of the support of diverse private companies and kayak clubs, which can guarantee us all kinds of services, such as material hire, transport between towns, information about leaving points in case of need, and even guided routes along some of the sections.

Wind force scale 1- 2
(5-10 kph)
Suitable for beginner level

Wind force scale 3 - 4
(10-30 kph)
suitable for advanced level

Wind force scale 5 - 6
(30-50 kph)
suitable for expert level

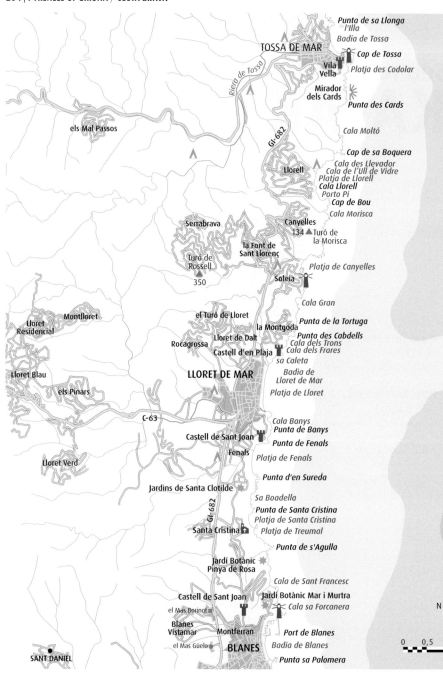

Punta de sa Llonga
l'Illa
Badia de Tossa
TOSSA DE MAR
Cap de Tossa
Vila
Vella
Platja des Codolar
Mirador
dels Cards
Punta des Cards
Cala Moltó
els Mal Passos
GI-682
Cap de sa Boquera
Cala des Llevador
Cala de l'Ull de Vidre
Llorell
Platja de Llorell
Cala Llorell
Porto Pi
Cap de Bou
Cala Morisca
Serrabrava
Canyelles
134 ▲ Turó de
la Morisca
la Font de
Sant Llorenç
Turó de
Rossell
Platja de Canyelles
350
Soleia
Cala Gran
el Turó de Lloret
Punta de la Tortuga
la Montgoda
Montlloret
Punta des Cabdells
Lloret
Residencial
Lloret de Dalt
Cala dels Trons
Rocagrossa
Cala dels Frares
Castell d'en Plaja
sa Caleta
LLORET DE MAR
Badia de
Lloret Blau
Lloret de Mar
els Pinars
Platja de Lloret
C-63
Cala Banys
Punta de Banys
Castell de Sant Joan
Punta de Fenals
Fenals
Lloret Verd
Platja de Fenals
Punta d'en Sureda
Jardins de Santa Clotilde
Sa Boadella
Punta de Santa Cristina
GI-682
Platja de Santa Cristina
Santa Cristina
Platja de Treumal
Punta de s'Agulla
Jardí Botànic
Pinya de Rosa
Cala de Sant Francesc
Castell de Sant Joan
Jardí Botànic Mar i Murtra
el Mas Borinot
Cala sa Forcanera
Blanes
Vistamar
el Mas Güelo
Montferran
Port de Blanes
BLANES
Badia de Blanes
SANT DANIEL
Punta sa Palomera

N

0   0,5   1 k

SEA ROUTES IN KAYAK

1 FROM BLANES TO TOSSA DE MAR 1

▲ **Beach of Porto Pi in the bay of Llorell**

BLANES   LLORET DE MAR   TOSSA DE MAR

Beach of Santa Cristina   Beach of Canyelles   Beach of Llorell

Distance
17 - 20 km
[9 - 11 nautical miles]

Despite the many tourist establishments, this section has some of the best spots of the Costa Brava, where we have many leaving points and lovely coastal paths to climb up to the cliffs on foot. We should pay attention to the large number of small passenger boats during the summer season.

ROUTE

Our starting point is from the emblematic **islet of Sa Palomera**, in the centre of the **bay of Blanes**. We should pay great attention to the entrance and exit of boats from the **sports and fishing port**, which has a kayak base throughout the year. The beginning is truly spectacular, since it goes all the way around the base of the magnificent **Puig de Sant Joan** (173 m), crowned by an old castle. This tour among sensational cliffs and islets introduces us to the wild corner of **Sa Forcanera**. Just above we can make out the romantic viewpoints of the **Mar i Murtra botanical garden**, created in 1921, which constitutes a veritable temple of world gardening, with thousands of species, within a marvellous geographical setting. Shortly after appears the pretty **beach of Sant Francesc**, very popular and accessible from the land, from where we get a fantastic perspective of the next section of wild coastline. Here is the **Pinya de Rosa botanical garden**, created in 1945 and also internationally renowned. We immediately pass close to the pronounced **point of S'Agulla**, which leads to the aesthetically pleasing **beach of Treumal**, from where the continuity of the pine woods over the coast and diverse connections of coastal paths invite us to make a stop. The neighbouring **beach of Santa Cristina**, with access from the popular

hermitage of the same name, is an excellent spot and logistic point in case of need, just before reaching the unspoilt **beach of Sa Boadella** (naturist area). Above this beach appears the complex of the **gardens of Santa Clotilde**, from 1919, from where a new line of cliffs begins that contrasts with the extension of the **beach of Fenals** and its bay. On the other side of the **bay of Fenals** is the dominant watchtower of **Sant Joan de Lloret**, with origins in the 10th century, announcing the final section of rocky reliefs before reaching the large beach of Lloret de Mar, where the beauty of **Cala Banys**, surrounded by pine and palm trees, stands out.

From Cala Banys we complete a lovely tour past small points and rocks, almost beside the coastal path that comes out on the busy **beach of Lloret de Mar**, the most international tourist resort of the Costa Brava, but in any case a Mediterranean enclave with a

▲ Cala de Sa Forcanera from the Mar i Murtra botanical garden

1

▲ Coast between Cala Moltó and the point of Es Cards

long history dating back to Iberian culture. The silhouette of the **castle of En Plaja**, built in 1935, marks the second part of the route towards Tossa de Mar. This new section includes many spots such as **Racó de sa Caleta**, **Cala dels Frares**, **Cala dels Trons**, **Punta des Cabdells**, **Punta de la Tortuga** and **Cala Gran**, all flanked by beautiful cliffs. Finally we discover the small sports port of the **beach of Canyelles**, a good escape route in case of need, since from here to the end of the route we are faced with the wildest stretch and therefore of greater physical commitment. It is a section where we can see for ourselves the magnitude and width of some cliffs with heights of more than one hundred metres, among which is hidden the small **Cala Morisca**, a wild corner that marks the limit between the municipalities of Lloret and Tossa, with craggy paths through dense woods.

A little further on we pass the cliffs of **Cap de Bou** and reach the fantastic **bay of Llorell**, where two large sandy beaches spread out, connected by the coastal path: the beaches of **Porto Pi** and **Llorell**, also accessible by car from several urbanisations. This space contrasts with the magical setting that forms **Cala Ull de Vidre**, **Cala Es Llevador** and **Cap de Sa Boquera**, with an old jetty between crags and rocks. Behind the Cap de sa Boquera we discover a large vertical cleft and the entrance to the remote **Cala Moltó**, the last reference point before a long stretch beneath an imposing wall of cliffs, from which stands out the **Punta des Cards**. The **beach of Es Codolar** immediately appears, with the old fortified precinct of the **old city of Tossa de Mar** in the upper part, a spectacular and thrilling end on going around the impressive promontory of **Cap de Tossa**, crowned by the lighthouse of the same name. We set our sights on the arrival at the **Platja Gran** of Tossa de Mar, enjoying unforgettable scenery.

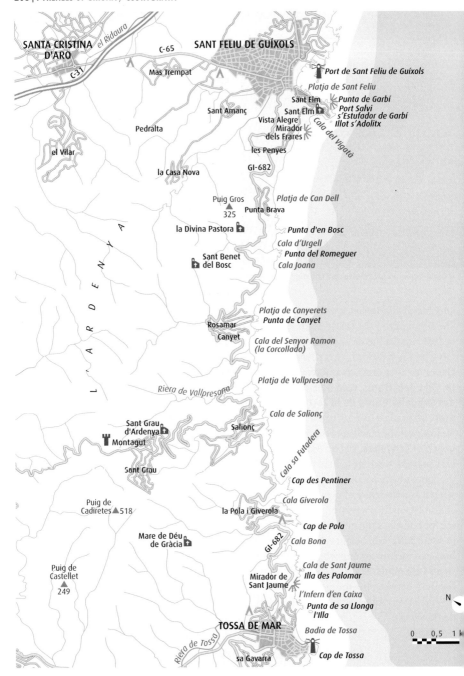

SANTA CRISTINA
D'ARO

el Ridaura

C-65

C-31

Mas Trempat

SANT FELIU DE GUÍXOLS

Port de Sant Feliu de Guíxols

Platja de Sant Feliu

Sant Amanç

Sant Elm
Sant Elm
Vista Alegre
Mirador
dels Frares

Punta de Garbí
Port Salvi
s'Estufador de Garbí
Illot s'Adolitx

Pedralta

les Penyes

Cala del Vigatà

el Vilar

la Casa Nova

GI-682

Puig Gros
325

Platja de Can Dell

Punta Brava

la Divina Pastora

Punta d'en Bosc

Cala d'Urgell

Punta del Romeguer

Sant Benet
del Bosc

Cala Joana

L'A R D E N Y A

Rosamar
Canyet

Platja de Canyerets
Punta de Canyet

Cala del Senyor Ramon
(la Corcollada)

Riera de Vallpresona

Platja de Vallpresona

Sant Grau
d'Ardenya
Montagut

Salionç

Cala de Salionç

Sant Grau

Cala sa Futadera

Puig de
Cadiretes ▲518

la Pola i Giverola

Cap des Pentiner

Cala Giverola

Cap de Pola

Mare de Déu
de Gràcia

GI-682

Cala Bona

Puig de
Castellet
249

Mirador de
Sant Jaume

Cala de Sant Jaume
Illa des Palomar

l'Infern d'en Caixa

Punta de sa Llonga
l'Illa

TOSSA DE MAR

Badia de Tossa

N

Riera de Tossa

sa Gavarra

Cap de Tossa

0   0,5   1 k

SEA ROUTES IN KAYAK

2

FROM TOSSA DE MAR TO SANT FELIU DE GUÍXOLS

2

▲ Cala Canyet

TOSSA DE MAR

SANT FELIU DE GUÍXOLS

Cala Giverola   Cala Salionç   Cala Canyet

Distance
14 - 17 km
[7 - 9 nautical miles]

This route coincides end to end with the maritime limits of the massif of L'Ardenya, a space full of craggy reliefs that plummet from heights of more than 200 metres, which has shaped an abrupt and almost inaccessible coastline. Only a dozen coves have diverse accesses from the spectacular coastal road.

ROUTE

The start from the Playa Gran of **Tossa de Mar** could not be more stimulating, since we slip our kayaks between a formidable series of islets and cliffs. This labyrinth of formations begins with the prominent islet of **L'Illa**, followed by the rocks of the **Punta de Sa Llonga**, the incredible cleft of the **Infern d'en Caixa**, the cliffs with caves of the **Punta de Sant**

Jaume and the paradise of seabirds around the **isle of Es Palomar**. A little further on we enter the wonderful **Cala Bona**, a small sanctuary of crystalline waters from where a delightful line of cliffs start covered by a dense Mediterranean wood until the sand if **Cala Pola**, frequented by clients of a nearby campsite. From here we make a tour beneath the large cliffs of Cap de Pola and we immediately come to the magnificent setting of **Cala Giverola**, which has an extensive sandy area, and as such the main attraction of a tourist complex located in the upper part. In any case it is worth continuing a little further and going around the cliffs of **Cap de Giverola** and the **Punta Es Pentiner**, behind which we discover a sensational spot. Here we come to an old fishermen's jetty of Tossa, with some long steps that allow access on foot. Then comes the **unspoilt cove of Futadera**, beneath majestic cliffs. The next

section, always at the foot of cliffs covered in woods, is only interrupted by **Cala Salionç**, another small spot of crystalline waters within the caprices of the coastal reliefs. The last stretch to complete the coastline of the municipality of Tossa de Mar culminates in the **beach of Vallpresona**, covered with pebbles, where one of the wildest streams of the massif of L'Ardenya comes out. From this beach, we navigate for a few moments within the coastal limits of the municipality of Santa Cristina d'Aro.

Just after the beach of Vallpresona, another unspoilt space appears, the **beach of Senyor Ramon** (naturist area), followed by a passage easily identifiable for a series of rocks and clefts around the **Punta de Canyet**, which stands out for the system of bridges and stone paths over crystalline waters. In a corner we discover the remains of an old lobster nursery, stuck beneath a crag with a view-

▲ Cala Futadera

▲ Beach of Els Canyerets

point above. In fact, we are now in **Cala Canyet**, which represents the end of the access road to the **Rosamar urbanisation**. This point is particularly known for the activity of an attractive farmhouse-restaurant, as well as for being the access to the sensational **beach of Els Canyerets**, the first in the municipality of Sant Feliu de Guíxols along our route. The setting is perfect for a welcome stop before starting the final part, along which there are small spots between cliffs, such as **Cala Joana**, **Cala d'Urgell**, **Cala d'en Pei** and **beach of Can Dell**, with the presence of chalets all around. This navigation brings us to an elegant line of cliffs, closed by the heights of **Puig Castellar** (99 m), crowned by the old **hermitage of Sant Elm** –patron saint of sailors and pilgrims -, where in 1908 the journalist Ferran Agulló was inspired to coin the phrase "Costa Brava", which some decades later would become a worldwide tourist brand. Here we can take in the spectacular **Cala del Vigatà**, with a surprising natural spring from which spouts water from inside the mountain. The final manoeuvre, with a notable presence of tourist establishments, enables us to enjoy a fantastic route across the **Marine Reserve of Sant Feliu de Guíxols**, passing close to the **islet of S'Adolitx**, the jetty of **Port Salvi**, the **islet of Es Freu** and **Punta de Garbí**. The final turns of the paddle, parallel to some pretty coastal reliefs, culminate in the extensive **beach of Sant Feliu de Guíxols**, flanked by its elegant esplanade.

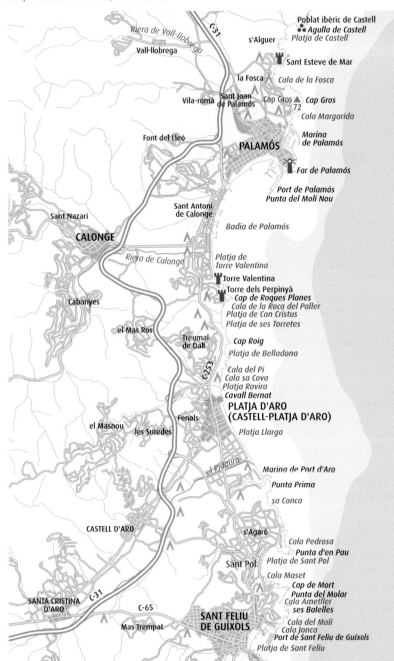

Riera de Vall-llobrega

C-31

Vall-llobrega

Poblat ibèric de Castell
Agulla de Castell
Platja de Castell

s'Alguer

Sant Esteve de Mar

la Fosca

Cala de la Fosca

Sant Joan
de Palamós

Vila-romà

Cap Gros

Cap Gros
72

Cala Margarida

Font del Lleó

PALAMÓS

Marina
de Palamós

Far de Palamós

Port de Palamós
Punta del Molí Nou

Sant Antoni
de Calonge

Sant Nazari

Badia de Palamós

CALONGE

Riera de Calonge

Platja de
Torre Valentina

Cabanyes

Torre Valentina
Torre dels Perpinyà
Cap de Roques Planes
Cala de la Roca del Paller
Platja de Can Cristus
Platja de ses Torretes

el Mas Ros

Treumal
de Dalt

Cap Roig

Platja de Belladona

C-253

Cala del Pi
Cala sa Cova
Platja Rovira
Cavall Bernat

el Masnou

Fenals

PLATJA D'ARO
(CASTELL-PLATJA D'ARO)

les Suredes

Platja Llarga

el Ridaura

Marina de Port d'Aro

Punta Prima

sa Conca

CASTELL D'ARO

s'Agaró

Cala Pedrosa
Punta d'en Pau
Platja de Sant Pol

Sant Pol

Cala Maset
Cap de Mort
Punta del Molar
Cala Ametller
ses Balelles

SANTA CRISTINA
D'ARO

C-31

C-65

Mas Trempat

SANT FELIU
DE GUÍXOLS

Cala del Molí
Cala Jonca
Port de Sant Feliu de Guíxols
Platja de Sant Feliu

N

0   0,5   1 k

3

3

FROM SANT FELIU DE GUÍXOLS TO PALAMÓS (beach of Castell)

▲ The spot of Castell with the Iberian settlement in the foreground

SANT FELIU DE GUÍXOLS

Sant Pol

PLATJA D'ARO

Sant Antoni de Calonge

PALAMÓS (beach of Castell)

Distance
19-22 km
[10-12 nautical miles]

Route of many contrasts between two of the most emblematic ports of the Costa Brava, where we alternate between wonderful coves and long areas of urbanised beaches. All in all, the rocky reliefs acquire a sublime expressiveness, with an initial wild part, a harmonious central part and a grand finish to savour the Mediterranean essence.

ROUTE

We leave from beside the **port of Sant Feliu de Guíxols**, being especially cautious for the passing of boats during the whole time we go round a long breakwater. Just behind we come to **Cala Jonca**, accessible on foot via some long steps that also connect with the fantastic coastal path to the beach of Sant Pol. The whole section concentrates one of the best series of cliffs of the Costa Brava, with islets and coves of true fantasy so it is worth going into them little by little to discover unforgettable small corners. We immediately reach **Cala del Molí**, where, between the cliffs, runs a popular iron way, an old railway track now used by walkers. We then navigate between the **islets of Ses Balelles**, the magical **Cala de L'Ametller**, the cliffs of the **Punta del Molar**, the sensational labyrinth of **Cap de Mort**, the corners of **Cala d'en Oliu**, the **cave of the Rates Penades** and **Cala del Peix**. Finally we discover the pretty **Cala Maset** and the spot of **La Caleta**, now beside the long **beach of Sant Pol**, which still recalls the times of splendour as a destination for the upper classes between the 1920s and 1930s (kayak hire centre). On the other side of its bay we follow the old **coastal path of S'Agaró**, where the initial part involves passing between an islet and the **Punta d'en Pau**. Further on we pass by **Cala Pedrosa**, which has a small beach with a jetty, and which precedes the large cleft of **Cala Vaques**, where we see the exemplary work of the most elegant pedestrian way on the Costa Brava. At last we reach the **beach of Sa Conca**, sheltered by the lovely promontory of the **Punta del Pinell**, with a pine wood on the upper part. Just behind this promontory we should pay great attention to the entrance and exit of boats from the **sports port of Platja d'Aro**. We soon come up against one of the main tourist complexes of the region, although we still have a few metres to cover across the **mouth of the river Ridaura**.

The next section of rowing, of more than 2 kilometres parallel to the esplanade of Platja d'Aro, provides many places to land in case of need. Once situated in the northern end of the beach, we begin a new section of rocky reliefs with numerous coves and points perfectly connected by the coastal paths between pine woods. We thus go past the **beach of La Rovira**, **Cala de Sa Cova**, **Cala del Pi** and the **beach of Belladona**, before arriving at the magnificent promontory of **Punta de Cap Roig**, which marks the entrance to the municipality of Calonge. From this point extend the **beaches of Ses Torretes** and **Can Cristus**, and a little further on

▲ **Kayak between Sant Feliu and Sant Pol**

we can take in a great view between the **unspoilt Cala Roca del Paller** and a strip of rocks around the **point of Roques Planes** (Flat Rocks) which as its name indicates, is an outstanding series of horizontal slabs of granite. This latter step introduces us to the emblematic **bay of Palamós**, known by sailors of all times, although the section we should follow is the long succession of beaches of the tourist resort of **Sant Antoni de Calonge**. In the distance we can now see the silhouette of the town and **port of Palamós**, where it is well worth approaching the wharves of the fishing boats, an activity still deeply-rooted here, as can be seen in the marvellous **Fishing Museum**, which also recalls the condition of royal port since 1279.

To complete the route we still have to pay great attention to the section that takes us, surrounding the long breakwater of the port, to the **Punta del Molí**, where the **lighthouse of Palamós** stands, and later, behind a large **sports port**, to the old houses of **Cala Margarida**. Once here we set off on the final section under the cliffs of **Cap Gros**, an interesting promontory of metamorphic rocks covered by a dense pine wood. In the back part appears a large vertical cleft of some 50 metres' drop, called **Rec de Fenals**. We then come to the **beach of La Fosca**, a popular tourist destination, with the remains of the medieval castle of **Sant Esteve de Mar** at the opposite end. Just after this enclave, we discover between a series of rocks, the romantic **Cala S'Alguer**, overlooked by a set of fishermen's cottages that date back to the 16th century. Half a kilometre further on, we

▲ Coast in the area of Cap de Mort

reach the sands of the **beach of Castell**, a setting of magnificence and beauty alike, sheltered by a dominant promontory that hides one of the best archaeological sites of the Costa Brava: the ancient **Iberian settlement of Castell**, from the 6th century BC. In summer there is a kayak hire centre. It is a great pleasure to stretch your legs along an excellent network of paths among fields and Mediterranean woods. A couple of nearby campsites complete the services.

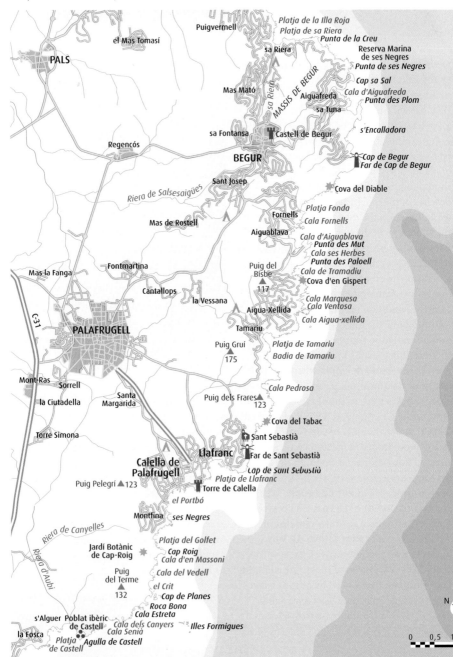

4

FROM PALAMÓS (beach of Castell) TO BEGUR (Sa Riera)

▲ Group of kayakers leaving Llafranc

PALAMÓS (beach of Castell) — CALELLA DE PALAFRUGELL — Llafranc — Tamariu — Aiguablava — Sa Tuna — BEGUR (Sa Riera)

Distance
20 - 23 km
[**11 - 13** nautical miles]

An exceptional section of coast that concentrates an enormous number of spots and provides an overdose of sensations. For many sea kayakers, it is one of the best routes you can do in all the Mediterranean, although on the other hand it requires good sea conditions to be able to pass through exposed points or to be able to enjoy the magic of unique corners.

ROUTE

We leave behind the **beach of Castell** and go around the promontory of **Agulla de Castell**, a memorable moment on reaching a small inlet of transparent waters beneath the remains of the old Iberian citadel and some fantastic cliffs. Just here it is well worth crossing the tunnel of natural rock of **Foradada de Castell**, a truly thrilling moment. At the exit, we follow the large line of cliffs covered with Mediterranean woods, beneath which follow a series of wonderful coves and points, decorated by many rocks. On the right and for quite a while we can take in the popular **Illes Formigues**, a wild series of islets populated by seabirds, which at the end of the 13th century was the setting a great victory by the Catalan armada against the French armada. We thus enter a fantasy route that connects the inaccessible **Cala Sanià**; **Punta Els Canyers**, with two small coves to either side; the wild **Cala Estreta**, with its old fishermen's refuge; **Punta de Rocabona**, reserved for naturism fans; **Cap de Planes**, with a wonderful setting among rocks; **Cala del Crit**, where the fabulous coastal path from the **beach of Castell** ends; **Cala del Vedell**, at the foot of some impressive cliffs, and finally **Cala d'en Massoni**, with a small jetty. In this latter cove you should look for a small tunnel of natural rock, known as the **Banyera de la Russa**, which recalls the couple of Anglo-Russian aristocrats who from 1927 created the current **Botanical Garden of Cap Roig**, one of the symbols of the Costa Brava, situated over marvellous cliffs. Just on the other side of the **point of Cap Roig**, we enter the municipality of Palafrugell, in a setting of wonderful scenery, embellished by the **islets of Castellets des Falcó** and **Cala del Golfet**. From this point on, we follow a coastline with residential chalets, under a pretty section of coastal path that connects Calella de Palafrugell and Llafranc.

From Cala del Golfet, the way is great fun between rocks and rocky points to the town of **Calella de Palafrugell**, where we have many sandy coves to land on, although we advise doing so on the old jetty of **Port Bo**, in front of a popular setting of arcades that conserve the full essence of yesteryear as the fishermen's district of Palafrugell. The continuation of the route continues across more series of rocks and rocky points, with the silhouette of the **watchtower of Calella** from 1597, which tells us of intense pirate attacks between the 16th and 17th centuries along the Catalan coast. We thus reach **Llafranc**, the second fishermen's district of Palafrugell, similarly developed into a select tourist resort due to its splendid sandy beach and small sports port. This is where we come to the foot of the **Puig de Sant Sebastià** (178 m), crowned by a series of elements of a rich historical heritage, among which features one of the most powerful lighthouses in the Mediterranean, a hermitage-guesthouse with a 15th-century watchtower, and even the remains of an Iberian settlement from the 4th century BC. For us, however, a section of very exposed coastline begins, at the foot of some formidable cliffs and some caves at the base, which only has a couple of escape points: when passing **Cala Gens**, which has a jetty and the protection of a pretty islet, and later in **Cala Pedrosa**, which connects with the coastal path between Llafranc and Tamariu. After this section, the coast levels out, but without losing the rocky nature until the thrilling entrance to the small **bay of Tamariu**, the third fishermen's

▲ Beach of Port Bo in Calella de Palafrugell   ▼ Calella de Palafrugell

▲ Beach of Illa Roja

district of Palafrugell, known by sailors from all times, since it was here where a good supply of drinking water was found. It has a summer kayak hire centre.

From Tamariu we still have a long section of coast left, full of incredible corners, with some new elevations of land and cliffs of great geological complexity. A series of fantastic formations and cavities fill the route towards **Cala d'Aigua-xelida**, of calm and crystalline waters, where we discover a space that has stood still in time, with an old fishermen's hut as a witness. From here we start off on an exciting trip that connects with the formidable **Punta des Banc**, **Cala Llarga**,

Cala Ventosa and **Cala Marquesa**. In this latter cove it is an absolute must to go in single file with the kayaks through a very narrow passage, between an islet and the walls of a gigantic cliff, which takes the name of **Rec dels Arbres**. At the exit of this unforgettable passage, we come to the **caves of Bisbe** and **Gavina**, both easily accessible in kayak. Immediately after appears the **cave of En Gispert**, which with its 150 metres' length is the longest on the Costa Brava; one of the best experiences we can ever have. We must go with great caution in these caves in the case of an agitated sea or seabed with currents, since it may make it difficult to get out.

Having passed the cave of d'en Gispert, we reach the municipal district of Begur. Surrounded by high cliffs of an unusual expressiveness, we continue past **Cala des Tramadiu**, the **Punta del Paluell**, **Cala de Ses Herbes** and **Punta des Munt**, to finally end before the beautiful **beach of Aiguablava**, situated in the shadow of the Parador Nacional hotel of the same name. This old hotel marks the entrance to the majestic setting of the **bay of Aiguablava**, beneath the heights of the **massif of Begur**. We then enjoy a series of small coves until the **port of Fornells**, a very romantic corner with an attractive coastal path that follows the outline of the coast until the neighbouring **beach of Fonda**, with blue and mysterious waters. From this beach we start the most exposed part of the route. In principle we must go round **Cap de Begur**, with some cliffs of over 200 metres high in some places. A first-class geographic extreme, where the dominant winds of the Costa Brava usually cross: the tramontana from the north or the lebeche from the southwest. You therefore need to grit your teeth to face a stretch of wild coast of 3.5 kilometres –almost 2 nautical miles–, which ends when passing the long **point of Es Plom** and the entrance to the **cove of Sa Tuna**. Here we discover another pretty fishing village of the municipality of Begur, where you will almost certainly feel like stopping off for a rest. Once we have set off again, it is worth following the beautiful reliefs until the solitary jetty of the **cove of Aiguafreda**, a space only spoilt by a large hotel that occupies the whole point of the

neighbouring **Cap Sa Sal**. Ahead of us remains the last section of 2 kilometres, also very exposed, at the foot of very elegant cliffs that mark the limits of the **Marine Reserve of Ses Negres**, where some beautiful rocks also stand out. Having reached the **point of La Creu**, it is now just a question of making the final push to the wide **beach of Sa Riera**, the last tourist centre of seafaring roots belonging to the municipality of Begur. We can complete this end with the view of the **beach of Illa Roja** (naturist area), easily identifiable for the spectacular islet that gives the name to the spot, before some large, broken up cliffs. A little further on begins the long stretch of the beach of Pals, until the town of L'Estartit and the massif of Montgrí.

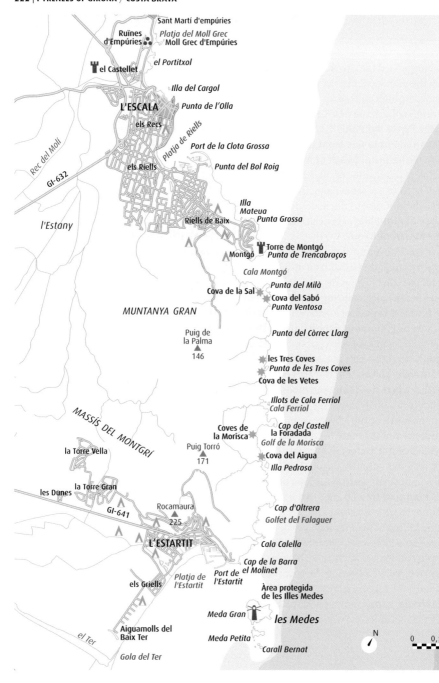

Sant Martí d'empúries
Ruïnes d'Empúries
Platja del Moll Grec
Moll Grec d'Empúries
el Castellet
el Portitxol
Illa del Cargol
L'ESCALA
Punta de l'Olla
els Recs
Platja de Riells
Port de la Clota Grossa
els Riells
Punta del Bol Roig
Rec del Moll
GI-632
Illa Mateua
l'Estany
Riells de Baix
Punta Grossa
Torre de Montgó
Montgó
Punta de Trencabraços
Cala Montgó
Cova de la Sal
Punta del Milà
Cova del Sabó
Punta Ventosa
MUNTANYA GRAN
Puig de la Palma
146
Punta del Còrrec Llarg
les Tres Coves
Punta de les Tres Coves
Cova de les Vetes
Illots de Cala Ferriol
Cala Ferriol
MASSÍS DEL MONTGRÍ
Coves de la Morisca
Cap del Castell
la Foradada
Golf de la Morisca
la Torre Vella
Puig Torró
171
Cova del Aigua
Illa Pedrosa
la Torre Gran
les Dunes
GI-641
Rocamaura
225
Cap d'Oltrera
Golfet del Falaguer
L'ESTARTIT
Cala Calella
Cap de la Barra
Port de el Molinet
els Griells
Platja de l'Estartit
l'Estartit
Àrea protegida de les Illes Medes
Meda Gran
les Medes
Aiguamolls del Baix Ter
Meda Petita
el Ter
Gola del Ter
Carall Bernat

N

0   0,5   1 k

5

FROM L'ESTARTIT (Islas Medes) TO L'ESCALA (Empúries)

▲ **Greek wharf of Empúries**

L'ESTARTIT
(Illes Medes)

Cala Montgó

L'ESCALA
(Empúries)

Distance
16 - 19 km
[8 - 10 nautical miles]

The fact that this is a coastline marked by a geological structure with a predominance of calcareous rock, cliffs with a height of one hundred metres' vertical drop, and very evocative reliefs with numerous cavities at the base make it incredibly attractive for sea kayaking. Nevertheless, optimum maritime conditions are required due to its great exposure to the elements.

ROUTE

The **port of L'Estartit** is a focus of great activity throughout the year, and we should find the starting point on a small beach that forms part of the wharves, which at the same time has direct access from the esplanade. Paying a great deal of attention to the entrance and exit of boats, we

▲ La Foradada

row the kayaks towards the **point of Molinet** –the end of the access road–, with the silhouette of the Illes Medes facing. We leave as optional a visit to the **Natural Park of the Illes Medes**, made up of seven islets of different sizes, among which the **Meda Gran** (72 m) stands out, crowned by a lighthouse dating back to 1866, and above all the majestic monolith of **Cavall Bernat**, 68 metres of vertical drop. If you want to make a tour around the amazing archipelago, protected since 1990 and a paradise for divers from all over Europe, you will have to add 4 kilometres to the route, 2.2 nautical miles. The straight route beneath the impressive cliffs of the **massif of Montgrí** is very evocative from the very beginning. At the start we pass by **Cap de la Barra**, **Cala Calella** and the **island of Dui** (diving area), the **Golfet del Falaguer**, **Cap de Oltrera**

and the **Racó de la Sardina** (diving area). We thus reach the **island of Pedrosa**, which marks the entrance to the sensational passage of **Cala Pedrosa**, the first stop-off point, where it is worth discovering the rich forest ecosystem concealed inside the ravines of the massif of Montgrí before setting off to sea. On leaving this cove, we reach the magnificent **gulf of La Morisca** (diving area), where we discover one of the most exceptional orographic accidents, formed by the large arch of natural rock of **La Foradada** through the **Cap del Castell**, which with 70 metres of tunnel allows even medium-size tourist boats to pass. A moment as thrilling as this gains intensity a little after, when we enter **Cala Ferriol**, between islets and crystalline waters, and a spot with more space to disembark than in Cala Pedrosa.

Located beneath the highest and wildest cliffs, one kilometre north of Cala Ferriol we come to another astonishing spot on the other side of the **point of Les Tres Coves** (The Three Caves), which as its name indicates houses three fantastic caves of different lengths that can be explored by kayak. The **Cova del Frare**, the largest of the three, is also a visiting point for tourist boats from L'Estartit. A little further on appears the wild **Cova Tomarràs**, identifiable by a large cleft. From here we still have to do a long stretch to come to the sensational series of cliffs that extends between **Punta Ventosa** and **Punta del Milà**, a reference point to start the entrance into the wonderful **bay Montgó**. Although this space could be crossed straight, it is well worth following its perimeter, populated by pine woods, in our direction of the route, since we can discover reliefs of great expressiveness, such as the **Cova de la Sal** (be careful of falling stones), as well as a group of inlets around which runs a lovely section of the coastal path over turquoise-coloured waters. We thus reach the **beach of Cala Montgó**, at the foot of a large urbanisation of residential chalets, where there is a popular summer kayak hire centre and other tourist services. After a stop-off, we complete the rest of the perimeter of Cala Montgó beneath the line of chalets of the urbanisation.

We then begin a spectacular section. We need to pay great attention to find the entrance to a cavity (be careful of falling stones), through which we can enter for 50 metres of amazing tunnel. This tunnel, known as **Les Cambres**, comes out via a second wider opening, beside the **point of Trencabraços**, where we make an exposed turn at the foot of a vertical wall of one hundred metres' height, called **Salt de la Deua**. Just at the top of these cliffs stands the **surveillance tower of Montgó** dated 1598, another of the many examples of this type of construction relating to pirate attacks in the past. We immediately complete the full turn of the promontory of Montgó to come to the quiet spot of the **beach of Illa Mateua**. From here, we go along an attractive line of small cliffs with pine trees and old dispersed military bunkers, where the coastal path also runs between Cala Montgó and L'Escala. The end of this section, at the **point of Bol Roig**, continues with the rounding of the large breakwater of the **port of La Clota**, in which are concentrated the sports and fishing boats of **L'Escala** (you should go carefully). At the other end of the port the large **beach of Riells** extends and the beginning of the long esplanade that leads to the old centre of the town. Between pretty rocks and reliefs, we progress towards the pretty **beach of Les Barques**, an old embarkation point for the fishermen of L'Escala. Our route, however, culminates in the lovely **beaches of Empúries**, beside the old Greek Wharf and the archaeological remains of the mythical **Greco-Roman city of Empúries**.

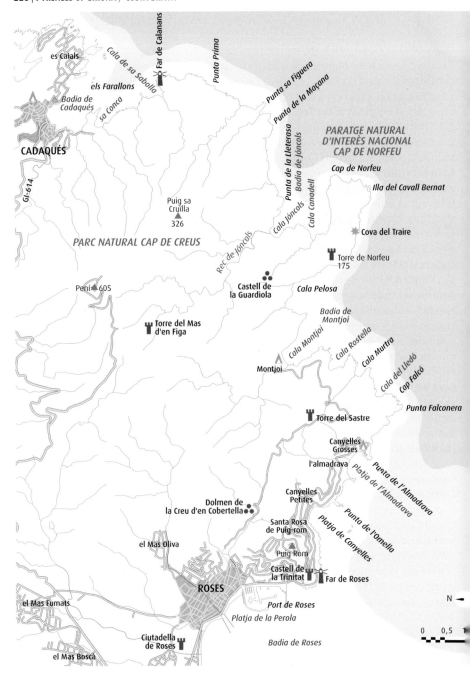

es Caials

Cala de sa Sabolla

Far de Calanans

Punta Prima

els Farallons

Badia de Cadaqués

sa Conca

CADAQUÉS

Gi-614

Puig sa Cruïlla
▲ 326

Punta sa Figuera

Punta de la Maçana

Punta de la Lleterasa

Badia de Jóncols

Cala Jóncols

Cala Canadell

PARATGE NATURAL D'INTERÈS NACIONAL CAP DE NORFEU

Cap de Norfeu

Illa del Cavall Bernat

PARC NATURAL CAP DE CREUS

Rec de Jóncols

Cova del Traire

Torre de Norfeu
175

Pení ▲ 605

Castell de la Guardiola

Cala Pelosa

Badia de Montjoi

Torre del Mas d'en Figa

Cala Montjoi

Cala Rostella

Cala Murtra

Cala del Lledó

Cap Falcó

Montjoi

Punta Falconera

Torre del Sastre

Canyelles Grosses

l'almadrava

Punta de l'Almadrava

Platja de l'Almadrava

Dolmen de la Creu d'en Cobertella

Canyelles Petites

Santa Rosa de Puig-rom

Punta de l'Omella

Platja de Canyelles

el Mas Oliva

Puig Rom

Castell de la Trinitat

Far de Roses

ROSES

el Mas Fumats

Port de Roses

Platja de la Perola

N →

Ciutadella de Roses

Badia de Roses

el Mas Bosca

0   0,5

6 FROM ROSES TO CADAQUÉS 6

▲ Coast in the bay of Montjoi

ROSES

CADAQUÉS

L'Almadrava   Cala Montjoi   Cala Jóncols

Distance
22-25 km
[12-14 nautical miles]

After a start in a landscape heavily influenced by mankind, the rest of the route goes along large bays flanked by magnificent cliffs. Accompanied by the memory of classical Greek mythology, here we find a coastline of pure and harmonious landscape, which culminates in one of the most romantic towns of the whole Mediterranean.

ROUTE

We leave from the **beach of Perola in Roses**, beside the **sports and fishing port** of a town with nearly 3,000 years of history since it was founded by Greek colonists, and has been a royal port since 1304. Paying attention to passing boats, we go straight towards the point of the **lighthouse of Roses**, from 1864, with the remains of the **castle of La Trinitat**, from the 16th century behind. Behind us we leave the sight of the **bay of Roses** to pass by the **beach of Canyelles Petites** and **beach of Almadrava**, along a pretty route between points, islets and rocks in the shadow a large urban extension. However, just after passing the **point of Almadrava** (a name that recalls the traditional fishing art, tunny fishing, almadraba in Spanish, to catch tuna fish during their migrations close to this coast), the landscape suddenly becomes wild and extensive again. A couple of small inlets of turquoise waters precede the passing by the large cliff of the **Punta Falconera**, with an old military settlement that controlled the access to the **bay of Montjoi**. Our route follows some coastal profiles of great richness, cove-

red with pine woods, where there is also a fantastic section of coastal path to go on foot. Between more points and rocks we pass the **Cala del Lledó**, **Cala Murtra** (naturist area), and **Cala Rostella**, before coming to the **beach of Cala Montjoi** and its popular holiday centre. At the foot of the mountains connected to the Pyrenean range, we continue ahead to come to the two pretty **beaches of Cala Pelosa**, just before the large promontory of **Cap Norfeu** (171 m), which we have had in our sights for some time, with its surveillance tower from 1598. This sensational geographic accident constitutes the largest calcareous rock mass of the **Natural Park of Cap de Creus** and involves a round trip of 4 kilometres of perimeter, at the foot of cliffs of more

▲ **Cadaqués with the beach of Sa Conca in the foreground**

6

than 100 metres in height, with many caves at the base and a large monolith of rock of 32 metres at the end, called **Cavall Bernat de Norfeu**.

After completing the full tour around Cap Norfeu, we come to the solitary **cove of Canadell**, a good point to enjoy the panorama in the centre of the **bay of Jóncols**, just before passing by the large cliff of the **point of Canadell**, with a couple of caves at the base. We then reach the **beach of Cala Jóncols**, a lovely spot where the forest track ends from Cala Montjoi, with an eco-tourism establishment that may be useful in case of need. This is the border between the municipalities of Roses and Cadaqués, historically a meeting point between the fishermen of both towns. Here we start the last part, with a stretch of nearly 5 kilometres beneath the line of the biggest cliffs of the route, which indicates that we have to face another area very exposed to the beatings of the sea. At the beginning we navigate between the **point of La Lleterassa** and the **point of Sa Figuera**, to complete the extraordinary perimeter of the bay of Jóncols. From the latter point, flanked by spectacular clefts, we set course northwards. We go beneath the cliffs of **Punta Prima**, until reaching the **point of Calanans**, which marks the entrance to the **bay of Cadaqués**, with a famous lighthouse from 1856 as our reference point. In the back part of the lighthouse we discover the **cove of Sa Sabolla**, which has a small sandy beach and a link to the coastal path from Cadaqués. Beside this spot we enjoy a delightful passage between the large **islets of Des Cucurucuc** and an extensive zone of rocks. A little further on we come to the **beach of Sa Conca**, the first urbanised point of the town of Cadaqués. The final navigation over the crystalline waters of the bay of Cadaqués is an unforgettable moment when we pass between the **point of Sa Conca** and the **islet of Sortell**, with a stone bridge that links these two elegant spaces. We then have before us the sight of the town of **Cadaqués**, overlooked by its church of Santa Maria and the other houses of the old quarter, a marvellous fishermen's town which, between the 18th and 19th centuries, traded directly with the far-off ports of Europe, Africa and Asia. This encounter with the most authentic Mediterranean is the best reward for the hardworking kayaker.

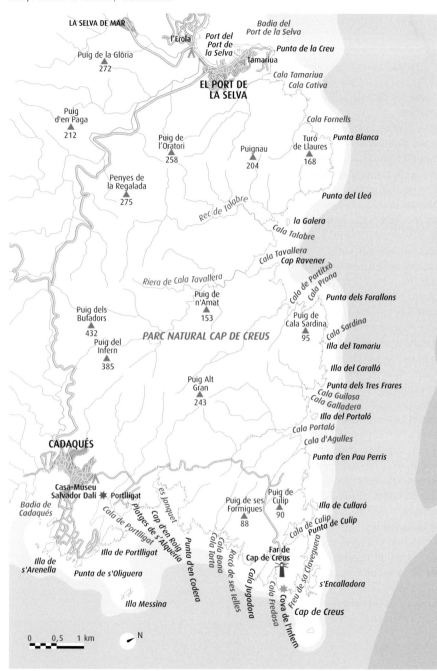

LA SELVA DE MAR

Badia del Port de la Selva

l'Erola

Port del Port de la Selva

Punta de la Creu

Tamariua

Puig de la Glòria
272

EL PORT DE LA SELVA

Cala Tamariua
Cala Cativa

Puig d'en Paga
212

Cala Fornells

Puig de l'Oratori
258

Puignau
204

Turó de Llaures
168

Punta Blanca

Penyes de la Regalada
275

Punta del Lleó

Rec de Talabre

la Galera

Cala Talabre

Cala Tavallera
Cap Ravener

Riera de Cala Tavallera

Puig de n'Amat
153

Cala de Portitxó
Cala Prona

Punta dels Forallons

Puig dels Bufadors
432

Puig de Cala Sardina
95

Cala Sardina

PARC NATURAL CAP DE CREUS

Puig del Infern
385

Illa del Tamariu

Illa del Caralló

Puig Alt Gran
243

Punta dels Tres Frares
Cala Guilosa
Cala Galladera

Illa del Portaló

Cala Portaló

Cala d'Agulles

Punta d'en Pau Perris

CADAQUÉS

Casa-Museu Salvador Dalí ✳ Portlligat

es Jonquet

Cala de Portlligat

platges de s'Alqueria

Cap d'en Roig

Puig de ses Formigues
88

Puig de Culip
90

Illa de Cullaró

Cala de Culip
Punta de Culip

Badia de Cadaqués

Illa de Portlligat

Punta d'en Codera

Cala Bona
Cala Torta

Racó de ses Telles

Far de Cap de Creus

Freu de sa Claveguera

Illa de s'Arenella

Punta de s'Oliguera

Cala Jugadora

Cala Fredosa

✳ Cova de l'Infern

s'Encalladora

Illa Messina

Cap de Creus

0   0,5   1 km

N

SEA ROUTES IN KAYAK

7

FROM CADAQUÉS TO PORT DE LA SELVA

7

▲ Cala Jugadora

CADAQUÉS   PORT DE LA SELVA

Portlligat   Cap de Creus

Distance
27-30 km
[**14-16** nautical miles]

During this route we navigate along one of the sections of the wildest coastlines of Europe, since it goes along nothing less than the easternmost end of the Pyrenees and the Iberian Peninsula. We should therefore be well aware of the untamed nature of a territory that requires optimum weather conditions and good planning.

ROUTE

From the **Platja Gran of Cadaqués**, we glide the kayaks over the marvellous waters of the 4 kilometres of the perimeter of its bay, a destination of sailors of all times. Our speedy progression follows some pretty coastal outlines with chalets, until passing the **point of En Perefet**, leaving on the right a structure with a permanent light, installed in 1933 and which has the name of **Es Piló**. We immediately pass between the coastline and the **islet of S'Arenella**, where we can appreciate the transparency and shallowness of the sea, as well as the old stone constructions on both sides. From here we advance along the extensive area of **rocks of Es Caials** and **Es Forallons**, and we must take great care to find the beginning of the **passage of Ses Boquelle**s, very narrow and shallow, which separates the coast and the **isle of Portlligat**. The landscape gradually gains width, until we reach the bay of Portlligat, an old Mediterranean paradise where the brilliant painter Salvador Dalí built his home and studio, today converted into the **Dalí House-Museum**. As well as the diverse

services and road link to Cadaqués, the spot has a summertime kayak hire centre. At the exit, heading north, we cross the **coves of S'Alqueria**, from where we begin to take in the first dramatic reliefs that typify the north coast of the **Natural Park of Cap de Creus**, marked by rocks of magmatic origin with extraordinary colours and formations. On passing between **Cap d'en Roig** and the **Illot del Jonquet** we can see for ourselves these characteristics, and at the same time start the tour of the **bay of Guillola**. This pleasant bay, with agricultural terraces above the coast, has a number of inlets and small beaches to the **point of Cudera**. On this point, some large vertical clefts advise us that the coastline is becoming more ir-

▲ **Jetty of Cala Culip**

7

regular and rocky, standing out on our route the deep entrances to **Cala Torta**, **Cala Bona** and **Cala de Ses Ielles**, all very interesting. Just past Cala de Ses Ielles, we come to the big cliff of **Ses Orgues**, identifiable for its relief, which simulates the structure of an organ manipulated by the wind. This point also marks the entrance into the fantastic **Cala Jugadora**, the destination of solitary sailboats, with a good space for landing. In fact this is the best place to do so if you want to visit the **lighthouse of Cap de Creus**, which is above us, due to the easy access to the old coastal path from Cadaqués. Also a little higher up, we come to the road that ends at the mythical lighthouse, opened in 1853 (bar-restaurant and information office). On the other side of Cala Jugadora is the wild **Cala Fredosa**, with the remains of an old jetty that was used to supply the lighthouse from the sea. On leaving this cove, we discover the **Cova de l'Infern** (Cave of Hell), which can be entered in kayak to take in the massive arch of natural rock with an access path from the lighthouse. A few metres further on we pass the **point of Cap del Creus**, full of emotion, leaving on the right the **isle of Massa d'Or**, which strictly speaking represents the easternmost fragment of the Pyrenees and the Iberian Peninsula. We thus reach the **Mar d'Amunt** (Sea of Above), named thus by the sailors of Cap de Creus, the point that receives all the violence of the tramontana, the feared northerly wind that is channelled through the gulf of León, responsible in this area for the highest concentration of shipwrecks in all the Mediterra-

nean since ancient times. On the right emerges the dramatic **isle of S'Encalladora**, which looks somewhat like a petrified boat, with its large colony of seabirds.

Navigating along what is called the **channel of Sa Claveguera**, we begin to contemplate the most impressive geological reliefs of the coastline of Cap de Creus. Then appears the irregular **bay of Cala Culip**, where it is worth approaching the old **fishermen's hut** hidden in one of its entrances. At the exit we come to a narrow channel between the coast and the **isle of Cullaró**, through which our kayaks pass tightly. This lovely pass places us within the precious **spot of Tudela**, which houses some of the best sea beds of the Costa Brava and where for more than 40 years there was a famous holiday centre, today totally demolished in order to recover all the landscape that at one time inspired some of the most famous works by the painter Dalí. Further on we come to the formidable **Cala d'Agulles**, where the combination of mineral fragments and erosion caused by the elements provide a stunning image. The neighbouring space we come to is the entrance to **Cala Portaló**, with a long passage that is highly recommendable to cover in its totality, as far as a delightful sandy beach, within an intact natural ecosystem. It is very important to be aware of this point before setting off on the rest of the route, knowing that in case of emergency we have a connection to the road, between the lighthouse of Cap de Creus and Cadaqués.

From Cala Portaló we enjoy a route full of wild inlets, where of note are the **isle of Por-**

taló, **Cala Galladera**, with an old jetty between ravines, the cliffs of the **point of Tres Frares**, with a cave at the base, **Cala del Molà**, of almost volcanic appearance, and the **islets of Cala Sardina**, which make a tempting and entertaining pass. Now inside the municipality of Port de la Selva, we reach the **point of Els Forallons**, which has some spectacular white seams of volcanic origin –called pegmatites–, with a pretty pass between rocks that leads us to the large **bay of Gou** and **Cala Prona**. This cove is known for its old jetty and a fisherman's hut that can be used as a refuge in case of need. From Cala Prona onwards, we can see an imposing mountainside, which falls forming several amphitheatres over the **coves of Portitxó** and **Ravaner**, respectively. We then reach the open space of **Cala Tavallera**, where one of the most important streams of the peninsula of Cap de Creus comes out, with a pretty pine wood and couple of old fishermen's huts that recall the times of a life in harmony with nature in its purest state. Cala Tavallera is a passing point of a branch of the old path between Cap de Creus and Port de la Selva.

The final part of the route begins in Cala Tavallera, passing by **Cala del Talabre**, which has a small beach at the foot of high cliffs. Before us emerges the **isle of La Galera**, which recalls the shipwreck, in 1654, of the galley Gran Pelicana. The grandiose setting is strengthened on passing in the shadow of the **cliffs of Figuerola**, the highest on the route, which fall from the heights of **Puig Gros** (168 m) and which close the bay

of Gou at its opposite end. Further on we discover **El Boc** and **La Cabra**, a place formed by an islet with an outstanding rocky formation and a very narrow passage to the foot of **Punta Blanca**, where the verticality of the cliffs is still overwhelming. After passing this point come **Cala Corquell**, **Cala Torta**, **Cala Fornells**, **Cala Cativa** and finally **Cala Tamariua**, the five of them accessible by land via a lovely coastal path from Port de la Selva. Cala Cativa features an old stone refuge and a series of rocks, and in Cala Tamariua there is a more extensive beach, just before making the turn round the **point of La Creu** and entering the **bay of Port de la Selva**. A series of small coves and the panorama of the **Rodes range** on the horizon close a route of great intensity and emotions. We should find the embarkation point a little further on from the busy fishing wharfs of **Port de la Selva**, a seafaring town with a lot of tradition since 1787, the year it was founded as a municipality.

▲ Cala Tavallera

▼ Port de la Selva

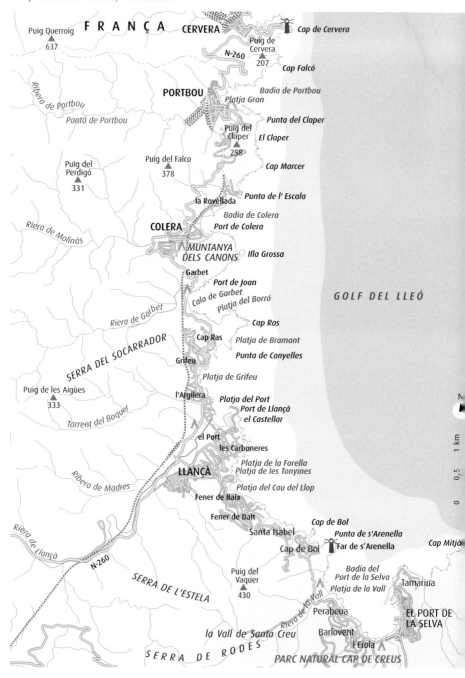

Puig Querroig
637

F R A N Ç A

CERVERA

Cap de Cervera

Puig de Cervera
207

N-260

Cap Falcó

PORTBOU

Badia de Portbou

Platja Gran

Punta del Claper

Puig del Claper
258

El Claper

Puig del Perdigó
331

Puig del Falco
378

Cap Marcer

la Rovellada

Punta de l' Escala

Ribera de portbou

Pantà de Portbou

Riera de Molinàs

COLERA

Badia de Colera

Port de Colera

MUNTANYA
DELS CANONS

Illa Grossa

Garbet

Port de Joan

Cala de Garbet

Platja del Borró

Riera de Garbet

Cap Ras

Cap Ras

Platja de Bramant

SERRA DEL SOCARRADOR

Grifeu

Punta de Canyelles

Platja de Grifeu

Puig de les Aigües
333

l'Argilera

Platja del Port

Port de Llançà

el Castellar

GOLF DEL LLEÓ

Torrent del Boquer

el Port

les Carboneres

LLANÇÀ

Platja de la Farella

Platja de les Tonyines

Ribera de Madres

Platja del Cau del Llop

Fener de Baix

Fener de Dalt

Santa Isabel

Cap de Bol

Cap de Bol

Punta de s'Arenella

Far de s'Arenella

Cap Mitjà

Riera de Llançà

N-260

SERRA DE L'ESTELA

Puig del Vaquer
430

Badia del
Port de la Selva

Platja de la Vall

Tamariua

EL PORT DE
LA SELVA

Riera de la Vall

Perabeua

la Vall de Santa Creu

Barlovent

l'Erola

SERRA DE RODES

PARC NATURAL CAP DE CREUS

1 km

0,5

0

SEA ROUTES IN KAYAK

8 FROM PORT DE LA SELVA TO PORTBOU

▲ Kayakers on the beach of La Vall

PORT DE LA SELVA   LLANÇÀ   COLERA   PORTBOU

Beach of La Vall   Beach of Garbet

Distance
19-22 km
[10-12 nautical miles]

Along what is called the coastline of La Balmeta we find a crescent full of coves and bays where the easternmost valleys of the Pyrenees come out. Although the roads run very close to the coastline, we enjoy a setting that breathes character, perhaps because it is border territory with the more poetic fusion of the Pyrenees and the Mediterranean.

ROUTE

We cross the **bay of Port de la Selva**, leaving the coastal path on the left, which will accompany us all along the way, until the town of Llançà. After enjoying some pretty rocky reliefs, we reach the **beach of La Vall**, with a popular campsite above and, a little further on, the **Els Lladres cave**, which has a small tunnel through which it is a great pleas-

▲ Cliffs of Puig del Claper

ure to pass with the kayaks. These coastal reliefs gain more beauty on turning around the **point of S'Arenella**, well visible thanks to its lighthouse, built in 1910. On the other side appear a small sandy cove and a notable series of rocks, which protect the **isle of Cap de Bol** like a belt, a regular destination for rod anglers. From this point we continue passing beautiful rocky points until the **beach of Cau del Llop**, where the extension of residential urbanisations is generalised, although this does not stop us from continuing to enjoy a very attractive coast. To go along the **beach of Les Tonyines**, **beach of La Farella** and the **point of Morer**, we must use all the skill we have to slip the kayaks between a vast expanse of rocks over shal-

low crystalline waters. We thus reach the **islet of Castellar**, with a cave at the base, a space which in bygone times was a separate point of the coast, but which now forms part of the protective breakwaters of **Port de Llançà**, a fisherman's district of the municipality of Llançà, with all kinds of tourist services. Always alert to passing boats, it is highly recommendable to take a good rest in the **beach of El Port**, where there is a large kayak centre that is open all year round, with a shop and material for hire. Setting off northwards, we pass in the middle of urbanisations of chalets the pretty **beach of Grifeu**, and immediately begin the turn around the perimeter of the large promontory of **Cap Ras**, covered by a thick pine wood in-

8

land, which contrasts with its craggy and rocky coast.

Before reaching the end of Cap Ras, we discover the surprising **Cala Bramant**, which has a narrow passage between rocky points. In contrast, at the other end of the cape, now in the **bay of Garbet**, we come to the **unspoilt coves of Borró** (naturist area), with old military bunkers around it. At the back of the fantastic bay which we are rowing round appears the **beach of Garbet**, which is an ideal space for taking in the lovely surrounding scenery. that surrounds. On the side is the jetty of **Port Joan** and a series of terraces with vines growing, once again offering a great contrast of forms and colours in the direction of **Cap Lladró**, some way further on, beneath which is the **isle of Grossa**, all surrounded by rocks and eroded crags. Just above this point stands the **mountain of Els Canons**, in reference to the iron cannons, installed as a type of viewpoint, that belonged to some vessels of the Spanish Armada that sunk before this coast in the winter of 1793. Immediately after we reach the small **port of Colera**, a quiet town which has all the services necessary, including a railway station of the line between Barcelona and the French border. On the other side of the **bay of Colera** we leave **Cala Rovellada**, the spot where there is a sudden rising of the cliffs, since the physical frontier of the Pyrenees is 3 kilometres as the crow flies from our position.

The prominent **Cap Marcer**, with a beautiful cavity at the base, marks the beginning of the biggest cliffs on the Costa Brava,

which drop dramatically from the heights of **Puig del Claper** (258 m). A little further on we discover some steps that drop to a small cove, from a viewpoint with access from the old road between Colera and Portbou. These cliffs mark the entrance to the wonderful **bay of Portbou**, but before finishing the route it is highly recommendable to row straight to **Cap de Cervera**, identifiable by its lighthouse, which represents the start of what is called the Côte Vermeille (Crimson Coast). Once at the foot of the equally stunning cliffs of **Puig de Cervera** (207 m), on the other side of the bay of Portbou, we reach what is officially the physical and political border of the Pyrenees. From here we go along the coastline via a series of small coves until the **Platja Gran of Portbou**. The final point of the route, in the last town of the Costa Brava, is also the end of the railway line from Barcelona. Portbou also offers some spectacular walks outside the town, on being the extreme maritime end of the **Natural park of L'Albera**. It is also an excellent stopping-off point before setting off on a final route by kayak along the entire Côte Vermeille, to the large town of Colliure.

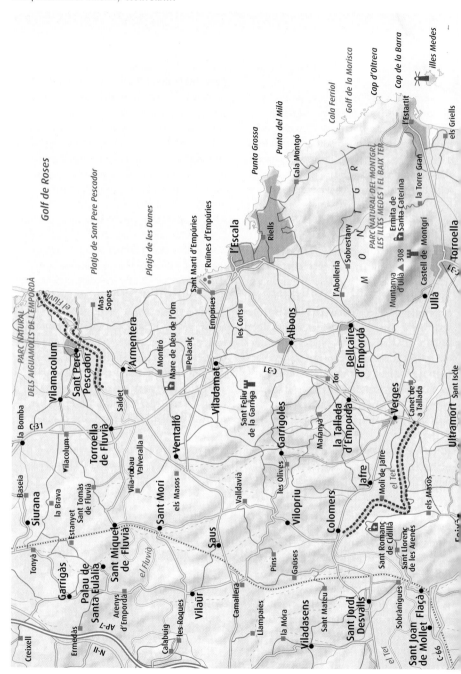

Golf de Roses

Golf de la Morisca

Cala Ferriol

Cap de la Barra

Cap d'Oltrera

illes Medes

l'Estartit

els Griells

Punta del Milà

Punta Grossa

Cala Montgó

PARC NATURAL DEL MONTGRÍ
LES ILLES MEDES I EL BAIX TER

M O N T G R Í

la Torre Gran

Ermita de
Santa Caterina

Muntanya
d'Ulla ▲ 308

Castell de Montgrí

Torroella

Ulla

Platja de Sant Pere Pescador

Platja de les Dunes

Sant Martí d'Empúries

Ruïnes d'Empúries

l'Escala

Riells

Sobrestany

l'Abolleria

Sant Iscle

Canet de
a Tallada

Verges

Ultramort

C-31

Bellcaire
d'Empordà

Tor

la Tallada
d'Empordà

Mafanyà

els Masos

Moli de Jafre

el Ter

Sant Romàn
de Cidillà

Sant Llorenç
de les Arenes

Colomers

Jafre

Feix

PARC NATURAL
DELS AIGUAMOLLS DE L'EMPORDÀ

EL FLUVIÀ

Golf de Roses

Mas
Sopes

l'Armentera

Montiró

Mare de Déu de l'Om

Pelacalç

les Corts

Empúries

Albons

Vilamacolum

Sant Pere
Pescador

Saldet

Viladamat

Sant Feliu
de la Garriga

Garrigoles

Vilacolum

Torroella
de Fluvià

Valveralla

Vila-robau

Ventalló

els Masos

els Olives

Valldavià

la Bomba

C-31

Baseia

la Brava

Siurana

la Brava

Estanyet

Sant Tomàs
de Fluvià

Sant Miquel
de Fluvià

Sant Mori

Saus

Vilopriu

el Fluvià

Tonyà

Garrigàs

Palau de
Santa Eulàlia

Arenys
d'Empordà

Vilaür

Pins

Gaüses

Sant Romàn
de Cidillà

Creixell

Ermedàs

N-II

AP-7

Calabuig

les Roques

Camallera

Llampaies

la Móra

Sant Mateu

Viladasens

Sant Jordi
Desvalls

Sobrànigues

Sant Joan
de Mollet

Flaçà

C-66

el Ter

KAYAK IN THE RIVERS TER AND FLUVIÀ

▲ Kayak in the river Ter

You can go kayaking in the final part of the two main rivers of Girona through well-conserved natural ecosystems. In both cases there service companies from which we can hire kayaks, material and transport.

RIVER TER

The most advisable section of the river Ter is concentrated between the towns of **Colomers** and **Verges**, with 8 kilometres of very spectacular rowing, which features the presence of wild fauna, such as turtles and many species of birds. Thick river vegetation and a succession of small currents among meanders make rowing in Colomers great fun, and the established company organises the trip with basic equipment.

RIVER FLUVIÀ

From the sports port of **Sant Pere Pescador** to the mouth of the river Fluvià, we enjoy 4 very attractive kilometres which we can repeat the other way, since the river current is minimal. There and back, then, we have 8 kilometres within the boundaries of the **Natural Park of the Aiguamolls de l'Empordà**, with stops by outstanding spots, such as the **isle of Caramany**, or different sections replete with the fauna typical of this type of ecosystem.

TOURIST OFFICES

COSTA BRAVA

Arbúcies
C. Major, 6
Tel. (34) 972 162 477
ofturisme@ajarbucies.cat
www.arbucies.cat/turisme

Banyoles
Pg. Darder - Pesquera, 10
Tel. (34) 972 583 470
turisme@ajbanyoles.org
www.banyoles.cat/turisme

Begur
Av. Onze de Setembre, 5
Tel. (34) 972 624 520
turisme@begur.cat
www.visitbegur.com

Blanes
Pg. Catalunya, 2
Tel. (34) 972 330 348
turisme@blanes.cat
www.visitblanes.net

Punt d'Informació de Blanes Pins
Pl. dels Càmpings, s/n
Tel. (34) 972 330 348
turisme@blanes.cat
www.visitblanes.net

Breda
C. Santa Victòria, 1
Tel. (34) 972 871 530
elsforns@breda.cat
www.breda.cat

Cadaqués
C. des Cotxe, 2 A
Tel. (34) 972 258 315
turisme@cadaques.cat
www.visitcadaques.org

Caldes de Malavella
C. Vall-Llobera, s/n
Tel. (34) 972 480 103
turisme@caldesdemalavella.cat
www.caldesdemalavella.cat

Calella de Palafrugell
C. Les Voltes, 4
Tel. (34) 972 614 475
turisme@palafrugell.cat
www.visitpalafrugell.cat

Calonge
Pl. Major s/n
Tel. (34) 972 609 445
turisme@calonge.cat
www.calonge-santantoni.com

Castelló d'Empúries
Av. Sant Francesc, 5-7
Tel. (34) 972 156 233
turisme@castello.cat
www.castelloempuriabrava.com

Colera
C. Labrun, 34
Tel. (34) 972 389 050
ajuntament@colera.cat
www.colera.cat

El Port de la Selva
C. Illa, 13
Tel. (34) 972 387 122
turisme@elportdelaselva.cat
www.elportdelaselva.cat

Empuriabrava
Av. Pompeu Fabra, 1
Tel. (34) 972 450 802
turisme@empuriabrava.cat
www.castelloempuriabrava.com

Figueres
Pl. del Sol, s/n
Tel. (34) 972 503 155
turisme@figueres.org
www.visitfigueres.cat

Girona
Oficina Municipal de Turisme
Rambla de la Llibertat, 1
Tel. (34) 972 010 001
(34) 972 226 575
turisme@ajgirona.cat
www.girona.cat/turisme

Punt de Benvinguda
Girona – Gironès
C. Berenguer Carnicer, 3
Tel. (34) 972 211 678
(34) 972 01 16 69
puntdebenvinguda@ajgirona.cat
centredevisitants@girones.cat
www.girona.cat/turisme
www.turismegirones.cat

Hostalric
C. Raval, 45
Tel. (34) 972 864 565
turisme@hostalric.cat
www.hostalric.cat

La Bisbal d'Empordà
C. de l'Aigüeta, 17
Tel. (34) 972 645 500
turisme@labisbal.cat
www.visitlabisbal.cat

Punt d'informació de la Bisbal
d'Empordà (Castell-Palau)
Pl. del Castell s/n
Tel. (34) 972 645 166
turisme@baixemporda.cat
www.visitemporda.com

L'Escala
Pl. de les Escoles, 1
Tel. (34) 972 770 603
turisme@lescala.cat
www.visitlescala.com

L'Estartit
Pg. Marítim, s/n
Tel. (34) 972 751 910
info@visitestartit.com
www.visitestartit.com

Llafranc
Pg. Cípsela, s/n
Tel. (34) 972 305 008
turisme@palafrugell.cat
www.visitpalafrugell.cat

Llagostera
Pg. Romeu, s/n
(Estació del Carrilet)
Tel. (34) 972 832 322
turisme@llagostera.cat
www.llagostera.cat

Llançà
C. Camprodon, 16-18
Tel. (34) 972 380 855
turisme@llanca.cat
www.llanca.cat

Lloret de Mar
Av. de les Alegries, 3
Tel. (34) 972 365 788
central-turisme@lloret.org
www.lloretdemar.org

Museu del Mar
Pg. Camprodón i Arrieta, 1-2
Tel. (34) 972 364 735
lloret-turisme@lloret.org
www.lloretdemar.org

Terminal d'autobusos
Av. Vila de Blanes
turisme-terminal@lloret.org
www.lloretdemar.org

Maçanet de Cabrenys
Aparcament del Pont, s/n
Tel. (34) 972 544 297
turisme@massanet.org
www.massanet.org

Mont-ras
Pl. de l'Ajuntament, 1
Tel. (34) 972 301 974
ajuntament@mont-ras.cat
www.mont-ras.cat

Palafrugell
Av. Generalitat, 33
Tel. (34) 972 300 228
turisme@palafrugell.cat
www.visitpalafrugell.cat

Palamós
Pg. del Mar, s/n
Tel. (34) 972 600 550
oficinadeturisme@palamos.cat
www.visitpalamos.cat

Moll Pesquer, s/n.
Edifici Museu de la Pesca
Tel. (34) 972 600 550
oficinadeturisme@palamos.cat
www.visitpalamos.cat

Pals
C. Hospital, 22
Tel. (34) 972 637 380
info@pals.cat
www.pals.cat

C. Aniceta Figueras, 6
Tel. (34) 972 637 857
info@pals.cat
www.pals.cat

Peralada
Pl. Peixateria, 6
Tel. (34) 972 538 840
promocio@peralada.org
www.peralada.org

Peratallada (Forallac)
Pl. del Castell, 3
Tel. (34) 872 987 030
turisme@forallac.cat
www.forallac.cat

Platja d'Aro
C. Mn. Cinto Verdaguer, 4
Tel. (34) 972 817 179
turisme@platjadaro.com
www.platjadaro.com

Portbou
Pg. Lluís Companys
Tel. (34) 972 125 161
turisme@portbou.cat
www.portbou.cat

Roses
Av. Rhode, 77-79
Tel. (34) 972 257 331
(34) 902 103 636
turisme@roses.cat
www.visit.roses.cat

Sant Antoni de Calonge
Av. Catalunya, 26
Tel. (34) 972 661 714
turisme@calonge.cat
www.calonge.cat

Sant Feliu de Guíxols
Pl. del Monestir s/n
Tel. (34) 972 820 051
turisme@guixols.cat
www.visitguixols.com

Sant Hilari Sacalm
Pl. Dr. Robert, s/n
Tel. (34) 972 869 686
oficinaturisme@santhilari.cat
www.santhilari.cat

Sant Llorenç de la Muga
C. Església, 2
Tel. (34) 972 569 140
ajuntament@santllorençdelamuga.cat
www.santllorençdelamuga.cat

Sant Pere Pescador
Ctra. de la Platja, s/n
Tel. (34) 972 520 535
(34) 972 520 050
turisme@santpere.cat
www.santpere.cat

Santa Cristina d'Aro
Pl. Catalunya, 1
Tel. (34) 972 837 010
turisme@santacristina.net
www.santacristina.net

Sils
Pl. de l'Estació, s/n
Tel. (34) 972 168 285
estany@sils.cat
www.estanydesils.cat

Tamariu
C. de la Riera, s/n
Tel. (34) 972 620 193
turisme@palafrugell.cat
www.visitpalafrugell.cat

Torroella de Montgrí
Espai Ter - C. Riu Ter, 29
Tel. (34) 972 119 100
info@visitestartit.com
www.visitestartit.com

Museu de la Mediterrània
C. Ullà, 31 - Can Quintana
Tel. (34) 972 755 180
(34) 972 755 182
info@museudelamediterrania.cat
www.museudelamediterrania.cat

Tossa de Mar
Av. del Pelegrí, 25 (Edifici La Nau)
Tel. (34) 972 340 108
info@infotossa.com
www.infotossa.com

Verges
La Placeta, 1
Tel. (34) 972 780 974
turisme@verges.cat
www.verges.cat

Vilobí d'Onyar
Aeroport Girona-Costa Brava
Tel. (34) 972 942 955
ot.aeroportgirona@gencat.cat

PYRENEES OF GIRONA

Alp
C. Nord, s/n
Tel. (34) 972 890 385
turisme@alp2500.cat
www.alpturisme.cat

Besalú
C. Pont, 1
Tel. (34) 972 591 240
turisme@besalu.cat
www.besalu.cat

Camprodon
C. Sant Roc, 22
Tel. (34) 972 740 010
turisme@camprodon.cat
www.camprodon.cat

**La Vall d'en Bas
(els Hostalets d'en Bas)**
C. Teixeda, 12
Tel. (34) 972 692 177
(34) 972 690 225
turisme@vallbas.cat
www.vallbas.cat

**La Vall de Camprodon
(Camprodon)**
Ctra. C-38 km 9,60
Tel. (34) 972 740 936
turisme@valldecamprodon.org
www.valldecamprodon.org

La Vall de Núria
Estació de Muntanya Vall
de Núria
Tel. (34) 972 732 020
valldenuria@valldenuria.cat
www.valldenuria.cat

**La Vall de Ribes (Ribes
de Freser)**
Ctra. de Bruguera, 2
Tel. (34) 972 727 728
turisme@vallderibes.cat
www.vallderibes.cat

Les Planes d'Hostoles
Pg. de l'Estació, 2
Tel. (34) 972 448 026
turisme@lesplanes.cat
www.lesplanes.cat

Les Preses
Antiga Estació, s/n
Tel (34) 972 692 023
(34) 972 692 020
otlespreses@gmail.com
www.lespreses.cat

Llívia
C. dels Forns, 10
Tel. (34) 72 896 313
patronat@llivia.org
www.llivia.org

Olot
C. Hospici, 8
Tel. (34) 972 260 141
turisme@olot.cat
www.turismeolot.cat

**Centre d'informació Casal
dels Volcans**
Av. Santa Coloma, s/n
Tel. (34) 972 268 112
pnzvg@gencat.cat
www.gencat.cat/parcs/garrotxa

Puigcerdà
C. Querol, 1
Tel. (34) 972 880 542
info@puigcerda.cat
www.puigcerda.cat

Ripoll
Pl. de l'Abat Oliba, s/n
Tel. (34) 972 702 351
turismeripoll@ajripoll.com
www.elripolles.com

Sant Feliu de Pallerols
Ctra. d'Olot, 43 (Antiga Estació)
Tel. (34) 972 444 474
turisme@santfeliudepallerols.cat
www.santfeliudepallerols.cat

Sant Joan de les Abadesses
Pl. de l'Abadia, 9
Tel. (34) 972 720 599
turisme@santjoandelesabades
ses.cat
www.santjoandelesabadesses.cat

Sant Joan les Fonts
C. Juvinyà, s/n
Tel. (34) 972 290 507
turismesantjoan@hotmail.com
www.turismesantjoanlesfonts.com

Santa Pau
Pl. Major, 1 (Can Vayreda)
Tel. (34) 972 680 349
turisme@santapau.cat
www.santapau.com

Setcases
C. del Rec, 5
Tel. (34) 972 136 089
info@setcases.cat
www.setcases.info

Vallter 2000
Pla de Morens s/n
Tel. (34) 972 136 057
comercial@vallter2000.com
www.vallter2000.com

Vallfogona de Ripollès
C. Puig Estela, 9
Tel. (34) 972 701 909
(34) 972 690 225
vallfogona@ddgi.cat
www.ddgi.es/vallfogona

COUNTY INFORMATION OFFICES

**Consell Comarcal
de l'Alt Empordà**
C. Clerck i Nicolau, 2 B
Tel. (34) 972 514 431
info@empordaturisme.com
www.empordaturisme.com

**Consell Comarcal
de la Selva**
Pg. Sant Salvador, 25-27
Tel. (34) 972 841 702
info@laselvaturisme.com
www.laselvaturisme.com

**Consell Comarcal
del Baix Empordà**
C. Tarongers, 12
Tel. (34) 972 642 310
turisme@baixemporda.cat
www.visitemporda.com

**Consell Comarcal
del Pla de l'Estany**
C. Catalunya, 48
Tel. (34) 972 573 550
turisme@plaestany.cat
www.plaestany.cat/turisme

**Centre de Visitants del
Gironès**
Avinguda de França, 221
Sarrià de Ter
Tel. (34) 972011669
centredevisitants@girones.cat
www.turismegirones.cat

Ripollès Desenvolupament
Polígon Industrial dels Pintors
C. Joan Miró, 2-4
Tel. (34) 972 704 499
consorci@ripollesdesenvolupa
ment.com
www.elripolles.com

**Patronat Comarcal de
Turisme de la Cerdanya**
Ctra. Cruïlla N-152 amb N-260
Tel. (34) 972 140 665
info@cerdanya.org
www.cerdanya.org

Turisme Garrotxa
Av. Onze de Setembre, 22, 2a
Tel. (34) 972 271 600
(34) 972 274 900
info@turismegarrotxa.com
www.turismegarrotxa.com

SERVICES COMPANIES

CYCLE-TOURING

Cea Alt Ter
Sant Joan de les Abadesses
Tel. (34) 972 721 317
info@alt-ter.org
www.alt-ter.org

Caiac i Natura
Banyoles
Tel. (34) 699 770 647
info@caiacinatura.com
www.caiacinatura.com

Burricleta
Girona
Tel. (34) 972 751 017
hola@burricleta.com
www.burricleta.com

Bikecat
Girona
Tel. (34) 639 829 272
info@bikecat.com
www.bikecat.com

Lloguer de Bicicletes CAT
Can Guetes - Fundació MAP
Ripoll
Tel. (34) 972 718 001
cat@fundaciomap.com
cat.fundaciomap.org

Ocitània
Gualta
Tel. (34) 972 755 082
info@ocitania.cat
www.ocitania.cat

Giroguies
Palafrugell
Tel. (34) 972 303 886
info@giroguies.com
www.giroguies.com

Taxi Bikes - Antoni Juanals
Sant Feliu de Guíxols
Tel. (34) 699 365 253
antonijuanals@gmail.com

Empordà Bike Resort
La Bisbal d'Empordà
Tel. (34) 972 641 820
info@empordabikeresort.com
www.empordabikeresort.com

Vida Bike
Llagostera
Tel. (34) 670 552 590
info@vida-bike.com
www.vida-bike.com

Consorci de les Vies Verdes
Girona
Tel. (34) 972 486 950
info@viesverdes.org
www.viesverdes.org

Bicicarril.com-Enjoy Pyrinees
Amer
Tel. (34) 972 430 013
info@bicicarril.com
www.bicicarril.com

Cicles JK
Palafrugell
Tel. (34) 972 610 709
info@ciclesjk.com
www.ciclesjk.com

Cicloturisme i Medi Ambient
Girona
Tel. (34) 972 221 047
info@cicloturisme.com
www.cicloturisme.com

ATMA - Bicycle Logistics Centre
Olot
Tel. (34) 972 692 023
atma@atma.cat
www.atma.cat

Happy Bikes Girona
Madremanya
Tel. (34) 648 100 001
happybikesgirona@gmail.com
www.happybikesgirona.com

Consorci del Ter - Ruta del Ter
Manlleu
Tel. (34) 938 507 152
comunicacio@consorcidelter.cat
www.rutadelter.cat

EO Bikes / Walk & Bikes
Figueres
Tel. (34) 972 673 950
info@eobikes.com
www.eobikes.com

Cycling in Costa Brava
Blanes
Tel. (34) 654 540 809
jordi@cyclingincostabrava.com
www.cyclingincostabrava.com

Centre BTT Salines Bassegoda
Navata
Tel. (34) 972 565 004
informacio@salines-bassegoda.org
www.salines-bassegoda.org/centrebtt

TREKKING

Trescàlia
Olot
Tel. (34) 972 90 38 22
info@trescalia.com
www.trescalia.com

Cea Alt Ter
Sant Joan de les Abadesses
Tel. (34) 972 721 317
info@alt-ter.org
www.alt-ter.org

Terramar, nature and culture
Palau de Santa Eulàlia
Tel. (34) 618 547 958
terramar@terramar.org
www.terramar.org

Giroguies
Palafrugell
Tel. (34) 972 303 886
info@giroguies.com
www.giroguies.com

Cicloturisme i Medi Ambient
Girona
Tel. (34) 972 221 047
info@cicloturisme.com
www.cicloturisme.com

Consorci del Ter-Ruta del Ter
Manlleu
Tel. (34) 938 507 152
comunicacio@consorcidelter.cat
www.rutadelter.cat

Les Guilleries Associació d'Educació Ambiental
Sant Hilari Sacalm
Tel. (34) 972 869 127
lesguilleries@gmail.com
www.lesguilleries.org

Camí de Ronda ®
La Bisbal d'Empordà
Tel. (34) 972 109 358
info@camideronda.com
www.camideronda.com

KAYAK

Sk Kayak
Llançà
Tel. (34) 627 433 332
info@skkayak.com
www.kayakcostabrava.com

Nautical Centre Roses - Cap de Creus
Roses
Tel. (34) 972 15 44 12
info@enroses.com
www.enroses.com

Nautical Centre Sant Feliu de Guíxols - Costa Brava
Sant Feliu de Guíxols
Tel. (34) 972 968 080
info@enguixolscostabrava.com
www.enguixolscostabrava.com

Nautical Centre l'Estartit - Illes Medes
L'Estartit (Torroella de Montgrí)
Tel. (34) 972 750 699
info@enestartit.com
www.enestartit.com

Agenda Gestió Esportiva
Banyoles
Tel. (34) 972 58 06 39
info@agendasports.com
www.agendasports.com

Caiac i Natura
Banyoles
Tel. (34) 699 770 647
info@caiacinatura.com
www.caiacinatura.com

Medaqua
L'Estartit (Torroella de Montgrí)
Tel. (34) 972 752 043
carme@medaqua.com
www.medaqua.com

Club Nàutic Port de la Selva
El Port de la Selva
Tel. (34) 972 387 000
nautic@cnps.cat
www.cnps.cat

Funtastic Empordà
L'Escala
Tel. (34) 639 313 138

info@funtastic-emporda.com
www.funtastic-emporda.com

Club Nàutic l'Escala
L'Escala
Tel. (34) 972 770 016
club@nauticescala.com
www.nauticescala.com

Kayaking Costa Brava
L'Escala
Tel. (34) 972 773 806
info@kayakingcostabrava.com
www.kayakingcostabrava.com

Kayak del Ter
Colomers
Tel. (34) 662 159 496
info@kayakdelter.com
www.kayakdelter.com

Kayak Palamós
Palamós
Tel. (34) 670 339 269
info@kayakpalamos.com
www.kayakpalamos.com

INDEX OF PLACE NAMES

© **Triangle Postals SL**
Sant Lluís, Menorca
Tel. +34 971 15 04 51
triangle@triangle.cat
www.triangle.cat

Text and photographs
© Sergi Lara

Graphic design
David Martínez
joan Colomer

Maps
Joan Esteve

Translation
Steve Cedar

Printed by
Vanguard SL

Printed in Barcelona
DL: Me 43-2016
ISBN: 978-84-8478-676-4

Published with the support of

WEBS OF INTEREST

Costa Brava - Pirineu de Girona
costabrava.org

Turisme Alt Empordà
www.empordaturisme.com

Consell Comarcal del Baix Empordà
www.baixemporda-costabrava.org/ca

Associació de Turisme la Selva
www.laselvaturisme.com

Turisme Garrotxa
turismegarrotxa.com

Consorci de les Vies Verdes de Girona
www.viesverdes.cat

Ruta Pirinexus
www.pirinexus.cat

Ruta del Ter
www.rutadelter.cat

Itinerànnia, xarxa de senders
itinerannia.net

Federació d'Entitats Excursionistes de Catalunya
www.feec.cat

Senders de Catalunya
senders.feec.cat